in print @ 1675

HANNIBAL'S LIEUTENANT
A UNIQUE BIOGRAPHY OF HANNIBAL

Robert S. Capps

A Manor House Publication

Alexandria, Virginia

Copyright © 1994 by Robert S. Capps
All rights reserved under International and Pan-American Copyright Conventions.

Published in the United States by:
Manor House Publications
P.O. Box 19427
Alexandria, Virginia 22320-0427

Library of Congress Catalog Card Number 94-75074

ISBN 0-9640665-0-5

Capps, Robert S. - First Edition
A biography of Hannibal that interprets historical facts and situations as Hannibal and his sympathizers would have viewed them, as seen through the eyes of an interesting fictional officer.
Includes bibliographical references and five maps.
1. Hannibal, 247-183 B.C. 2. Second Punic War
3. Generals - Carthage(Ancient) - Biography
4. Historical Fiction

ACKNOWLEDGMENTS

The author is indebted to Alisa M. Hoffman of APOSTROPHE PUBLISHING SERVICES who edited the manuscript in detail, gave valuable advice, and arranged to have it printed; to B. Leiter and Robert G. Martin of CARLTON PRESS, INC. who provided valuable editorial suggestions; to Mike Winton, my son-in-law and computer expert, who made the computerization of the manuscript possible; and to my wife, Eve, for her patience and encouragement. The author is also indebted to Mike Bowers, currently the Attorney General for the state of Georgia, for initiating an interest in Hannibal during conversations over coffee many years ago.

CONTENTS

FOREWARD 5
CHAPTERS:
1. Background and Early Years (244-222 B.C.) 9
2. Preparation for Italy (222-218 B.C.) 41
3. The March to Italy (May-November, 218 B.C.) ... 82
4. First Roman Encounters: Ticinus and Trebbia
   (November, 218 B.C. to May, 217 B.C.) 110
5. Lake Trasimene to Camp at Gerunium
   (June, 217 B.C. to July, 216 B.C.) 137
6. Battle of Cannae (August 1-5, 216 B.C.) 165
7. Stalemate (216-211 B.C.) 191
8. Hannibal Marches to Rome and Hasdrubal
   Marches to Italy (211-206 B.C.) 229
9. Bizarre Events Before Hannibal Arrives in Africa
   (206-203 B.C.) 261
10. Events in Africa After Hannibal Arrives
    (203-195 B.C.) 286
11. Events After Hannibal Flees Africa
    (195-182 B.C.) 316
12. Epilogue 342

MAPS

HANNIBAL'S ROUTE 94
HANNIBAL'S ITALY 113
BATTLE OF LAKE TRASIMENE ... 142
BATTLE OF CANNAE 180
HANNIBAL'S MEDITERRANEAN .. 318

FOREWORD

Hannibal's Lieutenant is a well-researched biography of the great Hannibal as seen through the eyes of a fictional officer. It closely follows known facts about Hannibal's life as handed down to us by ancient writers and by modern research. Most of what we know about his life and character was written more than two-thousand years ago by his bitter enemies, the Romans, or by Greeks who were intimately associated with Romans. Thus, while the writings show a grudging admiration for the brilliant Hannibal, they are oriented from the Roman perspective, with Roman prejudices. *Hannibal's Lieutenant* attempts to view the facts and situations as Hannibal and his supporters would have seen them, with their own prejudices.

The most respected ancient writing of Hannibal's war was written by the Greek, Polybius (circa. 203-118 B.C.). He was a teacher and companion of the Roman general, Publius Cornelius Scipio Aemilianus, who was responsible for ruthlessly destroying the city of Carthage almost fifty years after Hannibal had left the country. This Roman general caused the death or enslavement of all inhabitants of Carthage and the destruction of Carthaginian records. To gather material for his *Histories,* Polybius interviewed many particiants of Hannibal's war and he traveled many of the same routes that Hannibal traveled. He was able to consult official Roman records, and he found one of Hannibal's records of the war inscribed on a bronze tablet in the shrine of Juno near Croton in southern Italy. Although Polybius wrote his history fifty years after the war, it is the most respected writing on the subject.

The next most respected ancient history of Hannibal's

war was written by the great Roman historian, Livy (59B.C..-17A.D.). He wrote his voluminous history of Rome more than 150 years after the end of Hannibal's war, thus he was not able to talk to the participants. His purpose was to record the history of "the greatest nation in the world," Rome, for future generations. He could not be expected to present the Carthaginian cause in the best light. Although his writing displays a grudging admiration for Hannibal, he attempts to present him as an unprincipled barbarian. It was a Roman custom to label all enemies of Rome as "barbarians," although many of Rome's enemies were more cultured and civilized than Romans were at that time. In his *The War With Hannibal*, Livy did not attempt to view Rome's war with Hannibal in sympathy with the brilliant Carthaginian's just cause for his war.

Some of the Roman writers who were alive during Hannibal's time were L. Cincius Alimentus, who was captured by Hannibal and wrote his history afterward, Q. Fabius Pictor, and M. Porcius Cato. Unfortunately, many valuable records have been lost, destroyed, or have come down to us in fragments. Carthaginian writings, written mostly by Greek scribes in Hannibal's camp (e.g. Soslius, Silenus, and Chaereas), were probably destroyed by Romans. Almost without exception, ancient writers acknowledge Hannibal's exceptional military genius and his unusual leadership abilities. It is abundantly clear that he had great strength of character and that he was an unusually charismatic leader.

Hannibal terrorized Romans more than any of their other enemies. The Roman, Juvenal, wrote that as late as the second century A.D. (more than 350 years after the war) Roman mothers were playfully terrorizing their children with the words, "Hannibal is coming," implying that many elephants were coming, as well as the one carrying the one-eyed Hannibal along with his army horde.

Hannibal nearly changed the course of history of the western world. His war was one that decided whether the western world would be ruled by Roman militarism or by Carthaginian (Phoenician) merchant traders. The war could have been won by either side during the seesaw course of its eighteen years. Romans labeled the war "The Second Punic War" after the name "Punic" which they had for Phoenicians, because Carthaginians were descendants of Phoenicians. Carthage was originally a colony of the Phoenician city, Tyre, which is now in Lebanon.

Hannibal caused the Roman military machine to drastically improve its tactics and strategy, as Roman generals studied Hannibal's astute tactics and policies. Many tactics and policies developed by Hannibal are still used in modern warfare, and they are taught in military schools throughout the world. In modern warfare, mechanized tanks have taken over most of the functions that horses formerly performed in ancient cavalries. During his telecast to an audience of billions of viewers in January, 1991, the Commanding General of the United Nations Forces in the Gulf War, General Norman Schwartzkopf, mentioned that the successful encirclement tactics his ground forces had used to defeat the Iraq army were similar to those used by Hannibal at the Battle of Cannae.

The following sympathetic or Carthaginian view of Hannibal's life was developed by using an eclectic approach. That is, available records and translations of ancient writings, as well as many available modern histories written over the past hundred years were analyzed and interpreted to determine how Hannibal or his sympathizers would have viewed the situations he faced. Ancient writers, as well as modern ones, disagree on many aspects of his story, particularly on the number of troops that participated in the battles and the number that were killed. His exact route over the Alps is still in question, but modern researchers have narrowed his trip over the Alps to one that is the most probable route taken. A selected bibliography of some books that the author found useful are listed in the *Appendix* at the end of this book.

Hannibal's fictitious lieutenant, Gisco, performs many tasks and deeds that were actually accomplished by many unknown officers serving on Hannibal's staff. The logistics-planning standards that Gisco used for computing the supply requirements in *Chapter 2* were taken from the excellent study, *Alexander the Great and the Logistics of the Macedonian Army*, by Donald W. Engels, University of California Press (1978). They were used with permission of the publishers. It is presumed that Hannibal and his officers studied the exploits of Alexander in great detail (as well as the exploits of the great Greek king, Pyrrhus) as most other military officers of his time would have done. Thus, it is not unusual for Hannibal's lieutenant to have adopted the advanced, innovative, logistics policies that Alexander used. These contributed immensely to Alexander's ability to move his armies rapidly and enabled him to surprise his enemies.

Chapter 1

BACKGROUND AND EARLY YEARS
(244 - 222 B.C.)

Gisco the Greek sat watching as he waited for the venerable Carthaginian warrior to finish dictating final pages of his astounding saga. An eager scribe, fascinated by every sentence, struggled to scratch out the warrior's memoirs on papyrus. The old man's handsome, tanned face was animated, and his gray head moved emphatically as he dictated Greek words with a refined accent. He paced back and forth across the mosaic-tiled floor. Because his scarred hand carried an ornate goblet of wine, his energetic movements almost caused wine to spill on his bright, gracefully-draped tunic. Dictation was interrupted occasionally as he took time to go to a nearby window and look out, down an approaching road. He had been warned that Roman soldiers were in the neighborhood searching for him again, and he was worried. He had recorded his story in great detail before, but Roman soldiers slew his scribes and destroyed his scrolls. He didn't want that to happen again. The old Carthaginian had asked his trusted friend, Gisco, to wait until the manuscript was finished so that he could take it to the great library of Alexandria, Egypt. There it would be safe for scholars of the world to read. He wanted his own version of Hannibal's great war with Rome to become known. Gisco was also helping him remember many details of the campaigns. Elderly Gisco had served Hannibal and his cause for many years. He was reminded of many memories as he listened to the Carthaginian's words. While waiting, the Greek began to reminisce about his own exciting experiences with Hannibal. While reminiscing, he realized that he had been destined to join the Carthaginian army in Spain from the time he was eight years old. It was foreordained by a catastrophic event which occurred at that time in his life. The event was so traumatic for the impressionable youth that it radically changed his life and predetermined his future.

Gisco was born into a substantial Greek family on October 14, 244 B.C. He was welcomed into the family with widespread celebration because he was a robust baby, an only child, and his popular parents had considerable social fame and influence. Much of this family eminence was won by Gisco's great-grandfather, Strato, who was the last brilliant head of the famous Aristotle school, the Lyceum, located in Athens. Strato was a dominant influence on Greek thought and learning during his time, famous for scientific research and experimentation. This illustrious man passed along his valuable character traits to his children and grandchildren. Strato's heirs created a prominent construction business that was busy building public-works projects throughout the Mediterranean world. The projects included bridges and large buildings around Athens, irrigation systems in Egypt, military fortifications in Alexandria and Syracuse, and wharves in Piraeus. His heirs continued much of Strato's academic tradition, keeping a strong interest in science and experimentation. They maintained an active correspondence with many great Greek scholars, exchanging and testing new ideas of applied science to be used in the family business.

Gisco's place of birth was a peaceful, enclosed, family villa on the north side of the Acropolis, in a respectable part of the city. The view from his home was spectacular, with the exquisite Parthenon and its huge Doric columns in full view. Red, gold, and white tinted marble temples could be seen in the glow of the evening sunset. Gisco's father, Zeno, was a well-educated man who took an early interest in his only offspring's training. Gisco's mother, Procne, was not only beautiful, but unusually intelligent and gifted. Athenian women did not normally go to school, but Zeno hired a private tutor to teach his extraordinary wife to read and write. She was an able tutor for Gisco at an early age.

The family spent many cozy and enjoyable evenings together reading poetry aloud and singing together to the accompaniment of a servant playing a lyre. Gisco was not required by law to attend public school until he was six years old, but he was such a precocious child that his father decided to hire a private tutor for him during his third year. Soon, he was reading and writing at a level far beyond his years. When Zeno was home, he would help with his son's training, unconsciously passing along many of his valuable character traits to his adored son. Young Gisco poured out love for his doting parents with great effusion, to their delight. The young son was made to feel very secure and happy.

Gisco's private tutor began teaching him many things in addition to rudiments of reading and writing. He began developing the child's character with exercises that increased his self-reliance, obedience, patriotism, modesty, alertness, and appreciation of beauty and harmony in life. Gisco's training was at least two years ahead of his contemporaries by the time he was required to enter public school with other six-year olds.

There were no government-owned schools, but the law required attendance at one of many private schools from ages six through fifteen. Many wealthy families sent their boys for higher learning after age fifteen. Only boys attended school, while girls remained in their homes for domestic training. All boys who were citizens were required to attend military training for one year after they reached eighteen. After military training, male citizens were required to remain in the reserve army, subject to call to active service in emergencies. This was the legal environment facing young Gisco.

The lower schools of Athens were the world's best, and foreign potentates as well as wealthy families from far-away nations sent their children there. On entering formal school, it was customary for the family to give the boy a full-time slave called a pedagogue whose duty it was to accompany the young master everywhere when he was away from home. The pedagogue brought the boy to school, waited for him in a special anteroom, helped with his lessons, carried his books and writing tablets, taught him good social manners, answered questions for him, and when his father was not available, whipped him if needed. Gisco's father selected a slave from the family business for the young boy's pedagogue. He chose one who was trustworthy, cultured, intelligent, had proper zest, and most important, one who eagerly volunteered for the job. The chosen slave could read and write and he had high morals. Though a war wound left him with a slight limp, he was an excellent athlete, and he had a superb physique. Zeno promised to reward him generously. The pedagogue, a Numidian, was called Cirta, after the name of the African town of his birth (now called Constantine). The town of Cirta was an important metropolis in Numidia, a nation on the northern coast of Africa (now, roughly Algeria) west of and adjacent to the nation of Carthage. Numidia had a powerful cavalry with more than ten-thousand mounted troops. Cirta was twenty years older than Gisco, had nine years of experience with the well-trained Numidian cavalry, a comprehensive knowledge of horses, and much experience with the use of cavalry in warfare. While in the cavalry service, he received the thigh wound that caused him to limp slightly. Cirta's personal qualities were such that he became a treasured and constant companion of Gisco the rest of his life. He became accepted and loved as a regular member of the family, and Cirta came to love Gisco and Zeno's family as his own.

Slavery was to play an important role in Gisco's future in more ways than one. His father used many slaves in his business. He trained them as craftsmen and technicians. He also owned ten household slaves, whom he carefully picked, paying premium prices for the best. They were trained as maids, caretakers, cooks, nurses for Gisco, and house guards. Slavery was an accepted institution throughout the Mediterranean world. Great advances made by Greek society up to this time can be attributed, to a significant extent, to the fact that slaves performed most menial tasks, freeing Greek citizens to devote more time to cultural pursuits. About half of Athens' population was slaves. Athenians believed, as Aristotle had taught, that lower echelons of society and barbarians who were less trained and cultivated than Greeks, were naturally slaves. They believed, as irrational as it may seem today, that it was to the slaves' benefit that they were under the care and rule of a civilized master. Most slaves were of the white or oriental races, from the Black Sea area and Asia Minor. Greeks would never use other Greeks as slaves. Slaves were traded regularly in Athens' market place, the agora, and most families had at least one. Slaves were part of the spoils of war, and slave markets of the Mediterranean nations made it a profitable business for armies - not necessarily Greek armies - to enslave defeated populations and sell them on the ready market. Pirates made a lucrative business of kidnapping travelers at sea to sell them as slaves. Pirates also launched raiding parties on defenseless coastal towns to get slaves. In Syria and the east, bankrupt businessmen and their families were sold on the slave market to pay their debts. As immoral as the slave issue is to us today, these were the harsh facts in Gisco's life.

To their credit, many Athenians treated their slaves well, many paid them wages, and many slaves were treated as part of the Greek family. Slaves dressed the same as common citizens, and it was difficult to tell them apart on the street. The city police force consisted of more than one-thousand slaves owned by the city. Slave police arrested citizens and others who broke the law, and they kept order in the agora. Citizen-soldiers in the Greek army usually had one slave. Athenian law protected slaves and the way they were treated. Some slaves were allowed to operate their own businesses or work for wages, and there were instances where slaves became so affluent that they hired their masters who were poor.

Gisco's public school lasted from dawn to dusk,

with time out for lunch, eaten at home nearby. As was customary for schools of the gentry, only four students were in his class. The teaching master sat on a high chair, looking down on the young boys who sat on benches scratching out their lessons on wood tablets covered with wax. There was strict discipline in class, as the master was a tyrant and did not spare the rod. At age six, training of Greek children passed from the soft, loving care of the mother (and in Gisco's case, the patient private tutor) to the rough, harsh, masculine discipline of the formal school.

From academic training in reading, writing, and arithmetic in the morning, Cirta would take Gisco to the music school to sing and read poetry to accompaniment of a lyre, and then to the nearby gymnasium. Gisco welcomed the relief of going from academics to music and poetry lessons, then to the great new gymnasium of Ptolemy near the agora. The gymnastics teacher, another tyrant and strict disciplinarian, was a famous champion of the pentathlon at the great Panhellenic games in Delphi. Thus, as with all such champions, he was a great celebrity and famous throughout Greece. He systematically taught his pupils running, wrestling, boxing, jumping, and discus and javelin throwing. Greeks believed that physical training had an important influence on building character, the body, the mind; it also built and trained strong bodies for the defense of the country in wartime.

The gymnastics master soon noted Gisco's unusual, natural, athletic ability and coordination. He took extra time and care with him, hoping to make him into a future Panhellenic games champion, as he himself had been. The young man excelled in all athletic events, and he was also very graceful in the dance classes he was required to attend. Cirta was helpful by giving him additional instruction and by disciplining his practice, so that he got the most out of it. Historians are in general agreement that in intelligence, grace, taste, and enthusiasm, no society has come up to the Greek's high level of achievement, and Gisco gradually became an exemplary product of this system. It was in gymnastics that he began to develop a strong competitive spirit and zest to excel at everything he tried.

Zeno occasionally took Gisco and Cirta to the Ecclesia (public assembly) to learn how Athenian government worked. He also took them on visits to the agora to teach Gisco things about life that weren't taught in school. Most of the better Athenian families protected their young boys from the evil and ugly things they could see in the noisy, crowded marketplace, but Zeno believed it was an important part of his son's education. Zeno also took the two on sea voyages, on business trips, both for personal companionship, which he enjoyed, and to broaden the boy's education.

When Gisco was eight years old, his father took the two on a voyage to Carales (now Cagliari), then the most important city in Sardinia, on its southern coast. It had been a Carthaginian trading colony and Carthaginians had been fortifying the town with help from Zeno's associate group of experts. Carthage was forced to cede Sardinia to Rome in 238 B.C., before the project was finished, and so Zeno had ceased work on it. Carthage's mercenary soldiers who remained stranded in the town after it was ceded to Rome were disgruntled because they were owed back wages. They joined the local population in a revolt against their new Roman masters and took control of the port. The mercenary leader then requested that

Zeno return to Carales to give him advice about completing the harbor's defenses. He wanted local labor to finish the project. Zeno had not learned of the political revolt, suspected no danger, so he accepted the proposal. He expected the trip to take only four weeks.

The trip to Sardinia was a pleasant one, on a fast merchant ship chartered by Zeno, with balmy seas and excellent weather. It was little more than eight-hundred nautical miles from Athens' port, Piraeus. They traveled only by day, pulling to shore at night. Gisco brought reading and writing material, and Zeno helped him with his lessons. Cirta helped with gymnastics practice. Among the stops was one made at Syracuse, on the island of Sicily, where Zeno introduced his son to Archimedes, the great scholar and longtime friend of the family. Two days were spent discussing secret defensive fortifications around the city's harbor that Zeno's family of experts were helping to build under Archimedes direction. This great scholar designed the fortifications, but he was glad to let Zeno's associates do much of the actual construction and supervision so that he, Archimedes, could devote more of his time to scientific studies. Gisco was impressed by the unusual war machines being installed around the port's embattlements. Fate would have him return to Syracuse years later.

It was at Canales that Gisco suffered the brutal tragedy that profoundly influenced the rest of his life. He and Cirta were high up on the acropolis, overlooking the sheltered port below, practicing gymnastics. Zeno was down at the harbor's docks, discussing business with the mercenary leaders who were in charge of the construction. Unnoticed by anyone, a surprise landing party of Roman soldiers made a sneak attack on the unarmed men. It was a quiet part of the day, and most inhabitants were having lunch. But the commotion below attracted the attention of the young son and his pedagogue. They looked down in time to see a Roman soldier brutally decapitate their beloved Zeno while others slew the four mercenary leaders with him. The eight-year-old boy was shocked and stricken with grief at the appalling sight below. His entire life up to that time had been protected, serene, without violence of any kind. He was completely overwhelmed by the disastrous event and by the horror of seeing his adored father suddenly and so savagely destroyed.

Mercenaries quickly assembled their defensive troops and repulsed the Roman attack, which turned out to be the first of many, before Rome finally conquered the island three years later. Grief-stricken Gisco and angry Cirta prepared to sail back to Piraeus with Zeno's mutilated body in a casket. Before sailing, Gisco's grief began to change to deep anger against Romans. He and Cirta found a sacred temple and vowed at its altar, sealed with an animal sacrifice, an eternal hatred and vengeance against Rome. They vowed to focus all their skills, energy, and resources toward achieving that goal.

When the two companions sadly returned to their home with the mangled body in the wooden casket, Procne was overcome by grief, as were all other occupants of the household. News traveled fast outside the home, and that evening a reception was prepared for friends and relatives in the home. Women of the household placed Zeno's coffin on a bier in the courtyard and adorned it with wreaths of flowers. Professional dirge singers were hired. Many friends, relatives, business associates, and government officials attended the emotional gathering. The melancholic singing of dirge singers filled the air, and most men and women, citizens as well as slaves, shed tears as Zeno was widely loved. Young Gisco was profoundly shaken, and the experience reinforced his strong desire for vengeance against Roman perpetrators of this horror.

Early the next morning, a procession of flute players was followed by close relatives carrying the litter which held the casket, followed by the grieving widow and young son, close relatives, friends, then slaves. All marched to an open field on the edge of the city. A funeral pyre had been prepared there, consisting of cedar wood and other aromatic substances. The long procession gathered around as the casket was placed on the pyre, and it was ceremoniously burned to the doleful music of flute players. Afterward, the remains were put in a large ornate urn and taken to the family's private field near the Itonian Gate, along the road to Piraeus. A beautiful carved monument was erected over the urn.

On the evening of the burial, an elaborate funeral feast was provided by Gisco's grandfather, in his own home. Everyone drank and ate their fill under the superstition that Zeno was host for the last time.

Zeno had bequeathed ample wealth to care for his family. Gisco's grandfather, Archelaus, was still alive and in good health, able to husband the family resources and to care for the family business. In the years that followed, Gisco became more zealous and dedicated to his sacred vow. Cirta, who had a strong distaste for Romans from his earlier experiences with them in Numidia, was driven to rage against them. He was caught up in Gisco's emotional state, and his love and concern for his master's welfare made him as vengeful.

Gisco resumed his studies with greater obedience, dedication, and fervency. His vigor and tenacity at his work astonished those who knew him. The Greek government did not regulate schools or gymnasiums, thus families were free to select the type of training they desired for their offspring. As Gisco rapidly progressed in his school work, he outgrew the schoolboy's bench and graduated to more advanced studies, far ahead of his contemporaries. Advanced students stood in front of their master as he read and discussed scrolls written by many different philosophers. His grandfather, Archelaus, had many such scrolls which he had inherited in the library left by the great Strato. In addition, Archelaus collected many more during his own schooling. Gisco had access to these and he read them voraciously.

Archelaus used an eclectic approach for guiding Gisco's training, as his prodigy grew. He sent the young boy to various private tutors and to visiting philosophers who came to the beautiful painted stoa at the north end of the agora. He did this to give Gisco a well-rounded education and to bring him in contact with many great minds. Gisco was readily accepted in classes designed for much older boys because he was coming to be recognized, generally, as a precocious prodigy, and he was well-liked by all.

His personal tragedy caused him to rapidly become mentally mature. He adopted a private philosophy that synthesized many different Greek philosophical schools. From the Stoics' philosopher, Chrysippus, who took over the Stoic school in 232 B.C., he learned that achieving happiness is a serious business. Happiness is not a matter of sensual indulgence, which only lasts a short time. Real happiness comes from the deep satisfaction of achievement and virtue, which lasts much longer and is more richly gratifying. He taught that sensual passions were types of beliefs, thus they were subject to the rational control of the mind, by will power. Lasting, rich happiness does not come from warmth, security, and coziness: it comes hard-won, by great physical and mental effort. Chrysippus also taught Gisco that one's own constitution is the first necessary concern of a person, before all else. Gisco rejected hedonism and sensual pleasures, while he adopted parts of the Spartan philosophy with his willingness to sacrifice comforts to achieve his personal goals.

From his great-grandfather's school, the Lyceum, and the philosophy of Aristotle taught there, the young boy adopted a scientific, inquiring, and questioning attitude. He became interested in science and experimentation. From the Sophists, he learned that oratorical skills should be developed as the most practical path for achieving social power and influence, the logical way to fulfill personal ambition. This was confirmed for him by his visits to the Ecclesia, the public meetings where government business was conducted. He observed that the greatest orators became the most successful and that oratorical skills were a necessary prerequisite to being a leader. He admired their talent and he strove to emulate their ability to persuade others through speech.

Gradually, Gisco's consuming interest focused on military tactics and strategy as a way to avenge his father's death. He began to evaluate everything he learned in terms of its potential for contributing toward fulfillment of his sacred vows. He carefully studied the military exploits of Alexander the Great, memorizing all aspects of his great campaigns. This brought his attention to a void in his training thus far: he had ignored the value and uses of cavalry in modern warfare. A major reason for this was that the Athenian army had a weak cavalry and didn't fully utilize its potential. Gisco decided to do something about this. With Cirta's help, he bought some fine horses in Thessaly, a region to the north of Athens. He gave some of the beautiful animals to the Athenian military cavalry, a custom followed by much older boys. This ingratiated him with the troops, and he was able to talk about military tactics with them, and about the care, feeding, and breeding of horses. As it turned out, Cirta was a much more skillful and knowledgeable cavalryman than any of the Athenians.

Cirta showed Gisco why the cavalry of Athens was a feeble fighting force, compared with his old Numidian cavalry. He also showed him that Roman military doctrine, as depicted in military manuals they had studied, was also weak in its use of cavalry. Both, Athenians and Romans, used horse soldiers effectively for scouting enemy and for chasing routed soldiers, but cavalry did not play a major role in the grand offensive strategies of their armies. Both relied primarily on heavily armed foot soldiers who marched in close ranks abreast, with deep rows of them, a modified phalanx. Cirta knew from his experience with the powerful Numidian cavalry that the Greek army could improve its effectiveness in combat if it were to make better use of cavalry wherever the terrain permitted. Gisco also believed, from his studies of military tactics used by Alexander when he conquered the world (from Greece and Egypt to northern India), that better cavalry tactics could improve effectiveness of the army of Athens. Cirta began correcting this deficiency by giving instruction to the Greeks.

Soon, Cirta and Gisco became popular and very competent honorary members of the horse troops of Athens. The two were allowed to ride in the numerous ceremonial and religious processions, disregarding the fact that Gisco was much below the age for military service. The commander of the cavalry formally and publicly commended their significant contributions to his unit's capability, morale, and welfare.

Gisco's gymnastic ability and fierce competitive spirit continued to attract the attention of his long-time tutor, the celebrated Panhellenic Games Champion. The boy did not disappoint his master's hopes that he would develop into a new champion of the pentathlon. By seventeen, his body had grown into a tall, graceful, powerful, classical Greek physique. Handsome Gisco kept his body tanned and well oiled in the custom of the other young men. Like the others, he spent considerable time at the barber having his hair dressed in a stylish fashion, and he had the long locks of his younger days trimmed shorter. He kept his high-quality chiton spotlessly clean, and he reserved a couple of pastel-colored ones for wear on special occasions. All athletic events were accomplished in the nude and barefoot in Greece, thus his garments were not rumpled or dirty. He wore them in fashionable folds and gracefully draped around his body.

In the city-sponsored games, Gisco defeated all competitors by wide margins in the five separate events of the pentathlon: sprinting, wrestling, javelin throwing, long jumping, and discus throwing. Then, in the famous Isthmian games at Corinth, where all the best athletes from the entire Hellenistic world competed, he won the championship. Winning the majority of the five events was all that was required to win, but Gisco won all of the five events, a feat seldom accomplished. As do all winners of the celebrated games, Gisco became famous, an idol throughout Greece, and especially in Athens. There was great festivity in Athens as its proud citizens rejoiced that one of their homegrown boys had taken the championship by such a wide margin. The government formally recognized and rewarded him. A statue of Gisco throwing a discus was commissioned. Poets wrote flatteringly about him, and he was received with great enthusiasm and extravagant celebration wherever he went. His relatives took on proud airs, and his name became a household word in Athens. He became the idol of all young men and women.

After winning the championship, his grandfather decided it was time for Gisco to visit his old friend, Eratosthenes, head of the great library in Alexandria. He believed that this would relieve the young man from the distractions created by an adulating, doting Athenian populace. Furthermore, Gisco had rapidly progressed through much of the worthwhile reading available in Athens. The library in Alexandria and its associated university, called the Museum, had the finest collection of books in the world. Great scholars from all over the world gathered there to study and discuss them, and to do research. Alexander the Great had established the city as the capital of his empire. He planned to create the greatest library ever established and make it into the leading learning center of the world. Ptolemy, one of Alexander's leading generals, succeeded him as ruler of Egypt after his death, and he continued to implement Alexander's master plan for the city. Ptolemy II, ruler of Egypt when Gisco was sent there to study, continued to sponsor the plan enthusiastically.

Eratosthenes was a great academic leader while head of the library, and he became famous for many scientific studies and experiments. Among these was his accurate calculation of the circumference of the earth (1700 years before Columbus sailed to America). He did this by measuring the length of shadows cast at noon on the same day at different latitudes of the earth. From this information, he was able to calculate, using triangulation and mathematics, a reasonably precise circumference of the earth. Other great academic achievements were accomplished here. It was at Alexandria that Euclid wrote his "Element", the basic work in geometry. Here, also, Herophilus the famous physician pioneered the study of anatomy and medicine.

As Gisco and Cirta approached Egypt's capital city on a balmy evening, they could see light from the famous Pharos lighthouse many miles out at sea. The 400-hundred-foot-tall, magnificent structure was regarded as one of the Seven Wonders of the World. In the red glow of the setting sun, as they approached the city, they could see the beautiful royal palaces, the exquisite Poseidon Temple of the Sea God, a large theater, a huge gymnasium, and the most famous of all Alexandria's temples, the Serapeum. The harbor was filled with vessels from everywhere in the Mediterranean. The city was now the commercial metropolis of the world because it was on the new main trade route between India and the western world by way of the Red Sea. Alexander's corpse was brought here and put in a mausoleum that formed an elegant ring in conjunction with the mausoleums of the Ptolemys.

Eratosthenes enthusiastically welcomed the two men sent by his warm friend, Archelaus. He was quick to discern the unusual qualities of Gisco, which vastly exceeded his expectations. The young man's obvious acumen, zest, personal charm, and oratorical skills impressed the famous scientist. He took great pleasure in guiding Gisco in his studies. He introduced him to many researchers who were knowledgeable in Gisco's areas of interest who provided further guidance. They invited Gisco to discussion symposiums. Eratosthenes was forty-eight years old, and he took a fatherly attitude toward the talented young man, not yet eighteen.

The library and its associated Museum (which was equivalent in concept to modern universities) had been a high priority project of the Ptolemys. They assembled eminent scholars of literature, art, science, and philosophy here, providing them with the best facilities available for their research. Since the Macedonian conquest of Athens, and the loss of its city-state nationality, Athens gradually became second to Alexandria in advanced study and learning in the known world. The Alexandria school became an interface between oriental culture and that of the western nations. It became a melting pot for Platoism, Stoicism, Aristotleism, and the oriental philosophies - an intellectual crossroads.

Every vessel visiting the port of Alexandria was required by law to leave a manuscript for the famous library. Gisco and Archelaus had anticipated this, and they provided some excellent scrolls for the collection. The library had its literature indexed chronologically and by subject - one of Eratosthenes achievements. The original foundation of the library's collection was a purchase of Aristotle's library which had many foreign books. It had the Old Testament which seventy local Palestinian Jews translated into Greek (the Septuagent) in seventy days for Ptolemy II.

Because of family connections in the royal court, and Ptolemy's familiarity with the fine work Zeno and Archelaus had done for Egypt, much of it still in progress, the two visitors were provided luxurious accommodations. They were located in the Greek, or royal quarter, of the city near Ptolemy's palace. Their apartments were normally reserved for very important visitors, and they were provided seven household servants to cater their needs. The two men had an audience with the powerful ruler who wished them well in their endeavors, and he told Gisco that he was well aware of the valuable work his father and grandfather had done for Egypt. The visitors were impressed with the opulence and grandeur of the royal court, but they were more impressed by the efficient way administrative business was conducted.

Ptolemy II (Euergetes) and his close friends at court were stirred by the striking, handsome, young pentathlon champion who had displayed such intellectual and oratorical talent during his audience at court. All of them had mistresses, as was the custom. They searched for the most beautiful and charming slave they could find to give to Gisco as a mistress. They did this not only as a hospitable gesture for their esteemed guest whom they perceived, incorrectly, to be lonely, but they believed that two such magnificent people mating would produce an exceedingly beautiful offspring.

Until now, Gisco had been deeply preoccupied while pursuing his avowed goals. The psychological shock of seeing the brutal slaying of his father in Sardinia, events that followed, and his consuming drive to excel at everything he attempted, had driven him to an almost Spartan existence. As Chrysippus had taught him, sensual indulgence was not the path to true happiness. Gisco sincerely believed that the deep gratification derived from virtue and achievement was the only path to genuine happiness. Most important, that belief was consistent with his main purpose in life, the fulfillment of his sacred vows. His entire existence up to this point had revolved around that purpose. Furthermore, his mother, grandfather, his tyrannical tutors, and his father before, had guided him into a very chaste, disciplined existence. Gisco would not let anything distract him from his main goal in life.

When he first saw the mistress provided by Ptolemy, as she greeted him in his quarters, Gisco was stunned by her voluptuous beauty, charm, and grace. She was the most alluring woman he had ever seen. She stirred emotions that he had carefully controlled and had kept dormant within himself for a long time. He was embarrassed and perplexed. It was obvious that she, too, was uncomfortable and troubled by the situation in which she had been placed. She was embarrassed and obviously not accustomed to the role of a mistress. Gisco made no attempt to make love to her. He did not treat her as a slave, but treated her with the same respect and friendship that he would have shown the fine daughter of a family friend. As was the custom, she was called Tarra, short for Tarraco, the town on the northeast coast of Spain (now Tarragona) from which she came. She was seventeen years old and had been captured at sea with her older brother by pirates. Pirates sold the two captives on Alexandria's slave market a few days before she was given to Gisco. She had been bathed, royally dressed, bejeweled, anointed with exotic perfumes, given a beautiful coiffure, and her face was painted with enhancing cosmetics.

Gisco sincerely sympathized with her when she told him her story, and he promised to protect her from harm. He promised to have Tarra and her brother freed from slavery when it was politically feasible. He did not want to risk affronting the royal court so soon after his arrival. As days passed, Tarra's fear of him turned to affection. She had never seen such perfection in a man. He was handsome, charming, tender, intelligent, and he had a sincere interest in her welfare. She was intelligent, had a good sense of humor, and they had many enjoyable conversations. Her voluptuous charms, pleasant personality, exotic perfumes, and her constant, close proximity gradually caused him to fall in love with her, unwittingly, breaking through his strong psychological barriers against it. She reciprocated his love, and by the fourth week Gisco had lost his virginity and his heart.

During daylight hours, Gisco and Cirta focused their attention on studies they believed would help them achieve their avowed goals in some way. They had concluded earlier that some form of military action was the most logical course for them to take. They studied military tactics, strategy, weapons, science, military history, and fortifications as primary interests, but they also read about medicine, navigation, geography, engineering, architecture, and humanities as ancillary subjects. There was considerable information on all these subjects (although information was not necessarily filed under those modern categories). The original Ptolemy, Soter, was one of Alexander's principal generals during the great conqueror's campaigns, and Soter wrote his detailed history of those amazing military exploits. The two visitors studied his manuscripts intensely and memorized them.

Much time was spent exploring, as tourists, the

wonderful streets of Alexandria and its defensive preparations. The city had magnificent edifices and it was laid out in a gridiron of parallel streets, each of which had a subterranean canal. There were two 200-foot-wide streets that intersected the city, and they were lined with beautiful colonnades. There was a fortified wall around the metropolis. The two visitors were stimulated by the cosmopolitan nature of the city, with its Orientals, Greeks, Jews, Egyptians, Carthaginians, Syrians, Romans, and many other nationalities.

Gisco and Tarra lived together a year and a half before he had to return to Athens for his military training. He had made it clear to her that he could not consider marriage until his vows were fulfilled, and he had no idea how long that would take. However, he freed her from slavery and he arranged freedom for her brother. He booked a secure passage for them on a fast galley that was not vulnerable to pirates so they could safely return to Tarraco, Spain. Gisco told Tarra that he would come to see her after he had completed his military training in Greece, and that they may consider marriage at that time providing he was able to complete his plans for his future by then. Tarra and her brother were from an affluent family, and they insisted that they would be well cared for once they were home. The sad parting was very emotional as the ship for Spain left first. Gisco and Cirta left for home a few days later on a fast galley.

Greeks only sailed during the safe time of year when weather was expected to be good, as it was for their trip to Athens. Gisco missed Tarra constantly, but he had many important concerns on his mind that helped keep him distracted from his longing for her. First, he had already entered manhood, as he was almost nineteen years old. He was now an official citizen of Athens with attendant responsibilities. Under the law, he had to spend a year in military training, at the end of which he would be a member of the citizen-reserve army until age sixty. He would be subject to recall for active duty in emergencies during that time. That conflicted with his plans for revenge against Rome, unless Greece went to war with Rome, which seemed unlikely at that time. The government provided a way of avoiding military service, which he was reluctant to take at that time: a citizen could hire a mercenary soldier to take his place. Gisco was very patriotic and his status as a celebrity, hero of the pentathlon, and idol of Greek youth made him feel obligated to set an example for them. He decided to complete his military training and to continue his military obligation thereafter, until he could decide on a plan that would enable him to fulfill his vows. Sacred vows were very serious obligations in his superstitious society, and he did not want to risk an affront to the omnipotent gods that he believed were constantly watching over him.

From ages six through eighteen, Athenian boys' gymnastics training developed strong, hard, fit bodies as a resource for the military defense of their country. In their year of military training they were subjected to more intensive training and much more rigorous exercises. They had to learn to run for great distances in the hot sun while wearing 50 pounds of full armor, accurately throw spears, shoot arrows, fight with swords, and discipline themselves to adhere to fighting formations and military commands.

Gisco had completed his cavalry training long before he was eighteen, but he was required to take the formal basic training course of a foot soldier (a hoplite). All cavalrymen of the Greek (and Roman) army were expected to be able to take their positions as hoplites - heavily armed infantrymen - if needed. Each citizen soldier was allowed to bring along a trusted slave. Slaves were not normally given heavy armor, but Gisco treated Cirta as a brother. Both men participated in full regalia: the finest helmets, lances, swords, close-fitting breast plate armor, leg and knee armor, and a shield with the Greek letter alpha for "Athens" inscribed upon it. Cirta, the oldest of the trainees but well respected by the military authorities because of his demonstrated ability earlier with the cavalry, was allowed to participate. He was the most capable and knowledgeable of them all because of his years of fighting with the Numidian army. Heedless of his slight limp, he kept himself physically fit and athletically competent while helping Gisco. Of the forty new citizens in Gisco's class, and their forty slaves, Cirta was looked upon as the leader of the class, with Gisco following him as a close runner-up in the minds of the instructors and the students. Gisco found time to continue work on a plan for his future in tandem with his military training

After completing the arduous, compulsory military training, Gisco soon completed his master plan of action, which was to guide his activities for the next few years. International news about Roman expansionism in the west was beginning to concern many Greek citizens, particularly the army. In the barber shops and in the agora, which had contact with travelers returning from the western Mediterranean, there was much discussion about aggressive activities of the Romans. Many Athenians and other Greeks were beginning to view militant Rome as a menace to their freedom. After Rome had defeated the Greek, Pyrrhus, in 275

B.C., Greek settlements in southern Italy and Sicily were vulnerable to Roman aggression. In 238, Rome had annexed Corsica and Sardinia, after driving Carthaginians out of Sicily earlier. Again, it was military force that brought these people under Roman rule. It was the beginning of this last Roman campaign in Sardinia that resulted in the death of Gisco's father. Greeks looked on Romans as barbaric neighbors. Thus, when Gisco announced he was going to hire a mercenary soldier to free him from the remainder of his military duty, to enable him to go fight Romans, it was generally accepted as an honorable mission for the celebrity. He and Cirta had made many contributions toward improving the cavalry. They recently made many valuable suggestions for updating the local military doctrine, war machines, and tactics, as a result of their studies in Alexandria. Their energy, zest, and overall competence gave the Athenian army an impetus it hadn't had for many years. Their improvements were widely known and formally commended by the government. Athenians were aware of the brutal, unjust death of Gisco's father at the hands of the Romans, and of Gisco's vow for revenge at a sacred altar. By fighting Romans he would be helping Greece, though the country was not formally at war with Rome; Rome was a growing menace to the freedom of all Mediterranean nations.

Gisco had completed a definite master plan for implementing his vows. The plan, carefully researched in great detail for many months, required him to go to Spain and volunteer his services to the military commander, Hamilcar Barca, in that rich province of Carthage. He intended to try selling the commander, whom he knew was a bitter enemy of Rome, on a proposal for invading Italy by taking a land route from

Spain, through Gallia (France), over the Alps, then south into Italy, to conquer the hated Romans in their capital city, and stop Rome's oppressive military expansionism forever. Gisco had learned from his study that Hamilcar Barca was irate at Rome for driving him out of Sicily in 241 B.C. (ending the First Punic War), and for confiscating Carthaginian trading colonies in Sardinia and Corsica. Gisco believed that Hamilcar must be aware of the fact that Roman expansion would probably reach Spain's rich territory soon and that Carthage would have to fight Rome again. Gisco learned that Hamilcar had required his son, Hannibal Barca, to take an oath on a sacred alter in the temple of Melkart (Hercules) in Carthage, vowing eternal hatred of Rome, sealed with the boy's hand on a sacrificial lamb. The boy was only nine-year old. Hamilcar had taken the lad with him to Spain in 238, to train him to become a commander. Hamilcar went to Spain as governor and military commander of Carthage's few remaining trading colonies to protect them from the plundering by barbaric tribes. He also wanted to expand the rich trade there to compensate for the trading colonies lost to Rome.

Gisco expected his master plan to appeal to the Carthaginian officers in Spain, many of whom were veterans of fighting Romans in Sicily, for several reasons: it would avenge previous defeats at the hands of Romans; it would stop Rome's despotic expansionism which would surely reach Spain eventually; it would expand the wealth of Carthage at the expense of the hated Romans; and Gisco had convincing evidence that the plan would work.

The first piece of evidence that the plan would succeed was because the Roman army was unable to defeat the brilliant Hamilcar on land in Sicily during that war. The Carthaginian army was superior to the Roman army. Undefeated in combat on land by the Romans, Hamilcar was forced to sign an agreement that ceded Carthaginian colonies in Sicily to Rome because he was unable to obtain sufficient supplies by sea from Carthage to continue fighting. Rome's superior navy controlled the seas, and its stronger navy prevented supplies from being sent across the water. Rome's navy, not the Roman army, was the decisive factor in that war. Gisco's new plan eliminated need for support by sea from Carthage. Gisco's studies indicated that all logistics needed to fight the campaign - all soldiers, money, food, material, and animals - were already available in Spain or could be purchased in territories en route as the Carthaginian army marched from Spain, on land, to conquer Rome.

In addition, Gisco's studies had shown him that Roman military doctrine was highly vulnerable to modern concepts that he and Cirta had developed in Alexandria. The first weakness he noted in the Roman military establishment was its lack of competent, full-time, professional commanders at the head of its armies - as existed in the professional Carthaginian army. It was a policy of the Roman Government to elect two civilian consuls as co-commanders for its armies. These two commanders shared command in the field of battle when the combined armies were used. They were primarily politicians, not professional soldiers, and they were only elected for one year. Standards carried by Roman legions in battle were emblazoned with the letters "S.P.O.R." which stood for "The Senate and People of Rome." Traditionally, the Senate, whose members were aristocrats, elected one consul. The People of Rome, most of whom were not aristocrats and were represented by the Assembly of the People, traditionally elected the other consul. Consuls elected in this manner were usually civilian-politicians, not career military generals, and they typically knew only a limited number of parade-ground maneuvers. In combat, their reactions to various situations were very predictable, as outlined in the military manuals that Gisco and Cirta had memorized. Furthermore, because they often had opposing political views and were usually ambitious politicians, their military views often conflicted as well. (Note that this was not the Roman army that Caesar commanded much later, which learned much from his predecessors' mistakes).

Another important weakness of the Roman army was the lack of maneuverability of its massive formations of foot soldiers compared to the mobility of thousands of soldiers riding horses as used by the Numidian cavalry. Roman legions relied primarily on vast numbers of heavily-armed foot soldiers, highly disciplined to remain in formation in close and deep ranks, a formation called the manipular legion formation, a modification of the ancient Greek phalanx. They would be slow-moving and less flexible in combat when compared with a fast-moving, disciplined, and well-trained cavalry force. Romans relied on brute force, head-on fighting. Roman armies only used token cavalries, mostly made up of poorly-trained foreign troops, because Roman citizen-soldiers did not hold service in the cavalry with high regard. Cavalry did not play a decisive role in Roman military strategy. Gisco believed that maneuverability, as could be provided by large numbers of good horse-mounted soldiers, when combined with finessing tactics, could prevail over plodding Roman formations of foot soldiers. Each typical Roman legion employed 600 horse-mounted troops, and each army (usually four legions) had only 2,400. Gisco planned for use of four to five times that number of highly trained horse troops to support Hamilcar's experienced, professional Carthaginian army against the Romans.

Gisco's plan called for Hamilcar Barca to subdue and make allies of those wild territories of Spain that were not presently under Carthaginian control. Hamilcar was already doing this. This was necessary to make secure the rich Spanish silver mines, already owned by Carthage, that were being harassed by barbaric raiding parties. The silver mines would be an important source of money to finance the war. Furthermore, trade with the rich Spanish territories that Hamilcar subdued could provide war supplies for his army. Additional supplies could be obtained by purchases from tribes in territories outside Spain as the army passed through them en route to Rome. Gisco believed that Hamilcar already intended to subdue the wild tribes of Spain as part of his master plan for the Spanish peninsula.

Additional troops for the Carthaginian army could be recruited and trained as mercenaries, from tribes in Spain and from Celtic tribes in northern Italy. Many Spanish tribes had served as mercenary soldiers for centuries. The Celtic tribes in northern Italy had been fighting Roman occupation of their lands for many years. Northern Italian Celts (called Cisalpine Gauls by the Romans) bitterly disliked Romans, and they should be anxious to help Hamilcar's army defeat Rome.

In summary, Gisco reasoned that his plan would appeal to Hamilcar Barca because it would stop Roman expansionism which would have to be stopped anyway; it would avenge the defeat of Carthage in Sicily and the losses of Sardinia and Corsica; and it would expand the wealth of Carthage at the expense of the hated Romans. Gisco saw this plan as a means of fulfilling his own sacred vows.

Gisco and Cirta decided to travel with four horses to Spain overland from southern Italy to the Alps, then over the Alps through Gallia (France) to Spain, with an important stop at Tarraco on the way, to see his beloved Tarra. The trip was about 1,200 miles on horseback. Traveling this route allowed them to reconnoiter the proposed invasion route, gather information about Roman military installations and stockpiles of food, and assess the prospects for foraging the land by the invading Carthaginian army.

They left Athens early in 223 B.C. There were many Greeks throughout Italy, and Greece was not at war with Rome. Romans had a high regard for the more cultured Greeks, thus Gisco was able to mingle freely with Romans as he collected data. Gisco had studied the native tongue of Rome (Latin), and he had much practice using it. He found many Greek teachers, artists, and tradesmen who provided information, and Gisco obtained some reliable sources of information (spies) which would be useful in the future. He arranged for agents to send him a steady flow of information about the Roman Senate's actions affecting Roman military forces. He also arranged for a steady supply of dossiers on top commanders, describing their strengths and weaknesses. He paid his agents generously, with a promise of steady payment for information received from them in the future. He told the agents that he would have them contacted during the next year by crews of merchant trading vessels which plied the Mediterranean ports regularly.

The two travelers criss-crossed Italy, being careful

to visit major military forts and grain storage sites. They examined the rich Padus (now called Po) valley, and examined a route over the Alps to the Rhone River which the Carthaginian army could take. They contacted leaders of many important tribes of Cisalpine Gauls, assessing their potential as allies against Rome for future reference. As expected, these tribes hated Romans, they had a long history of fighting them, and they would welcome any help in their continuing fight. Gisco was encouraged by the many rich Roman military storehouses he found, which he judged to be vulnerable for plunder, to provide supplies for the Carthaginian army. After passing over the Alps, the two companions followed the Rhone to Massilia (now Marseilles). As they left Massilia, finally headed for Spain, Gisco became excited by the prospect of seeing his beloved Tarra again. They reconnoitered the southern coast of Gallia, then passed over the Pyranees to Tarraco, Spain, reaching it by late fall, 223 B.C.

Tarraco was a rich seaport village because of its flax trade and other products. It had a large population of Massiliote Greeks - Greeks from Massilia. Tarra and her brother were Massiliote Greeks. If authorities in Alexandria had known this earlier, she and her brother would not have been sold as slaves. Greeks did not use other Greeks as slaves. However, the swarthy complexions that Tarra and her brother had acquired from their sea voyage, and their unfamiliar accents, caused authorities to disbelieve their story. Tarra and her brother were operating a profitable third generation trading business, trading in flax and other commodities in the busy trade center of the popular seaport.

Tarra was in the lovely garden of her villa when

Gisco surprised her with his sudden appearance. The two embraced enthusiastically, and the beautiful Tarra nearly fainted with delight. They had much to talk about, as it had been two years since they had parted.

A few minutes later, Tarra called to a maid and whispered something in her ear. The maid soon returned with a little boy, able to walk by himself. Tarra introduced Gisco to his son, Gisco II. Overcome with happiness, Gisco picked the boy up and hugged and kissed him. Tarra and Gisco were married, and they spent an enjoyable four months together before Gisco and Cirta had to continue their journey. Tarra and their son taught Gisco how to laugh again and how to relax, something he had forgotten. They had many amusing stories and hearty laughs together.

He told Tarra that once he was established with the Carthaginian army, he would visit her as often as possible. Gisco suggested that if Carthage and Rome should go to war in the next few years, she should plan to take the young boy to Athens where they could be cared for by his family in a comfortable and safe fashion. Tarra's parents were deceased. Gisco II could attend school in Athens, and they could live with his mother, Procne, who would be anxious to see them. They would be safe from the war, far away from the potential battle zone.

After another emotional farewell, the two crusaders mounted their horses and continued south toward the Carthaginian army's winter quarters at New Carthage (now Cartagena), on the southeast coast of Spain. They left in the early spring of 222 B.C.

Chapter 2

PREPARATION FOR ITALY
(222 - 218 B.C.)

The spring weather was magnificent. The two travelers rode their horses south, down the picturesque east coast of Spain in March of 222 B.C. Heavy winter clothing was no longer needed because the sun was so bright and warm. Wild flowers were beginning to bloom in masses of color, birds were singing, farmers were plowing their fields, and people were tending grapevines and olive groves. They followed the coastline trail, keeping the beautiful blue Mediterranean constantly on their left. They passed many small villages as they made the 275-mile journey from Tarraco to New Carthage, the Carthaginian winter camp on the southeast coast.

Road traffic and dust increased as they approached the huge Carthaginian army camp in the fertile valley northeast of the splendid harbor of New Carthage. The enormous camp was a spectacular, colorful sight bursting with activity. It had thousands of brightly-colored tents, thousands of soldiers in many different, vivid costumes, and many campfires cooking spicy noon meals. More than sixty elephants were performing various chores around camp as expert mahouts rode on their backs and guided them. Thousands of horses were seen in a separate area at the edge of the campground. There was an occasional trumpet of an elephant, neighing of horses, cursing of mule drivers, shouting of orders by commanders, murmured voices of soldiers, and intermittent blasts of military trumpets. The spicy aromas, sights, and sounds caused excitement to permeate the air as Gisco and Cirta rode their horses through the immense camp. The two men were impressed by the industry, energy, and obvious enthusiasm of soldiers they passed. The scene intoxicated them with eagerness and hopeful anticipation. Soon they would learn if their plan could be accepted by the Carthaginians.

Gisco obtained directions to the headquarters pavilion where he located the administrative officer responsible for arranging audiences with the army commander. The officer turned out to be a Greek from a small village near Athens who recognized Gisco's name and fame. He gave Gisco a warm welcome, and after a short discussion, he escorted Gisco and Cirta to be introduced to a charming, handsome, commander named Hasdrubal Pulcher. Gisco later learned that the commander was popularly called "Hasdrubal the Splendid" and that he was the son-in-law of the deceased Hamilcar Barca. The administrative officer gave Gisco an adulatory introduction to his busy commander after which Gisco explained the purpose of their visit - to volunteer their services to his army. He gave a brief summary of their military qualifications, and he also explained that he had developed an important military plan and interesting information that he believed the commander would want to hear. Hasdrubal was very polite, but he said that he was too busy to hear the plan. He said that he would listen to it the next morning. He had already scheduled a meeting of his close advisers for the morning, and he invited Gisco to attend that meeting. He told Gisco that he could meet many of the officers of the army at the same time that he made a brief summary of his plan for them. The two visitors were ushered to temporary quarters in a nearby tent.

Gisco was curious about Hasdrubal, and he wanted to learn more about him, including the background concerning how he came to be governor of the Carthaginian province in Spain and commander of its army. The last he had heard, Hamilcar Barca held those positions. That evening Gisco sought out some Carthaginian officers whom he found sitting around a nearby campfire, and he was invited to join them.

From his reading in Alexandria, Gisco already knew that Phoenicians had established trading centers along the coasts of Spain long before 800 B.C., and Phoenicians were the first people in history to establish colonies overseas, away from their homeland in Tyre (now in Lebanon). That was done by free enterprise; that is, it was done by individual merchant traders who were anxious to make a profit by expanding their trade, not by the planned direction of the Phoenician government. Merchants seeking to expand their trading businesses created trade centers around the coasts of the Mediterranean to trade with local inhabitants for products that could be transported in Phoenician ships and sold elsewhere.

Many of these trade-centers were on Spanish coasts and the richest of them was Carthage, on the African coast (now in Tunisia). Over the centuries, many Phoenician merchants gradually expanded their trade-centers inland, and many took control of mines and agricultural areas in the rich Spanish interior to provide a steady supply of commercial goods for trade. One of the richest and earliest Spanish trading colonies was Gades (now Cadiz) on the southwest coast of Spain which became a base for Phoenician exploration in the Atlantic region. Phoenician traders ventured as far north as Iceland and as far west as the Canary Islands seeking trade. When the Phoenician motherland, Tyre, was conquered by Persians, it lost hegemony over its far-flung trade settlements, and the richest Phoenician settlement, Carthage, became dominant over remaining trading centers.

After he returned from the war in Sicily (First Punic War), Hamilcar Barca saw that many rich Carthaginian settlements in Spain were being harassed by raids from unruly, barbaric tribes coming from the interior of Spain. The raids were destroying the flourishing trade of Carthage at a time that its economy was already suffering from the costs of the Sicilian war and from the loss of trading colonies in Sicily, Sardinia, and Corsica to the Romans. Hamilcar went to Spain, organized an army, and he put down the uprisings, making the trade-centers secure. He brought stability and order to one-third of the Iberian peninsula, and he began to develop the rich territory for Carthage by importing engineers and craftsmen from Africa. He built canals, developed many mines, cut timber, and built an economic infrastructure for the new province. Natives were recruited and trained in various skills and trades, and many tribes that had recently been fighting Carthaginians were happily integrated into the new economy.

Hamilcar had three sons: Hannibal the oldest, Hasdrubal (another Hasdrubal), and Mago the youngest. The brilliant general carefully trained his sons for war and to hate Romans. He taught them that Rome would be the most important enemy of Carthage, and that Rome's insatiable appetite for expansion would eventually reach the rich territory of Spain. Hamilcar, a visionary, instilled in his sons the conviction that war with Rome was inevitable, but that this eventual conflict was in the national interest of Carthage, not a conflict to satisfy personal ambition or aggrandizement. The oldest son, Hannibal, became obsessed by the strategic issues his father taught him. He hated Romans, but his hate was more intellectual than emotional, as he was a very intelligent, mentally-balanced lad. Hamilcar paid special attention to training his oldest son, whom he kept at his side from the time he was a small child, grooming him to succeed his father as commander. Unfortunately, Hamilcar was killed in battle at the early age of 42, in 228 B.C., and Hannibal was only eighteen, too young to assume his father's responsibilities. Command of the army and rule of the province was given to Hannibal's brother-in-law, Hasdrubal the Splendid, who had married Hamilcar's older daughter.

Hasdrubal was an owner of mines, a competent manager and capitalist, rather than a dedicated military leader. He had quite a different temperament from either Hamilcar or Hannibal. He was a charming, handsome, natural diplomat, disposed to accomplish his goals by diplomacy and negotiation rather than by military force. He didn't have the deep hatred for Romans that the Barca family had. Although he was a competent military commander, he didn't participate much in warfare with his army once he became commander, preferring to delegate that task to others. He spent most of his time managing the administrative affairs of the province. He concentrated on developing Spain's profitability by expanding its mining, agricultural, and fishing production and its trade.

Hasdrubal made strategic alliances that obviated the need for use of military force whenever possible. Though he did not fully trust Romans, and he was aware of the lingering feelings against Romans that veterans of the Sicilian war still harbored, he made a treaty with Rome. The treaty provided Rome all claim to territory north of the Ebro River that runs across northern Spain, and he agreed not to take his army north of that river. In return, Romans agreed to allow Carthage all claim to territory south of the Ebro. Neither Rome nor Carthage had conquered much of the territory agreed upon at the time of the treaty.

In view of his recent agreement with Rome, and his general inclination toward diplomacy rather than war, Hasdrubal could not be expected to favor Gisco's plan for attacking Rome. However, Gisco did not know about Hasdrubal's treaty with Rome as he prepared to present his plan to the commander and his staff of officers.

The next morning, the charming Carthaginian commander and governor of the province greeted Gisco in the army headquarters pavilion where he had assembled his most trusted officers for a routine meeting to discuss daily problems. When the routine business was concluded, Hasdrubal introduced Gisco to his men and told them that the young Greek would present a military plan that he had developed over many years of intense study. The handsome, athletic, erudite Gisco became as charming as the commander, and he made an eloquent, stirring presentation of his plan, supporting every major aspect of it with logic, backed with statistics and calculations. As a prelude, he also made a convincing argument showing why it was expedient for Carthage to stop Roman aggression soon. It was inevitable, he said, for Rome and Carthage to eventually be at war.

The entire audience, including Hasdrubal, was moved by his brilliant, stimulating, incisive analysis.

They admired his oratorical skill and his obvious superior knowledge of military tactics and strategy. His detailed, practical planning for logistics, particularly, was a masterpiece and it astounded the listeners. Gisco's genius was obvious to all. After many questions by officers concerning the plan, which he adroitly answered, Hasdrubal expressed his admiration and appreciation for Gisco's great work. He patiently explained why he could not adopt such a plan so soon after making his agreement with Rome. If Rome should attack Carthage, then Gisco's plan would be a serious consideration. Hasdrubal was quick to perceive Gisco's unusual qualities, and he invited him to join the many other Greeks already in his growing army. He told Gisco that he was expanding his army for security reasons, to subdue the barbaric tribes south of the Ebro so the economy of Spain would be secure. He wanted to develop the entire Spanish peninsula south of the Ebro.

Hasdrubal acknowledged the potential threat of further Roman aggression, as Gisco had made very clear, and he stated that a larger Carthaginian army would be a safeguard against such an eventuality. He told Gisco that he had a great need for a man with Gisco's superior qualifications, and he asked the Greek to consider joining his army. Hasdrubal asked Gisco to give him a decision within the next few days.

Gisco was deeply disappointed by this turn of events. He had high hopes of fulfilling his vows by fighting Romans with the army of Carthage, but with Hasdrubal's treaty with the Romans, that did not appear possible. He was feeling deeply depressed and perplexed as he and Cirta headed toward the temporary quarters that Hasdrubal's staff had prepared for them. As they were approaching their assigned tent, a very tall, handsome, young Carthaginian approached them. He said his name was Hannibal and that he was among the officers who had listened to his presentation. He told Gisco, privately, that he and most of his fellow officers thought it was a sound plan, particularly because it eliminated the need for a strong navy, Carthage's prime weakness. Speaking excellent Greek with the refined accent of a highly-educated man, he explained that he and many of his fellow officers had discussed a similar plan, although they had not developed it in as much detail as Gisco had achieved with his plan. Most of his fellow officers believed that it could be successfully accomplished. Hannibal was quick to perceive Gisco's discouragement and depression because Hasdrubal couldn't use his plan so soon after making a treaty with Rome. Hannibal reminded Gisco that his plan required that Carthage control all wild Spanish country as a prerequisite to making war on Rome, to secure the necessary resources to support the war. Hannibal told Gisco that at the present rate progress was being made, it would take at least two years to achieve. He urged Gisco and Cirta to accept Hasdrubal's invitation to join his army for two years, as they could get some practical training in the field while they helped Carthage achieve its current goals. Hannibal said, further, that during that time the untrustworthy and expansion-minded Romans could possibly renege on their treaty, causing Carthage to be at war with Rome again. If that were to happen, Gisco's plan would be useful. After discussing the matter between them, Gisco and Cirta decided to join the army as the only practical alternative available to them.

    Hannibal and Gisco had an immediate professional affinity for each other. Hannibal took an instinctive liking for the talented, well-spoken, personable Gisco, and Gisco was electrified by the obvious and powerful charisma of this tall, dark, steely eyed, twenty-five-year-old son of Hamilcar. Gisco had never met a man like him. Hannibal had intense, penetrating, fascinating eyes; he was powerfully but gracefully built; he was mentally quick; he had a deep, commanding, cultured voice; and he appeared sincerely interested in what happened to Gisco and Cirta. Hannibal was billeted near them and acted as Gisco's sponsor by introducing him to the other officers and orienting him within the organization. Gisco soon learned that although this tall Carthaginian was very energetic, determined, and intense, he had an enjoyable gift of laughter and a sardonic sense of humor.

Gisco was impressed by the number of languages Hannibal spoke fluently as he introduced the young Greek to the different tribes as they journeyed around camp during the next few days. He spoke excellent, cultured Greek, as he had a private Greek tutor most of his life. He spoke his native Phoenician, he spoke many dialects of the Iberian tribes as he had lived among them for many years, and he was able to converse with Gauls. The son of Hamilcar was a popular charmer and he had a great rapport with everyone they met in camp. It was clear he was sincerely devoted to them, they to him, and that he was an unusually charismatic leader.

As they toured the huge camp, Gisco noticed there were many ethnic groups, each in its separate part of the camp, speaking its own language, wearing its own colorful costume, and flying its own brightly colored standards and banners. There were thousands of cloaked Numidian cavalry soldiers from Africa with their fast Arabian horses; thousands of Celtiberian cavalry troops with their sturdy, stocky Iberian horses; tens of thousands of foot soldiers from various Iberian and Celtiberian tribes of Spain; proud slingers from the Balearic Islands - who were getting slinging practice by launching missiles from leather slings at distant targets; and a small core of Carthaginians, mostly officers, wearing their distinctive crimson capes. On the outskirts of camp was an area where innumerable cattle, oxen, mules, elephants, and large war machines were situated.

Hannibal's attire, when he was not wearing his distinctive battle armor, was much the same as his fellow Carthaginians, except that he wore special Spanish riding boots that the others did not. He and his fellow Africans were wearing their typical, plain Tyrians (long, straight, woolen robes with long sleeves as worn in Carthage) during the cold weather. Hannibal and others were beginning to adopt Spanish riding costumes during warmer weather. Their clothing was drab and crude compared with the refined quality of the attire worn by Gisco and Cirta. This caused the two newcomers to appear much different from the others. In the spring and summer, the Greek and his companion wore stylishly draped chitons which were lengths of fine, bright white, silk material without seams, fastened by ornate gold clasps so that arms and legs were left bare.

Gisco hadn't given his dress much thought until he and Hannibal came upon a group of Carthaginian troops that were watching a wrestling match. A huge, 300-pound, muscular Carthaginian had just defeated one of his fellows as he looked up to see the nattily dressed Gisco watching the match with Hannibal. The enormous wrestler made a loud, snide remark to

Hannibal about Gisco's femininity, and he questioned Gisco's value as a soldier and his fighting ability. In a good-natured manner, Gisco loudly stated that he admired the wrestling skills of the man, and that he would like to test his own limited fighting skills against such an accomplished wrestler, who was much larger, more powerful, and obviously more talented than himself. A loud cheer went up from the raucous crowd of spectators that encircled them, as the 190-pound Gisco quickly disrobed and stood in the ready position to engage the obvious bully. The large wrestler took the challenge and rapidly moved toward Gisco. The pentathlon champion, using his years of experience gained from competing against more formidable opponents than this one, moved faster than the Carthaginian hulk could react. Gisco adeptly and effortlessly used the momentum of the oncoming hulk to quickly catapult the tyrant violently to the ground, on his back. Gisco rapidly jumped on top of the stunned bully, pinned him to the earth, and grasped him in a tortuous lock of his giant arm, causing him to shout his surrender, in agony, to the tumultuous cheers of the soldiers watching the spectacle. Gisco got up, helped his dazed opponent to his feet, then dressed without having ruffled a hair of his neatly arranged coiffure. Then, he and the amazed Hannibal continued their inspection tour of the camp, leaving the dumbfounded wrestler and the admiring audience watch them depart. Hannibal was impressed.

Hasdrubal was committed to expanding the size of the army, and he gave much of the responsibility for recruitment and training, as needed to meet its growing size, to Hannibal. This allowed Hasdrubal more time to administer the province. Busy Hannibal relied heavily on the talents and experience of Gisco and

Cirta to help him carry out his duties, and he made Gisco his trusted lieutenant, giving him more responsibility when new campaigns were initiated in the spring of 222 B.C.

Hannibal was recognized by all as the most capable, courageous, and energetic commander available to Hasdrubal. He had been well trained and groomed for command all his life by the best teacher available, his father, one of the great commanders of all time. Hannibal had lived among the Iberians and other troops since the age of nine. He spoke their languages fluently, and was intimately familiar with their customs. He enjoyed the loyal support, trust, confidence, and admiration of all allied ethnic groups, including the Carthaginians. He had dauntless determination, was the first to make contact in battle, and was the last to leave the battlefield. He was always trying to recruit and train new soldiers and improve the combat effectiveness of the army. He appreciated the sound advice that Gisco was able to give him regarding alternative tactics and weapons, and the two spent many hours discussing military matters.

Hannibal learned much from Hasdrubal about the power of diplomacy and the use of emissaries. He learned to send agents into a wild territory well in advance of his intended annexation of it, to gain its acceptance by local leaders, either by gifts, promises, or by subtle threats. His agents would reconnoiter the territory, bringing back many facts about strengths and weaknesses of the local army, the type of terrain, resources available, animal foraging areas, and other detail before he marched his army into the area to take control. As was true of most Carthaginians, Hannibal did not enjoy war. That was the most important reason Carthage, a nation of traders, had to hire mercenary soldiers to do their fighting. Hannibal only resorted to force as a last resort, and he never committed his troops to battle unless there was no reasonable alternative and the odds were in favor of his winning without heavy losses to his troops.

As progress continued with the pacification of the wild territory south of the Ebro River, force was not often necessary. However, when force was necessary, and the local tribe resisted with force, Hannibal would make a horrible example of it for other barbaric tribes that might have been contemplating resistance. He would devastate the capital of the tribe that resisted. This reduced the amount of bloodshed by both sides over the long run because it reduced the number of wild communities willing to resist with force. News of the devastation traveled fast to other territories of Spain, after being greatly exaggerated in transmission, causing other leaders to be more disposed to diplomatic solutions.

Once a territory was annexed, Hannibal would make a further, more favorable example for leaders of other territories that were not yet annexed. He would treat annexed tribes very fairly and humanely and establish a profitable trade with them. Hannibal was shrewd enough to ensure that allied tribes enjoyed economic profit as a result of their allegiance to Carthage. A profitable trade relationship was usually established with each territory to create a viable economic base for Carthage, as well as for his army. He generally made three demands of tribes: pay a tribute (tax); supply needed provisions or trading items in return for just payment in silver; and supply strong men for his army, also to be paid regularly in silver and other booty. The young men Hannibal recruited from families of recently annexed tribes would later return home on furloughs from the army with money, good clothes, and tales of adventure and success, attractive examples for other young men. Recruits taken from the tribes greatly reduced the tribe's ability and desire to make war in an uprising against Carthage. Losing their young men reduced the tribal army's manpower, and the recruited men also served as hostages against tribal revolts.

Gisco learned much by watching Hannibal in action. Hannibal stimulated an electric synergism felt by all around him particularly in the heat of combat. He had a dynamic personality, and his presence made his men feel insuperable against what sometimes appeared to be great odds against them. They had confidence in knowing that he would not take them into battle unless he believed the odds were strongly in their favor. They always knew Hannibal had some master plan that usually had a surprise in it. This confidence was nurtured by Hannibal over many years of fighting hand-to-hand with his soldiers, and his past track record supported their confidence. Hannibal left very little to chance, and he seldom engaged in battle without detailed reconnaissance of the enemy, the battlefield, and without first planning to put the terrain, weather, and psychological factors in his favor. He usually trained his men thoroughly, and each man knew exactly what he was supposed to do before each battle. Each man was thoroughly indoctrinated to have the discipline to do what was expected of him because he knew that success of the entire campaign depended upon each one of the team doing his part. Hannibal always tried to plan a surprise or an ambush for his enemy. Hannibal seldom did what his enemy expected him to do. Doing the unexpected to confuse the enemy became his trademark. Gisco and Cirta soon succumbed to the charm, competence, and selfless devotion of the cultured, wise Hannibal, and they became his devoted servants.

Gisco was beginning to make significant contributions to the military efficiency and success of campaigns. He was becoming known as the "miracle worker" among the superstitious troops. His wide knowledge enabled him to produce results that amazed and mystified most of the officers and men because they did not understand the scientific principles underlying his inventions and solutions to problems. Hannibal, too, was impressed by Gisco's achievements; however, Hannibal knew from his many conversations with Gisco that these "miracles" were not the result of some supernatural power he possessed, but the result of logical application of extensive knowledge gained from his intensive studies and experience. His father and grandfather had nourished in Gisco the ability and the desire to make practical application of what he had learned. He was constantly searching for ways to make improvements. For example, he was able to improve the smelting and forging techniques of the metal workers, allowing the metallurgy and design of shields, armor, spears, and swords to be enhanced. The Spanish swords were made superior to any used by Romans (or any other army) by Gisco's selection of exceptionally pure Spanish iron. He showed the blacksmiths how to cold hammer the swords into double-edged swords that had such hard, sharp blades they would cut through shields and helmets, through to the bone, without losing their edge.

The swords were so successful that Hannibal adopted them for his Carthaginian troops. These swords would later be given a major share of the credit for many victories. Gisco made catapults more accurate, with longer range - more than 300 meters - by improving materials used in their construction and by improving their mechanical advantage. Leather armor worn by elephants on their heads and sides was also improved by Gisco. He was able to build siege towers that were lighter, more mobile, quicker, and easier to build. He improved the missiles that were thrown by catapults, adding fireballs, lead balls, and metal darts as ammunition.

Hasdrubal and Hannibal were among Gisco's growing number of admirers. They recognized his ability to inspire and lead troops in combat. Many new recruits for the army were trained by Gisco and Cirta, and they fought shoulder-to-shoulder with them in numerous battles and sieges. Gisco and his companion gained wide respect and confidence throughout the army. Their ability and courage in combat was widely recognized, as Gisco emulated his idol, Hannibal.

By late fall, 222 B.C., the army returned to its winter quarters in New Carthage after a successful campaign season. Many of the Spanish troops were released to return to their homes for the winter. Gisco and Cirta returned to Tarraco for a joyful reunion with Tarra, little Gisco, and Tarra's brother. They spent many happy days together, and Gisco told Tarra of their campaigns. One campaign had taken Gisco near the mines of the Silver Mountains (now called Sierra Morena) to pacify some of the barbaric Carpetanians to the north. They had passed near the citadel of Castulo. Tarra excitedly told Gisco that the ruling family of that fortress was closely related to her family. The colony had been founded by Greek immigrants from Delphi, and the present king, ruler of the Olcades, was her uncle. She asked Gisco to give a letter to her cousin, princess Imilce, when he passed through Castulo again. They were close friends.

In spring, 221 B.C., Gisco and Cirta returned to New Carthage and a joyous reunion with their combat comrades. They had developed a rich camaraderie, and there was a festive celebration. There was much training to be accomplished before the new year's campaign could begin because there were many new recruits from tribes that had recently been fighting Carthaginians. After being conquered, or annexed by peaceful means, recruits were lured into the army by the pay, food, clothing, adventure, and colorful pageantry of the awesome, victorious spectacle they beheld in their hometowns and villages as Hannibal's army paraded by them. Going into the army saved many from a fate of dull, drab, poverty filled lives in their crudely developed home towns where life was very harsh.

There was a huge problem of coordinating actions and commands that Hannibal wanted to give this polyglot army. Hannibal normally gave his commands in Phoenician for his officers, mostly Carthaginians, who were immediately below him in rank. Then, the command or instructions had to be restated by officers down the organization in many different languages. After much training and practice, officers of different tribes came to know the meaning of commands in Phoenician before they were restated in their own language, reducing the reaction time required. Routine maneuvers were announced by trumpet calls as much as possible. Hannibal would visit each tribe during training and explain the tactics in the tribe's own language for the routine actions. Gisco and Hannibal were planning ahead to the day they may be fighting Romans, and speed of maneuver was one of the advantages they were depending upon against the truculent, slower-moving Roman legions.

Hannibal and Gisco gradually learned they had much in common. First, each had sworn eternal hatred of Romans on a sacred altar at a young age. Each had developed a real, consuming hate of them. The two warriors reaffirmed their common vows together, many times, at sacred altars in religious temples, and they began to worship the same gods together. Hannibal transported a shrine and carved idols of their common gods in a small tent when they traveled. Hannibal had originally sworn his vows before the god Melkart, but he had recently adopted Greek gods, in addition to traditional Carthaginian gods.

The two often discussed Gisco's plan for invading Italy, frequently debating various aspects in minute detail. Both viewed the plan as a means of fulfilling their vows, and as a means of stopping Roman expansion in the Mediterranean that both believed was inevitable. Both believed Rome's aggressive expansion was a long-range threat to their homelands, Greece and Carthage. Both men had superior intellects and they normally thought and planned far ahead of their fellow officers. Hannibal, three years older than Gisco, began treating his trusted lieutenant with the affection of an older brother and Gisco warmly responded. Gisco carefully avoided being disobedient, presumptuous, or otherwise taking advantage of their close rapport. Hannibal had no one he could confide in or trust as much as he could Gisco. His only other close confidant, Hasdrubal, did not come on military campaigns with them, and he was usually preoccupied with affairs related to ruling the commercial and political affairs of the province. Hannibal's brothers had other duties that kept them busy.

Hannibal and Gisco had much the same work ethic: they worked long hours while their fellow officers often debauched with wine and women. Both men were sexually abstemious (and later, both were monogamous in marriage). Both were highly cultured and educated. Since Gisco was so widely read and knowledgeable about many subjects, Hannibal enjoyed picking his brain for information and for testing his own plans and theories. Both were superior athletes, hand-to-hand fighters, and they enjoyed competing with each other in games as a means of keeping fit and proficient, a necessity for survival in combat. They ate food only when necessary to retain their health, and they could sleep anytime they chose, on any surface, including hard ground in cold weather. Both enjoyed mingling with their troops, and eating and sleeping among them. Hannibal often wore different wigs and attire so that he wouldn't be recognized by his men, so as not to inhibit their conversations. He wanted to keep in touch with their true sentiments and thoughts. The two warriors indulged in one ostentation: they wore the most exquisite, gold-inlaid armor into combat, and their horses were the most magnificent, well-groomed animals available with the finest silver and gold trappings, making them conspicuous during maneuvers. As did the other Carthaginian officers, Hannibal and Gisco wore brilliant crimson capes and plumes on their helmets.

One of the first campaigns in 221 B.C. took them north of the Silver Mountains. As they passed near Castulo, Gisco told Hannibal about his wife's request that he deliver a letter to her cousin, Imilce, at the citadel. Hannibal decided to accompany Gisco, because his father had been an acquaintance of the king and he had met the king many times. Hannibal vaguely remembered meeting a small girl named Imilce. The two rode up to the citadel, which was built of massive stone blocks. Wearing their magnificent combat armor, they identified themselves and were admitted inside the fortress walls by the steward. Gisco announced that he had a letter for princess Imilce, and she soon appeared. Imilce immediately impressed both men with her mature beauty, grace, and excellent Greek. She was now eighteen years old, no longer the small child that Hannibal had remembered. Imilce read the letter happily, and thanked Gisco. She introduced him to her father, the king, and he invited them join them for supper then stay the night. The two men bathed, put on clean clothes and perfume, then joined the family for a sumptuous meal. Imilce was allowed to join the group because Gisco, who was married to her close friend and cousin, was there. At supper, Hannibal displayed his good sense of humor by telling many stories that made them laugh heartily. Afterward, all of them relaxed, exchanged stories, drank wine and sang songs to accompaniment of a lyre. Imilce had a beautiful singing voice, and she was a very intelligent girl. Hannibal was deeply affected by her charms, and he told Gisco about it. Gisco commented that Imilce would make a good wife for him, not only because of her physical beauty, charm, and intelligence, but because a political alliance in the area, which bordered between territory occupied by Carthage on the south and barbaric tribes to the north that had a rapprochement with the king, would be politically advantageous. Another factor, the fact that Imilce was a Greek, would also add an advantageous political dimension because there were many Greek settlements in the part of Spain south of the Ebro.

The two warriors had to depart very early the next

morning before the rest of the household was awake. However, Imilce met them as they were leaving to give Gisco a letter for Tarra. It was obvious that Imilce warmly reciprocated Hannibal's feelings for her, and it was obvious to both men that the letter was not the only reason she arose so early in the morning to see them off. She could have had a servant perform that chore.

Hannibal gave Gisco more responsibility that season, putting him in charge of many smaller military operations. He was becoming more confident of Gisco's competence, courage, and energy in planning and leading combat campaigns. He noted how warmly the polyglot assortment of troops, most of whom Gisco and Cirta had trained, responded to his fiery leadership. Gisco developed a reputation among the soldiers for his competence, as his success was becoming an unbroken habit. It was the custom for armies of all nations to share part of the plunder gained from combat victories with their soldiers. It was a means of motivating them to victory. Enemy tribal leaders who had resisted pacification were required to surrender their wealth to the victors. Gisco won much booty in this manner for his troops. Gisco learned to speak their languages, to learn their customs, and to know what stimulated them. Hannibal was a great teacher for Gisco in developing these skills. Though the troops were mercenary, Hannibal's army was admirably disciplined, and the mercenary spirit was subordinate to the spirits of camaraderie, loyalty, and professional, unselfish cooperation. Carthaginians, Celts, and Iberians had servile attitudes toward those in authority. Although the Celts were less so, most of the troops were humble, superstitious people, and they looked upon the great talents of Hannibal and

Gisco, as well as the other officers, as powers provided by their supernatural gods. Most of the soldiers were in awe of their gods and in great fear of their omnipotent, supernatural powers. Thus, they were disposed to be obedient and respectful.

Hannibal and Gisco were returning from a routine skirmish when they were greeted by a special messenger from New Carthage. They were given the shocking news that Hasdrubal had been killed by a disgruntled native. They returned to New Carthage where they were met by a gathering of officers. The officers elected Hannibal, unanimously, to be their new commander. This decision was quickly confirmed by the government in Carthage. Thus the twenty-five-year-old suddenly became ruler of this Spanish province of Carthage and commander of its army.

Hannibal was quick to act. The early deaths of Hamilcar and Hasdrubal convinced him that he may not have much time left to invade Rome and fulfill his sacred vows before his own death. He discussed his intentions with Gisco, then he called his trusted officers to a meeting. He knew the temperament of most of them, veterans of the war in Sicily, and others who had heard Gisco's plan. He believed that a vast majority would be in favor of the invasion of Italy, and those few that would be against it could remain behind as a garrison in Spain. He told his officers that he was planning to implement Gisco's plan for invading Italy, and he explained his reasons. As expected, there was general acceptance, but a few officers had reservations about the chances for its success. Hannibal's quartermaster, in particular, said that he could not possibly feed the size of army needed on such a long march. He said, sarcastically, that it could only be done if the troops resorted to cannibalism. Gisco quickly and cleverly countered his allegations with numerous accurate, obvious facts and calculations about daily sustenance rates for men and animals, as shown by the records used over the last two years. He showed how much the pack animals could carry and how much could be purchased from tribes en route to Italy. Gisco made it clear that it could be done with much to spare, provided ample preparation was made in Spain before beginning the march. Everyone agreed that once they were in Italy, they could get adequate supplies from their allies. Foraging on Roman land and plundering military storehouses that the Roman army situated every day's march from Rome would provide more.

The vast majority of officers were convinced it could be done, and they were anxious to start preparations. They had to obtain an ample supply of silver, oxen, corn, and other supplies available in Spain before beginning the march. Gisco listed names of tribes and their leaders who would provide additional troops and provisions along the intended marching path. It was generally conceded that Hannibal would have to complete annexation of remaining territories south of the Ebro before leaving for Italy. This was necessary to make the rich silver mines and other needed supplies secure and to recruit additional soldiers that would be required for the campaign.

An army of at least 140,000 men was the initial estimate of what was needed to keep Spain secure against attack, keep lines of supply and communication with the expeditionary army open to Italy, and send to Carthage to help with defense of the motherland, guarding against an invasion by Rome. The officers established a target size of the army of 124,000 foot soldiers; 16,000 cavalry; and 60 elephants.

These, with additional allies acquired en route to Rome, were expected to be enough to accomplish the task. Fifty warships were planned to be built in New Carthage to maintain communications between Carthage and Spain. Everyone agreed that secrecy was the most important aspect of their plan: Rome must be surprised and not given the opportunity to prepare. It was desired that Rome learn about the invasion only after Hannibal's troops arrived in Italy. It was agreed that no one outside the present close circle of trusted officers would be told of the plan. Soldiers would not be told of the plan until they were well on their way to Italy.

Gisco's previous reconnaissance of Italy had given Hannibal a general estimate of resources available en route, as well as names of Cisalpine Gauls in northern Italy who had expressed a desire to have Carthaginians help them in their long fight against Rome. This information was a few years old, so Hannibal immediately dispatched emissaries to contact them to verify their current intentions. Emissaries were also dispatched to other tribes that resided along the intended marching path to Italy, to learn their reactions to his plan. As he had learned from Hasdrubal, Hannibal sent valuable gifts to encourage favorable support, with promises of more rewards later. He promised no harm to inhabitants or their property if they did not resist. He promised fair compensation in gold and silver for supplies and for mercenary soldiers that they may provide his army. He wanted to fight Romans, not Gauls in his marching path. Hannibal instructed his agents to return home by next year with all information. Hannibal estimated that he could complete the pacification of remaining Spanish territories located south of the

Ebro by 220 B.C. and that this would not prematurely alarm Rome.

Gisco had given Carthalo, Hannibal's chief of intelligence, the names of Greek agents in Italy whom he had contacted during his trip to Spain. Carthalo had established relationships with them long ago. Before he added Gisco's contacts to his list, he already had a substantial spy network. A steady flow of information was now coming to New Carthage on reliable Greek and Phoenician commercial trading vessels that regularly plied Mediterranean ports, including the Roman ports of Ostia (Rome's home port), Neapolis (Naples), Pisae (Pisa), and Genua (Genoa). A large number of these vessels were chartered to stop at New Carthage. Special crew members of these ships were bringing regular reports about actions of the Roman senate, particularly those affecting military forces. Spies also provided detailed dossiers about top Roman military commanders and proconsuls, including their strengths, weaknesses, experience, and personal foibles which interested Hannibal very much. Much information was provided about forts, military grain-storage sites, military strengths, and location of Roman legions. Most of this information was readily available in Italy. A staff of Greek administrators in New Carthage was keeping Hannibal apprised of latest changes by updating detailed maps that reflected recent changes and displayed location of Roman legions.

Conquest of remaining tribes below the Ebro - the Carpetani, Vaccei, and Celtiberi - took much longer than Hannibal expected. By winter 221-220 B.C., when his Spanish troops were allowed to return to their homes and African troops returned to winter quarters in New Carthage, it had not been completed. However, considerable progress had been made and substantial portions of these nations had been acquired.

Hannibal had noticed that the few Celtiberians who had already joined his army were making very good cavalry troops. He believed that they could be trained to help bring the size of his cavalry up to the required strength of 16,000. Celtiberians were a racial mix created in ancient times by merging Celtic immigrants from the north with native Iberians in central Spain, and they were taller and stronger than Iberians. They had large herds of beautiful, stocky Iberian horses that were superior as war horses because of their individual strength and agility. Celtiberians used two-foot-long, curved, double-edged swords, and they rode their horses using reins, something his African cavalry had not learned to do, as a matter of choice. His Numidians preferred to control their horses with their knees, something they had become expert at doing, thus freeing their hands to use weapons. Hannibal was training a large, fast-moving, powerful cavalry in which he allied Celtiberians with his Numidians. The well-groomed Numidians rode fast, slender, nimble Arabian horses, as they sat on leopard skins for saddles, and they used long, sharp spears. They were commanded by Maharbal, one of the greatest cavalry commanders of all time. A small nucleus of Carthaginian officers, all noblemen and well-educated, were mounted on excellent animals, and they completed Hannibal's cavalry.

From the Balearic Islands, Hannibal imported more slingers who could accurately cast projectiles from leather slings of three different lengths, depending on the distance of the targets. Foot soldiers were from Africa, Phoenicia, and Spain, and he was planning to add Cisalpine Gauls as allies after crossing the Alps.

Of his sixty elephants, most were smaller ones (nine-feet tall) from Africa, and a few were larger ones (twelve-feet tall) from India. All were driven by well-trained mahouts, and they carried huge baskets on their backs. The baskets bore archers, slingers, or javelin throwers. The scent and sight of elephants usually caused enemy horses to panic and bolt if they were not familiar with them. The sight of these huge beasts, charging forty abreast at them, usually terrified enemy soldiers who feared being trampled by them. Elephants were also useful for doing heavy work for the army when they were not in combat.

Spanish forces of this polyglot army were composed of Tartessians and Iberians from southern Spain and its coasts; the long-limbed, emotional, and less dependable Celtic barbarians from northern Spain up to the Pyranees, who wore tartan cloths and played bagpipes; and from the land in between these two areas, Celtiberians from plains around the head of the Tagus River (near Toledo today).

Greeks on Hannibal's staff worked as scribes and administrators, charged with bringing the latest intelligence information to his attention. Three Greek scribes, Chaereas, Sosilos, and Silenos, recorded extensive details of the campaigns. At Gisco's recommendation, the Greek, Synhalus of Alexandria, was recruited as the army's medical director.

Hannibal, Gisco and the staff worked long hours planning the Italian campaign, down to its most insignificant minutiae. The talents of Hannibal and his lieutenant complemented each other. Hannibal had a lifetime of practical experience with combat command, warfare, and human relations with soldiers. He had studied Greek texts on warfare, but Gisco was a veritable encyclopedia of information about Roman and Greek military strategy, tactics, armor, war machines, and logistics. Both men were dedicated, hardworking prodigies with much in common, and each had great respect and affection for the other. They abided little indulgence for weaknesses of the flesh. They both knew that it would require unusual talent to keep their army's strange coalition of divergent cultures together, motivated for war, and their actions coordinated.

As winter set in, Gisco helped make plans for the industrial support needed to provide the army with war material. Supplies of grain, oxen, wine, metals, leather, horses, glass, textiles, terra-cotta, timber, and such had already been arranged. However, large numbers of smelters and forges were needed to arm the huge army. Gisco enlisted natives to be trained by African craftsmen. He became the overseer for establishing 300 forges with five workers per forge. The monthly capacity of these forges, when in complete operation, would produce 2,500 shields, 8,000 swords, 13,000 spears, and 25,000 catapult darts.

Subordinates were left in charge of these activities, as Gisco returned to Tarraco with the intention of bringing Tarra and his son back to New Carthage, so that he could work through the winter on final planning and preparation. New Carthage had grown to a town of whitewashed houses with flat roofs and narrow, twisting streets, similar to those in Carthage. Gisco had obtained a suitable abode for his family and servants.

When Gisco returned to New Carthage with his family, he learned that Hannibal had married Imilce. Tarra was delighted, and the two cousins, glad to see each other again, spent many happy hours together while their great men were working. Hannibal told

Imilce, over her strong protests, that she could not plan to come along on the campaign to Italy because it would be too dangerous. He also told her that when they left for Italy she would have to go to his family home in Carthage, as the safest and most comfortable place to be during the war. Gisco told Tarra that she and young Gisco should go to Athens, a noncombatant zone, where the boy could be educated and she could be well-care-for by his mother and grandfather who would be anxious to see them.

There were a few campaigns to complete before Hannibal could be ready to take his army to Italy. His army resumed its task of conquering the few remaining tribes below the Ebro that were not under control of the Carthaginians. A typical example of Hannibal's military genius was a tactic he used in the climactic battle that took place on the Tagus. It was typical of his planning, as he used similar tactics many times. It was the battle that concluded the conquest of tribes south of the Ebro.

Parts of three tribes, the Carpetani, Olcades, and Hermandicas had split from their main forces to oppose Hannibal's impending rule of their territories. They formed a strong force of 100,000 troops, which was more than twice as many in Hannibal's army at the particular site at that time. Hannibal's army, returning from other battles, was tired and heavily laden with spoils from recent northern victories when they were confronted by this huge renegade enemy army. Hannibal's officers wanted to attack the enemy, head-on, immediately. Against the advice of his officers, Hannibal ordered his army to retreat across the Tagus, putting the river between his army and the hostile army. The enemy thought that Hannibal was running away from battle because of fright, as he was so vastly outnumbered. They started to pursue him by crossing the river. The river turned out to be surprisingly deep and swift flowing. All of that was part of Hannibal's plan. As soon as the enemy had committed itself to crossing the river, Hannibal halted his retreat, turned his army around, and attacked the fierce tribes while they were dispersed, crossing the treacherous river. The enemy troops were caught defenseless as they could not use their weapons effectively while they were floundering in the deep, fast-flowing river. Hannibal's elephants and cavalry killed many as they struggled out of the water. The Carthaginian army slaughtered many while they were helpless in the water by launching clouds of arrows, spears, and metal darts on them, and others drowned in the fast-flowing river as they panicked on seeing the elephants and the approaching cavalry. The result was a rout, with Hannibal's army losing few soldiers. His prestige and image, greatly exaggerated in stories told by fleeing, terrified soldiers as they returned to their homes in all parts of the central plains up to the Ebro, resulted in an end to armed conflict in the last remaining hostile region.

Roman administrators had made a serious blunder when they signed the agreement with Hasdrubal, giving Carthage all territory south of the Ebro. They did not realize, at the time of the agreement, that the rich colony of Saguntum was situated south of the Ebro, on the northeast coast of Spain. They assumed it was north of the Ebro. Rome had a long-standing agreement to protect Saguntum, considered to be Rome's major foothold in Spain. When Hannibal's army began conquering tribes located in areas surrounding Saguntum, its inhabitants became alarmed and petitioned

Rome for protection. Roman administrators finally realized their error and rapidly sent envoys to New Carthage in the spring, 219 B.C., to request that Saguntum be left unharmed and free. Unknown to these envoys, Hannibal's planned invasion route to Rome passed by Saguntum, and he had no intention of leaving this ally of Rome to remain free to threaten his lines of communication and supply once war was started. Saguntum was the only community south of the Ebro that was not under his control.

Hannibal's loathing for Romans caused him to treat their envoys rudely. In private consultation with Gisco, Hannibal told him this was the golden opportunity they had been waiting for - an attack on Saguntum would certainly cause Rome to declare war on Carthage. It would provide the two compatriots a legitimate reason for fighting Romans. The colony of Saguntum had recently been maltreating some of Carthage's allies, and Carthaginian subjects had been harmed during internal political strife in Saguntum. It was an ancestral tradition of Carthage to take up the cause of victims of injustice. The colony of Saguntum would provide rich booty to help finance a war with Rome, and a large share of the spoils could be sent to Carthage to mollify their government's reaction to the conquest. Anyway, they had a legitimate right to conquer Saguntum under Hasdrubal's pact with Rome, which gave Carthage all claim to territory south of the Ebro.

Hannibal brusquely told the Roman envoys that Carthage had a right, under their treaty, to take Saguntum, and he told them about the harm that had come to Carthaginian subjects living in the colony. He also stated that the long-standing tradition of Carthage was to take up the cause of victims of injustice.

Incensed by Hannibal's remarks and by his obviously intolerant attitude, the arrogant Roman party left for Carthage, intending to bring the issue to Hannibal's superior government for settlement. They hoped to coerce Carthage into overruling Hannibal by threatening them with war. As they left, Hannibal decided to take Saguntum quickly, before his government could tell him not to do it.

Luckily for Hannibal, incompetent politicians in the Carthaginian government took many months debating a decision on the matter, because the siege of Saguntum took much longer than Hannibal had expected, eight months. This was due to the heavy defensive fortifications of the colony. Hannibal was wounded slightly during the fighting and he used it as an excuse to return to New Carthage where Imilce was giving birth to their son. He left Maharbal in command during his absence. After more than six months of trying to conquer Saguntum, soldiers were growing impatient, and they requested that their "miracle man," Gisco, do something to speed up the operation.

Hannibal's lieutenant had noticed that walls of the town were constructed of huge stones which were not fixed in place with mortar. They were held in place with ordinary mud, making them easy to dismantle. To enable his soldiers to dismantle the wall, he designed and constructed a multistoried siege tower on rollers. The tower was much higher than the walls defending the colony. He designed special catapults for some of the stories of the tower which threw projectiles weighing several hundred pounds. On other stories of the huge machine, he installed large ballistae that projected massive numbers of iron darts as well as ten-foot, iron-tipped spears. When this mobile tower was moved up to the wall of the town, it swept away all defenders on the wall. This allowed 500 troops to use pickaxes and a huge battering-ram to break a large gap in defender's wall. Massive numbers of soldiers poured into the colony and it surrendered. This ended eight months of toil.

The sack of Saguntum was lucrative, as expected. Hannibal sent a large share of the rich spoils to the government in Carthage, as part of his plan, hoping that the riches would reach decision makers in Africa before they gave Roman emissaries an answer to their protest. The plunder sent to Carthage included much gold, silver, jewels, expensive furniture and materials. As was the custom of the age, all prisoners taken were made slaves of Hannibal's soldiers in proportion to each soldier's contribution to the fray. Hannibal also gave them a share of the silver booty. A large share of the booty taken, including considerable gold, was used to enrich the war chest for the campaign to Italy. Success of this venture, and its enrichment of the soldiers, made the troops enthusiastic for new campaigns.

The Carthaginian government in Africa engaged in a long, drawn-out debate that delayed, considerably, their decision concerning how they would answer the Roman protests. After they heard of Hannibal's sack of Saguntum, the Roman emissaries were outraged. They demanded that Hannibal's action be denounced and that Hannibal and his brothers be turned over to Rome's authorities for prosecution as war criminals. They said that if this were not done, Rome and Carthage would be at war, and the choice was up to the Carthaginian government. After another prolonged debate, and after receiving the rich booty sent by

Hannibal which heavily influenced the decision, his government decided to go to war.

Rome had envisioned the war, if it came, to be conducted entirely in Spain and Africa. If it knew of Hannibal's plans to invade Italy, Rome may have been more cautious with its actions. Roman planners never considered such a possibility as a serious threat. Hannibal now had official backing to fight Romans, although he had not yet received word about the decision. The decision came months after he had sacked Saguntum. Nevertheless, Hannibal and Gisco anticipated consequences of the sack long before they received official notification from Carthage and the army had begun all final preparations for the war. Emissaries that Hannibal had sent out earlier to Italy and Gallia had soon returned with good news by winter, 219 B.C., reporting that all tribes in territories they planned to pass through on the way to Rome were cooperative except a few small ones that would not commit themselves. Agents returning from the Padus valley in northern Italy said that two tribes of Cisalpine Gauls, the Boii and the Insubres, had enthusiastically welcomed them as allies in their own long struggle against Rome, and that they promised soldiers and supplies. Hannibal had promised that Carthage had no territorial claims to make after the defeat of Rome. The sole purpose of the war was to destroy the tyrannical Rome which was a threat to all Mediterranean nations, after which Carthage would leave Italy. This news from agents was the last link in the chain of events that Hannibal required to clear the way to Rome, except for receipt of official authorization from Carthage.

When the army returned to New Carthage from its successful conquest of Saguntum in the winter, 219 -

218 B.C., Hannibal assembled his soldiers to address them. The troops were flush with victory, their pockets were full of money, and their morale was high. He told them that now, with all Spanish peoples south of the Ebro united in the Carthaginian province, they had two alternatives: they could stop fighting and live in peace; or they could come back in the spring and pursue further conquests elsewhere. He said that the obvious choice should be the latter, as it would provide renown and spoils from conquests in distant lands, while their homeland could enjoy peace. Because they would be fighting in distant lands, and nobody knew when they would see their loved ones again after the campaign began, he told them he would grant a leave of absence to any man who wanted to visit his family. He ordered them to return from their vacation by the beginning of spring. In parting, he said, "With the help of the gods, we will begin a war which will fill your pockets with gold and carry your fame to the world's end."

He didn't tell them they were going on a long crusade as far as Italy to make their homeland secure from the Romans. He intended to tell this to them at the last minute, as they left Spain. Hannibal's speech was welcomed by loud cheers from the soldiers. They returned to their homes for a much needed rest, intent on coming back in the spring.

Hannibal called his officers together to summarize his latest plans and emphasize that a crucial part of the success of the plan was the requirement to keep it secret. He wanted Rome to believe that Hannibal planned to fight the war on Spanish soil. He told them not to divulge the plan to the soldiers until he told them to do it to reduce the risk of the secret falling into Roman hands.

With most of the detailed planning completed and all preliminary actions taken, Hannibal and Gisco were able to spend much more of the last few remaining months with their families. They also visited the sacred temple in Gades to renew their vows, sealed it with an animal sacrifice, and prayed for success in their coming campaign.

Roman envoys sailed from Carthage, returning to Rome during March, 218 B.C., and the Second Punic War was soon officially started. Carthage sent a fast messenger to Hannibal, notifying him of the decision for war. Hannibal's agents soon reported that Rome was not planning to fight battles on Italian soil. It was planning one front, with consul Publius Cornelius Scipio in command, to sail to Massilia to start the Spanish campaign (because the Roman foothold in Spain, Saguntum, was no longer available). A second front was to be an attack on Carthage in Africa with consul Tiberius Sempronius in command. Rome's planned Spanish expeditionary forces were reported to be composed of 22,000 infantry soldiers, 2,400 cavalry, and 60 warships. Its planned African forces were reported to be composed of 24,000 infantry, 1,800 cavalry, and 160 warships.

News that they now had official approval for war on Rome reached the delighted planners in New Carthage during April, 218 B.C. The troops had reassembled in March and were nearly ready to march. They wanted to get over the Alps before winter snows closed the passes to Italy. Based on the disposition of Roman forces as reported by spies, Hannibal divided his force into four separate parts. First, under the capable command of his brother, Hasdrubal, whom he had trained in the rudiments of administering the Spanish province, he allocated 14,000 infantry, 1,200 cavalry, and a fleet of 57 warships to defend southern Spain. Second, he sent 16,000 Spanish troops to augment the army in Carthage. Third, to keep the passes of the Pyranees open and meet Scipios legions, he allocated 10,000 foot soldiers and 1,000 cavalry under the command of the veteran Hanno. The fourth residual part, was to be what he took to Italy, an unknown number, since he wanted volunteers among the best fighters. He intended to select the best fighters of the remaining forces when he reached the Pyranees. For purposes of planning, Gisco had made provision for 50,000 troops to leave Spain and travel for 45 days to Italy.

Hannibal had been made acutely aware of the fact that the most crucial aspect of his job as commander of the army was his task of planning, organizing, and managing the logistics for each army campaign. That is, the solution of problems dealing with the procurement, maintenance, and transportation of the army's materiel, money, and personnel for each combat operation was crucial to his success. Hannibal realized that supply had to be the crucial basis of his military strategy, and he understood that movements of his army were limited by capabilities of his supply system. He spent the largest share of his time on each aspect of these tasks because his father, Hamilcar, had emphasized this part of his job during his training to become a commander. In addition, Hannibal had learned about the revolutionary changes that Alexander the Great had made to reduce his army's supply requirements (by drastically reducing the number of slow-moving baggage carts used by his army, by reducing the number of pack animals, and by eliminating non-fighting servants, slaves, and women from his marching army from those considered necessary by contemporary armies of Greece and Persia). Hannibal was convinced that these changes were the most important reason Alexander's army was able to move faster and be more mobile than his enemy armies. This action had allowed Alexander to outmaneuver his opponents and terrify them by his speed.

Before Gisco arrived in Spain to present his logistic plan to Hasdrubal and his staff, Hannibal had been working on problems of making the Carthaginian army more mobile and its movements more rapid, by reducing the size of his army's baggage train and the number of non-fighting people that marched with the army. However, when he observed Gisco's brilliant presentation to Hasdrubal, and noted how far Gisco had gone to apply scientific methods to the computation of the logistics requirement for the Carthaginian army, Hannibal realized he could learn much from the talented Gisco. Soon afterward, Hannibal and Gisco were working together to collect detailed records about every aspect of supply and transportation that was required by the Carthaginian army. They had collected records for more than two years before they began their trip to Italy, and they had made many reductions in nonproductive resources used by their army. For example, Gisco began comparing what he had learned about the logistics of the Carthaginian army with those of Alexander's army, as a goal that he expected Hannibal's army to achieve. After much work, the Carthaginian army was almost as efficient as Alexander's.

Gisco developed detailed standards for supply requirements of the Carthaginian army that he used in his presentation to Hasdrubal. Gisco determined, from his studies at Alexandria, that the optimum daily food and water requirement for soldiers averaged three pounds of grain and two quarts of water. The optimum daily consumption for horses and mules, in addition to their normal forage from suitable land where grass and water was available, was ten pounds of grain; the eight gallons of water and ten pounds of straw or grass consumed by each animal each day, in addition to the grain carried by the baggage train, was planned to be obtained by foraging from the land along the marching route.

Gisco's studies indicated that the average horse or mule could carry 200 pounds of baggage. From this information he computed the amount of food the pack animals could carry for the men and animals, in addition to the pack animals required to carry other necessary military equipment, tents, silver and gold. A policy of eliminating servants, slaves, and women from the marching army after it left Spain at the Pyranees, enabled a vast reduction in the number of human and animal mouths to feed each day. Nevertheless, after these economies were realized, the number of pack animals required to carry essential supplies for the army on its trek from the Pyranees to Italy was calculated to exceed 90,000 animals. This was a prohibitive, unwieldy, number. Gisco solved this problem by using the same tactics for supply that Alexander had used: supplies were pre-positioned in advance of the marching army along its intended marching path up to the Alps. The supplies, often purchased from local tribes by Hannibal's emissaries, were protected by garrisons of soldiers until the marching army reached them. Using all measures they could think of, Gisco and Hannibal were able to reduce the number of pack animals to the minimum number required for the short trek over the Alpine mountains, where emissaries were not able to get cooperation from the local, hostile tribes. No forage was available above the tree line. They reduced the number of animals required for the baggage train to a minimum of 25,000.

Hannibal and Gisco decided that, based on their calculations for the climb over the Alps, the policy for the marching army after it left the Pyranees would be one where no servants, slaves, or women would be allowed to march with the army. Slaves who were good fighters could come on the trip. Each soldier was required to carry three day's rations, his own weapons and armor, and his own utensils on the climb over the Alps. Only enough slow-moving carts would be brought along as was necessary to carry heavy materiel such as tents, heavy military supplies, and to act as ambulances. Pack animals would be used in lieu of carts wherever it was possible to reduce the number of slow-moving carts. The route to Italy was to be selected by scouts so that ample water would be available and there would be ample grass for animals and sufficient trees available for elephants to eat, except for the short part of the trek over the Alps that took the army above the tree line and over snow-covered land. As an additional measure, to reduce the number of pack animals required, emissaries were to be dispatched (to procure necessary supplies) well before the marching army reached the Alps. A strong garrison of soldiers would protect the supplies until the army arrived to take them. These restrictions were to apply to the army after it left the Pyranees, but there were no restrictions on the army while it was marching in Spain from New Carthage before reaching the Pyranees.

Hannibal did not expect Scipio's forces, as Rome had planned for Spain, to reach Spain after they learned that Hannibal had crossed the Alps on his way to attack them. He expected a large portion of Roman expeditionary forces to be recalled to Italy to defend Rome once it was known that Hannibal had crossed the Alps.

Hannibal planned to take the remaining 102,000 troops to the north Spanish border (this included Hanno's 11,000), and it was there he intended to cull out poor fighters and non-volunteers for the trip to Italy. He intended to leave Hanno with a strong force of 11,000 soldiers who did not want to go to Italy to defend the north. Hannibal intended to send some soldiers back to Hasdrubal, dismiss some, and take the rest to Italy. On the recommendation of Gisco who had read about policies of other armies, Hannibal adopted a policy for assigning troops that was later used extensively by Romans. Spanish soldiers were sent to Carthage to defend the mother country, and African troops were left in Spain to defend it and keep order. This tended to unify the Spanish province with the mother country, and Spanish men in Africa also served as hostages as a guard against an insurrection by the tribes in Spain from which they came.

Tearful good-byes were given to Imilce, Tarra, and the two young sons as they were put on fast vessels to take them to Carthage and Athens, respectively. Both wives made emotional pleas to be taken on the campaign, but they had to be refused because of the great danger and hardships expected, and because of the policy of bringing no women on the journey over the Alps.

Chapter 3

THE MARCH TO ITALY
(May - November, 218 B.C.)

As the enormous army marched out of New Carthage in May of 218 B.C., culminating months of planning and preparation, masses of spectators gathered along the road to watch the colorful pageantry. The six-mile-long column of marching soldiers from many nations was a feast for the eyes of all who watched. There were 90,000 infantry; 12,000 horse cavalry; thirty-seven elephants; and thousands of pack mules, cattle, oxen, carts, war machines, and supplies. It was a bright spring day and colors glistened in the sun. Warriors were grouped by nation, each with its own vivid banners, dress, and armor. Leading the way were magnificent, meticulous Numidians wearing large gold earrings and garish jewelry, white mantles, with leopard skins hung over their shoulders. They were seated on leopard skins, with javelin streamers whipping in the breeze and pipes wailing as they rode their sleek Arabians without reins. They were in the lead so they could scout ahead and guard the flanks of the enormous parade of fighting men.

Next came Hannibal, who was late catching up with the front of the column, with Gisco, Cirta, and other officers at his side. They wore their gold inlaid armor, helmets with bright red plumes gleaming in the sun, and brilliant crimson capes as they proudly rode magnificent, spirited animals, leading the massive column.

The heterogeneous assortment of nations making up the thousands of troops that followed Hannibal was a spectacular sight. For example, the Vaccaei and Urama tribes wore wolf and lion heads for helmets, and another tribe wore metal-studded leather helmets that covered their heads down to their shoulders. Another tribe wore polished iron helmets that glistened in the sun. There were many sizes and shapes of shields, made of many materials, many different types of body armor, and weapons. Balearic slingers carried leather slings of three different lengths coiled over their shoulders, which they used for slinging missiles of flaming pitch or heavy lead balls that could smash bronze shields and helmets. Spanish cavalry rode beautiful, strong Iberian horses with reins, carried colorful banners, wore crimson and white tunics, and leather armor. The lumbering elephants had leather nose and side armor, fitted boxes on their backs, brightly colored plumes on their heads, and were guided by brightly dressed, proud mahouts. There were enormous chests full of silver and gold in wagons, well-guarded by the more reliable Iberians with their standards of crescent moons and rayed suns. Trailing the column were thousands of pack animals, supply carts, slaughter oxen, and mobile war machines such as battering rams, storming towers, and siege machines, all disassembled and strapped on pack animals.

There was considerable clamor, with military trumpets blaring, officers shouting orders, neighing of horses, elephants trumpeting, chattering of troops, braying of pack animals, and stomping of hooves as the procession wound its way up the east coast of

Spain, strung out for many miles. Some veterans of the First Punic War were included in the army, such as Maharabal, Hert, and Hanno. The astrologer, Bog, was near the head of the column, available to give his forecasts for the superstitious soldiers.

After crossing the Ebro, the army was in hostile territory, inhabited by the Ilergetes and some coastal tribes, but these presented no serious opposition to the awesome army. Hannibal spent more than three months between the Ebro and passes of the Pyranees to evaluate his soldiers, selecting those with the highest morale and fighting ability. He spent time building roads and bridges from the Ebro through the eastern passes of the Pyranees (through le Perthus today), taking control of the territory by skirmishing with hostile barbarians, and sorting out and organizing the equipment he intended to take over the Alps. He was leaving Hanno all heavy equipment for his defense of northern Spain, expecting Gisco to build more in Italy if necessary. Gisco made a visit to Tarraco during this time to see his brother-in-law and friends.

Tribes of the Bargusii, Ausetani, and the district of Lacetania gave unexpected heavy opposition, causing considerable delay and severe losses in the area near the Pyranees. Since time was growing short before fall arrived, with snows that would close the Alpine passes, Hannibal left the task of pacifying the remaining tribes to Hanno. He departed for Italy with his army. By now, most of the rank and file soldiers had heard rumors that Hannibal intended to cross the feared Alps, a thought that terrified many of the superstitious men. Three thousand Carpetani deserted one night near the Pyranees. Instead of having them brought back and punished, Hannibal decided to forget them and to dismiss another 7,000 whom he knew to be of low morale; he intended to keep a core of highly motivated, obedient, strong fighters whom he believed to be willing to make the trip. Hannibal selected a total of 50,000 infantry and 9,000 cavalry to take through the Pyranees and on to Italy. These were particulary well-trained, experienced, and proven fighters. He left Hanno with 10,000 infantry, 1,000 cavalry, and all of the heavy equipment to assist him in his job of defending the passes of the Pyranees and northern Spain. Remaining soldiers were sent to Hasdrubal for defense of the south. These were good, loyal soldiers, but they did not want to march so far away from home as the Alps. There were abundant rumors circulating among the superstitious soldiers about evil demons that dwelled in the mysterious Alps and this terrorized many Spanish soldiers.

The army had already traveled half the distance to Rome, entirely in Spain, but the most difficult part was to come. As it was now mid-August, with little time left before snow would close the Alpine passes, Hannibal exhorted his men to make a great effort to move the long column faster. They responded by traveling thirty-five miles a day across southern Gallia (France), following the Mediterranean coast to the Rhone River, reaching it in four days at a point that scouts had selected as the best site for making the difficult crossing (at Tarascon). Thanks to Hannibal's gifts and diplomacy, that portion of the trip was made without opposition from local tribes. The selected crossing point on the Rhone was only fifty miles north of Massilia where, according to agents, the Roman consul Scipio had just landed with 24,000 soldiers, intending to invade Spain.

Hannibal made friends with inhabitants of the village on the west bank of the river, and he called upon his "miracle man," Gisco, to determine how to get the huge army across the Rhone, particularly the elephants. Gisco began by buying all the boats and canoes possessed by the natives, which was a considerable number because it was a seafaring tribe. In addition, Gisco purchased numerous logs from the natives and he enlisted their assistance in helping the soldiers build temporary rafts to carry themselves and their baggage across the river. Local natives were anxious to help the crossing, not only to be rid of their disturbing presence, but to earn scarce silver at the same time. Within two days they had sufficient water transport to move the soldiers across. The problem of moving the elephants was to be handled separately.

While all this activity was in progress, a new problem began to develop. A hostile tribe of Volcae were strung out along the opposite bank of the Rhone in a menacing manner, shouting and brandishing their weapons. Hannibal held a meeting of his trusted officers to discuss tactics for defeating the hostile tribe that appeared to be opposing their crossing. It was decided that Hanno (another Hanno, son of Bomilcar, nephew of Hannibal), would take a strong party of Spanish cavalry up the river a day's journey, leaving after nightfall on the third night so as not to be detected by the Volcae. They crossed the river upstream, rested a day, then headed downstream on the morning of the fifth day. On a prearranged signal, which was a huge smoke fire, they planned to ambush the enemy from the rear while it was distracted by the simultaneous crossing of the river by Hannibal's army.

Hannibal's army saw the giant smoke signal sent

up by Hanno's troops on noon of the fifth day, and Hannibal gave the order for his army to start crossing the river with trumpets blaring and men shouting war cries, to distract the hostile warriors waiting for them on the opposite bank of the river. The ambush worked perfectly, as Hanno's horsemen had approached the Volcae unseen in the rear, before Hannibal's forces reached the shore. The result was a rout, and most of the surprised tribe that were not killed fled in terror. Very few of the Carthaginian troops were injured. A camp was established on the east bank while the rest of the men, animals, and supplies began crossing the river unopposed.

Elephants were a problem. Gisco, working with their mahouts, designed a workable system to get the huge beasts across the rapidly flowing water. A seventy-yard pier was constructed to extend out into the river, stabilized by a network of cables that were anchored onto the shore. Rafts were built, then moored temporarily at the end of the pier. Next, earth was piled on all surfaces of both, pier and rafts, with the intent of deceiving the elephants into believing they were still on firm earth, rather than being out on the water, as they were led out onto them by female elephants. When the elephants were finally on the rafts, the rafts were disconnected from the pier and pulled to the opposite shore by cables. Only a few of the pachyderms panicked and fell into the water, but once in the water their huge hulks floated and they swam safely to shore. Only one of the elephants that panicked died of injuries it sustained.

While this elaborate elephant crossing was in progress, Hannibal sent 500 Numidian cavalry to scout the location of the Roman army. He wanted to avoid fighting Romans in Gallia, saving the fighting for

Italian soil, so he instructed his horsemen not to become embroiled in a prolonged battle if they encountered Romans. The Roman commander, Scipio, had already dispatched 300 cavalry north from Massilia to discover the whereabouts of the Carthaginians, because his agents had reported that they were in the vicinity. The remainder of his army was resting in Massilia, recuperating from its tiring sea voyage from Italy.

When the two cavalry forces met, cagey Numidians riding much faster horses, used a ploy that they normally used in battle. They bloodied the Roman troops, using hit and run tactics, then abruptly retreated as their leader, Maharbal, had instructed them to do because Hannibal wanted to save the fighting for Italian soil. The sudden retreat by Numidians caused Romans to believe, erroneously, that they had won the skirmish and had defeated a much larger force of African cavalry. The Romans returned to report to Scipio that they had defeated a larger force of Numidians, and that the Africans were afraid to fight Romans because they fled after a short skirmish. The tactic used by the Numidians had left Romans with a false sense of superiority that was intended as part of Maharbal's plan. He would make good use of that Roman overconfidence in future battles.

In the meantime, Hannibal had moved his forces north, as though he was headed into the heartland of Europe, and Scipio's scouts reported that movement to him. Hannibal had made this feint to the north deliberately to mislead Scipio from his true intentions because he did not believe Scipio would expect the Carthaginian army to be able to cross the Alps from that position. Hannibal's assumption was correct, as

Scipio was not expecting such a crossing, and Scipio believed that even if Hannibal were to try such a crossing, Hannibal's army would be destroyed in making the attempt. However, Hannibal's move to the north caused Hannibal to plan an Alpine crossing that his agents had not reconnoitered, one that would be more difficult. Whenever he had alternatives, Hannibal usually chose the one that was least expected by the enemy, even though it meant a great increase in the effort required by his army.

After Scipio's scouts reached Hannibal's crossing site on the Rhone, they reported back to Scipio that Hannibal had left the site, headed north, three days earlier. Scipio couldn't believe the speed with which the large Carthaginian army had moved. In the meantime, couriers from Italy reported that Gauls in northern Italy had begun a new uprising. Scipio decided to send the mass of his army on to Spain as originally ordered by the Roman Senate, but he left it under the command of his brother, Gnaeus Scipio. He, Consul Publius Cornelius Scipio, decided to return to northern Italy to take command of the legions in that area, in operations against the Gauls.

Hannibal's army reached the juncture of the Rhone and Drome Rivers, a land of the Allobrogues' nation, as many more of Hannibal's Spanish soldiers defected and other soldiers elected to return to Spain. The army was now down to 30,000 infantry, 8,000 cavalry, and thirty-six elephants.

Two brothers were fighting for the throne of the Allobroges as the Carthaginians passed through their territory. Hannibal helped the older brother, Brancus, to establish firm control as the ruler of the nation. In gratitude, Brancus provided supplies of all sorts to Hannibal's army, particularly heavy winter clothing that Brancus knew Hannibal's army needed to cross the Alps. This included wool outer garments, leg wrappings, and fur-lined boots. Hannibal paid for these in silver, hoping to keep good relations with the natives, as a part of his plan to keep an open line of communications with Spain.

As Hannibal turned his column eastward, and his superstitious Spanish troops began getting a view of the awesome Alps which they had never seen before, and which they had to climb to get to Italy, more and more of them were becoming intimidated. They imagined all kinds of demons and hazards lurking in the unknown snow capped mountains. Hannibal and Gisco always kept in touch with the mood of the soldiers, and they soon detected their growing fear. Angrily, Hannibal gathered each Spanish group of soldiers together, by nation, and he spoke to them in their native dialects. He told them that they had fought many tough battles together and that they had always been victorious. Now, they were near the gates of Rome, the mightiest and richest city in the world. Pointing to the Boii delegates who were at his side, and who could not understand the language, he said that the Gauls had just come over the Alps and that Gauls had once captured Rome. Hordes of Gauls, including women and children, had safely crossed the Alps in the past; the Alps are nothing more than tall mountains. Angrily and more heatedly, he told his men that they had two choices: either they had to admit they had less courage than Gauls, a race they had defeated in battle many times, even less courage than Gaul women and children; or they must march over the Alps, stopping only at the walls of the Roman capital. Furthermore, he told them, since they were at war with Rome, a return to their Spanish villages now would mean that Roman legions would soon be sacking their homes to obtain Spanish riches. If, instead, the Spanish marched over the Alps to sack Rome, they would eliminate Rome's ability to make war and they would obtain Rome's riches. Afterward, they could return to their homes as rich men and live securely the rest of their lives in a world free from Roman aggression.

Hannibal's emotional address had the desired affect. His proud Spaniards saw that there was no viable alternative, and they eagerly marched on through a driving rain toward the mountains along the valley of the Drome. They reached the steeper foothills without opposition from local tribes. As the long line of water-soaked soldiers and animals moved in constant rain up to the first steep slopes, they could see a tribe of wild men with shaggy heads standing on top of the ridges of both sides of the ravine ahead. The army had to pass through the ravine, and the wild men, wearing animal skins, were brandishing weapons in a threatening manner. They were in a position to ambush the long marching column. There was a narrow gorge in the ravine ahead which appeared to be the most dangerous ambush point. Hannibal saw this, called a halt to the march, and ordered his men to rest. Then, he sent Gisco to reconnoiter the situation ahead, accompanied by some guides who were of the same race as the wild men, and who spoke their language. Gisco had learned the Celtic language and he had been practicing the dialect of the guides since his first meeting with them. The guides had been provided by Brancus, King of the Allobroges.

Gisco's small party passed through the narrow gorge without incident while the huge army rested behind. Gisco's small party did not disturb the wild men because they were used to seeing small groups of travelers pass through their land on their way to Italy, to trade in their village which was ahead. Only Hannibal's huge army disturbed them. Gisco's group traveled up the trail to the main village, home of the wild men where they searched for the village elders to negotiate safe passage for the army. Gisco soon learned that all elders were out manning the ridges of the pass and that they returned to the warmth of their houses every night, along with the rest of the tribe. The wild men could not stay on the mountain ridges at night because as soon as the sun went down the temperature quickly dropped to severely low levels, and they could not survive the night. Furthermore, they did not believe that anyone would attempt to pass through the treacherous narrow gorge at night. Gisco and his party waited until nightfall when the tribal leaders returned, and he attempted to arrange safe passage for the column. He promised abundant compensation in silver for the privilege. He also promised no harm to the villagers if they cooperated. The tribal leaders were arrogant and hostile. They did not trust the intentions of such a huge, menacing army and believed that they could take most of Hannibal's rich cargo through plunder on the narrow trails ahead. When Gisco offered to increase the amount of silver he was willing to give them, they still wouldn't settle, and they rejected Gisco's proposal at any price he offered.

    Gisco and his guides returned to Hannibal's camp that night, passing through the narrow gorge in darkness, and he reported the news to his commander. Gisco said that since he and the guides had successfully negotiated the trail from the village in darkness, he was convinced that the guides could safely lead a strong group of hand-picked troops through the narrow pass at night, to secure its exit on the other side. Next, select groups of light armed Celtiberians, whom he knew were used to climbing steep cliffs in their native lands, could climb the steep walls of the gorge at night, one group on each of the two sides of the gorge, to secure the dominating positions on the tops of the hills that the wild men normally occupied during the daytime. The wild men would not be able to return to their threatening positions in the morning, because they would be occupied by Hannibal's men. This action would allow safe passage of the rest of the army through the narrow pass the next day.

Hannibal agreed to the plan and ordered his army to spend the next day fortifying their positions to make it appear that they were digging in to fight the tribe, thus concealing their real intentions. Before the next dawn, Gisco led a select group of tough fighters, who were also good mountain climbers, up one side of the ravine while Hannibal led a group up the other side. Each of the two night climbs was treacherous, resulting in deaths of a few men when they lost their footing in the darkness and tumbled down the steep precipices, rolling hundreds of feet below over sharp boulders. Finally, when both teams were in position, a prearranged signal was given with torches, and guides below led a group of better fighters through the narrow pass of the gorge in darkness. As planned, they left many campfires blazing to make it appear that all soldiers were still in camp. Soon it was dawn and the strong infantry was through the pass, guarding the other side, and the remainder of the army was able to start through.

When the sleepy, hostile tribesmen returned in the

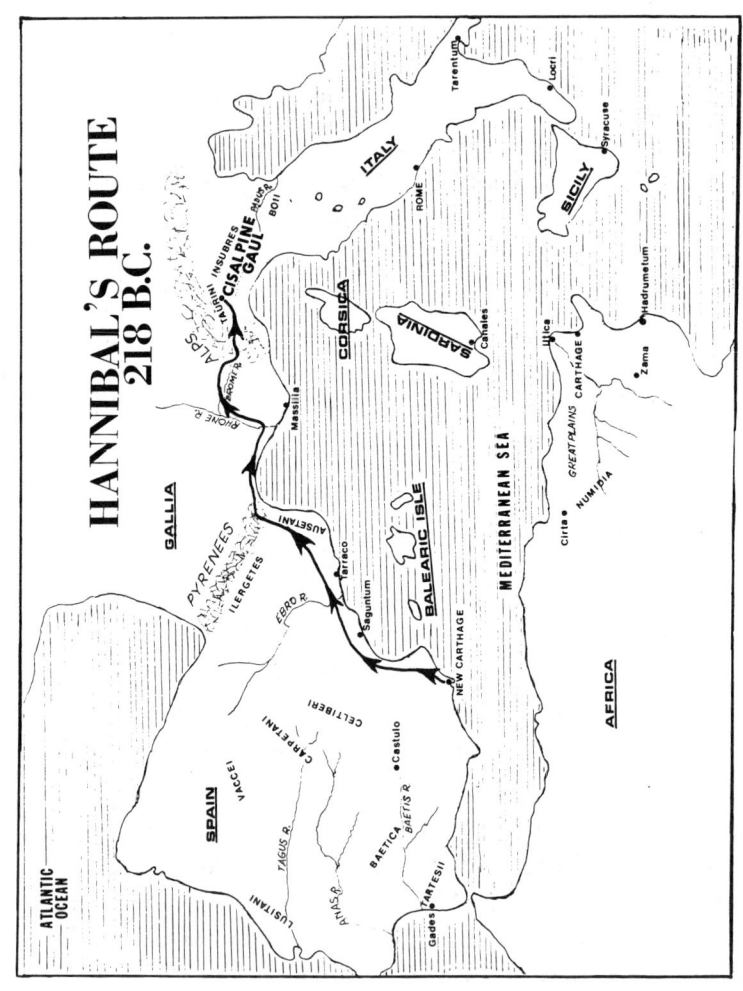

morning, they saw their previous positions on the mountain top occupied and Hannibal's army moving through the pass below. They were perplexed and uncertain as to what they should do until they observed disorganization and confusion in the army passing along the narrowest and most treacherous part of the trail. Part of the trail was uneven, running above river rapids, with a precipitous drop many hundreds of feet down into the icy river below. A couple of animals lost their footing, stumbled on the rocky trail, and plunged down the precipice with their riders and packs. Screams of animals and riders echoed throughout the canyon as they tumbled down the mountain crag, causing tumult among those still precariously picking their way along the rocky trail. Some horses panicked at the sights and sounds of those plunging down below, threw their riders, reversed direction on the trail, and wildly charged head-on into the narrow column struggling up the trail behind.

This confusion caused more animals to bolt, as many more plunged down the steep drop, screaming. The wild tribesmen observed this turmoil, and, motivated by the rich spoils on backs of the pack animals, they decided to add to the confusion. Ignoring dangers involved, they attacked the column, traversing the steep cliffs with the agility of mountain goats. They began hurling huge boulders down the mountain onto the helpless riders below, from positions halfway down the slope, under the positions held by Hannibal's troops. This caused avalanches of boulders which completely wiped out large sections in the middle of the column of pack animals that were carrying valuable supplies. Men, animals, and supplies were strewn all over the steep slope below. It created havoc. Carts and more pack animals, horses and their riders began hurling down amid screams of terror from men and animals. Added to the tumult was the thunderous sound of rocky avalanches. Emboldened, the wild men increased the confusion with their loud war shouts.

From high above, Hannibal was watching this. He had been reluctant to interfere previously for fear of adding to the confusion, thus causing more of his valuable resources to be lost. Finally, he could take no more, and the confusion was so great that it couldn't be increased by much. He ordered his men to attack the wild men below, and his archers and swordsmen plunged down the cliffs with an agility that matched that of the wild men. They massacred all in their path. The natives scattered over the mountain and disappeared after a single charge. What remained were hundreds of dead and wounded men and animals for miles along the gorge. Hannibal restored order as his men helped the wounded and salvaged some of the valuable supplies from backs of dead and wounded animals. There were serious losses, in the thousands, to the river below.

Afterward, the weary, bedraggled, rain-soaked army was able to pass unmolested through the trail, and it soon reached the main village of the tribe that had attacked them. The village was left unprotected because the wild men were dispersed in the mountains, still fleeing. The Carthaginians found sufficient grain and cattle in the village to provide needs of the army for three days. Though it was tempting to rest in the village longer, Hannibal ordered his men to remain in the village for only one night because rain was beginning to change to intermittent snow flurries. He was worried about getting over the pass before it was closed by snow. They continued their journey the next day, finding it more difficult to move their sore muscles and to breath as they climbed to higher elevations into the cold, oxygen-thin air of the high mountains.

In a few days, the weary travelers encountered another large mountain tribe that provided no resistance at first. Elders of the tribe approached the Carthaginians and feigned cooperation, offering to provide guides and supplies. They offered to provide hostages to Hannibal as guarantees of their good faith. Hannibal's guides provided by the Allobroges decided to leave abruptly, explaining they knew of no landmarks from that point onward. The departing guides merely instructed Hannibal to follow in the direction of the morning sun, saying that they didn't know the best passes to follow. This route that Hannibal had elected to take, in his attempt to deceive the Romans, was a more difficult one than any of his troops had ever taken. All of his agents, including Gisco, had scouted Alpine crossings that were farther south because they had been recommended as the easier crossing routes. Thus, since he had no guides, Hannibal accepted the mountain tribe's guides as a last resort, but he was highly suspicious of their behavior. He purchased much needed supplies from them, then continued his journey. Because he was suspicious, Hannibal organized his column in a more battle-ready formation than normal. He put his elephants and cavalry in the lead of the column to protect the front, and he remained with the strong infantry in rear guard, protecting against an assault from the rear.

Soon they reached another part of the trail that was rocky and narrow, high up a precipice, with a sheer drop hundreds of feet below. His mountain guides suddenly disappeared along with his hostages, and the long column was attacked in front, rear, and the middle. Again, huge boulders came raining down on the middle of the strung-out army as Hannibal and Gisco turned the rear guard infantry around to face attackers in the rear. While Hannibal was defending the rear, local tribesmen assaulted the middle of the column, cutting Hannibal and his rear guard off from the elephants, cavalry, and the supply train which were in front. The rear guard infantry had to spend the night separated from the others, but it fought its way back to rejoin the main army in the morning. The hostile tribe was not successful with its frontal assault on the column because it was intimidated by the elephants. Soon, enemy resistance ceased, and the bedraggled army continued its trek up the cold mountain with great difficulty because oxygen was becoming more scarce due to the increasing altitude. The primitive path they were taking required more and more effort to travel along because it hadn't been used very often. This required the army to hack out a pathway over very rough terrain. In some areas, elephants and other wounded animals, and carts had to be hand-lifted over the particularly rough parts, using huge straps and winches. More soldiers and pack animals were lost in the last skirmish, and many of the wounded soldiers unable to keep up with the rest of the army had to be left behind. They died on the trail or had to continue to move forward at their own pace. The security of the entire army could not be compromised by the delay necessary to help them. Hannibal did not want the army to be trapped on the mountain by a snowstorm, possible at any time.

From then on, no major opposition was encountered because elephants were leading the way and local natives were afraid of them. Elephants were slow and cumbersome to guide along the narrow, treacherous track. Infantrymen had to clear a path for them with picks and shovels. Sleet started to change to snow. As they climbed above the tree line there was nothing for the elephants to eat. There was no grass for animal forage on the snow-covered ground. Hannibal's officers estimated that their animals could not survive without forage for more than another three days. Most of the animal feed the army had brought with it was either eaten already or had been lost down ravines in skirmishes. Each morning as they broke camp, they left a few more dead or dying men and animals on the trail behind. The thinning ranks of soldiers were becoming disillusioned, sore, tired, cold, and they were gasping for oxygen. They struggled painfully to put one foot in front of the other to climb up the steep mountain. They were nearing the 10,000 foot elevation. Most troops were losing their enthusiasm for the campaign. Somehow, Hannibal was able to keep his shaggy, discouraged army together. He and Gisco kept their own vigor and ebullience as they passed up and down the long column giving words of encouragement to the weary soldiers. The men's faith and confidence in their leader was all that kept them going.

By the last week in October, the ninth day after starting into the foothills of the Alps, leading scouts reached the summit and were traveling on level ground (at the 9,500 foot level, south of Montegenevre). Hannibal called for his top officers to march on ahead of the column, to gather at a rise where they could see the green valley, cultivated fields, and the thick forest below them in northern Italy. He raised his jeweled sword, motioning in the direction of the pastures below and told his officers that they had reached the walls of Italy and Rome. He told them they had made it to the top and waiting for them below were wealthy cities full of gold, meat, wine, and women to pour it. He said they had only to ride down to reach them. His officers passed the good news down to the last man of the slowly moving line of soldiers who were still striving to reach the top. Spirits were raised and loud shouts of joy echoed through the mountains. Hannibal ordered a rest at the summit to allow stragglers to catch up, and a new spirit swelled within the ranks. Many riderless animals, thought to have been lost, caught up with the army as it rested.

But their celebration was premature. They soon discovered the path down was steeper and more treacherous than the climb up as they started down the south side of the Alps. It had been three days since the animals had sufficient food. Weak and weary from hunger and cold, they struggled down the icy, slippery, precipitous path.

On the way down the arduous path, the army came upon what appeared to be an insurmountable obstacle. A landslide had lodged a huge boulder the size of a house on the trail ahead, blocking the way. Some of the more agile soldiers were able to climb up and around the boulder, but it was impossible to get the animals and carts past it. The entire column was stopped for a day without progress. Animals and men were too weak to go back up the mountain to take another route down. It was now four days since animals had eaten, and the weak animals and men were cold as snow began to fall. Finally, the troops started to call for their "miracle man," Gisco, to do something. In desperation, Gisco decided to try something he had read about many years before, in Alexandria. He asked volunteer soldiers who could climb around the rock to descend the mountain down to the timberline, cut trees, then carry them back up the mountain. As difficult as the task was for the weakened men, it was finally accomplished. Gisco used the timbers to build a gigantic fire around the boulder, with the intent of oxidizing it and vaporizing the minute particles of water that may have been trapped within it. Gisco hoped that this would cause the huge boulder to crumble. When the boulder was heated to a high temperature, Gisco directed soldiers to pour a vast amount of cold, spoiled, vinegar wine on it. Amazingly, the rock began to split apart with huge cracks running through it. Men with picks and sledgehammers were able to break larger stones, along the cracks, into smaller ones and carry them away. This took much time to accomplish, and the army was delayed, disastrously, for four days at this site. Many more of the starving animals died before the army was able to descend to rich forests and meadows below. Hannibal ordered a well-earned rest at a suitable meadow below, where there was plenty of wood for fires and food and water for the animals that had survived the ordeal.

Fifteen days had elapsed from the time the army started its climb in the Alpine foothills to the day they reached the rich meadows of northern Italy. It had only been five months since the huge army left New Carthage, but the trip took a terrible toll on Hannibal's forces. When an accurate count was made at the campsite in the meadow, it was learned that

12,000 soldiers had been lost since leaving the Rhone river. These soldiers had been killed, severely wounded, died of cold and disease, or deserted during the Alpine crossing. Hannibal had only 26,000 tired, bedraggled troops left: 12,000 African infantry; 8,000 Spanish infantry; 6,000 cavalry; and fifteen elephants. This was all he had left to fight the potential 700,000 soldiers in Roman legions. By now snow had closed the passes behind them and there was no turning back. There was no hope of getting reinforcements or supplies from Spain until spring, because the only route that these could take was by water, until Alpine passes had been thawed along the land route. The strong Roman navy had cut off the water route to Spain. Additional troops had been promised by the Boii and Insubres who were in the rich valley below their present campsite, but Hannibal wasn't certain how many soldiers of these tribes would be joining him, nor how capable their fighters were.

It was early November. Hannibal ended his army's short rest in the foothills. He decided to find a more comfortable camp for his troops in the fertile valley of northwestern Italy below them, to continue their rest and recuperation. His soldiers looked more like wild animals than people. They had shaggy hair and beards, dirty and worn animal hides for clothes, and they were thin and drawn from their ordeal. The animals, particularly, were in very bad shape; those that were able to survive the obstacles were skinny and tired. The army was in no condition to fight soon. They finally reached the valley thirty days after leaving the Rhone.

The first tribe of Gauls they met in northern Italy was the Taurini, a tribe that happened to be feuding with Hannibal's allies, the Boii. Taurini were primitive people. Their men wore bronze helmets with large horns attached to them, long straggly hair, thick mustaches, and thick gold chains around their necks. As soon as they learned that Carthaginians were to become allies of the Boii, the Taurini treated them with hostility. Hannibal, who was in no mood to bicker with them, responded to their hostility by taking their main town (now Turin). Here he allowed his soldiers to continue their much needed rest to regain their vitality, to restore the health of the surviving animals, and to bring their equipment back to its original fighting order. Many were becoming worried because there was no sign of the tribes that were supposed to reinforce their army, the Boii and Insubres.

Gisco found some miniature, sample models of monuments that the Taurini had taken from a Greek merchant passing through the territory. The models were found by Carthaginian soldiers among the plunder when they took the town. Gisco volunteered to disguise himself and Cirta as a Greek salesmen of statues and monuments, then scout ahead while the army was recuperating. They planned to reconnoiter Roman forces by infiltrating their camps. He knew much about the camps in the area from his travels four years before and from reports that secret agents had made to New Carthage. Hannibal agreed to let him do it, and he told Gisco that he would accompany the two Greeks part of the way, incognito. He wanted to explore the terrain ahead for possible battle sites in the event that a fight should soon become necessary. He would wear one of his many wigs and disguises.

While Gisco and Cirta were visiting Roman camps, Hannibal made contact with the Boii and Insubres during his exploration of the terrain. He found the emissaries that each of the two tribes had sent to meet him in Gallia before he had crossed the Alps. They verified for their leaders that this man in disguise was actually the great Hannibal. He learned from them that they had received reports about the decimated state of the Carthaginian army after its trip over the Alps, and that they were no longer anxious to join his weak, reduced army in a fight against Scipio's powerful Roman legions. Afterwards, when Hannibal returned from his exploration to his camp, he didn't tell his troops about this new development because he thought it would be too much of a blow to their morale in their present weakened condition. He intended to tell them after they had fully recovered from the trip.

It was getting cold as Gisco and Cirta rode their horses to the Roman forts of Cremona and Placentia (Piacenza now) in northern Italy to gather information concerning enemy forces, grain storage sites, and forage areas for the animals. While posing as a Greek vendor of monuments, Gisco was recognized by a Cisalpine Gaul who had joined the Roman army along with thousands of his countrymen. The soldier had been in a group that Gisco and Cirta had met nearly four years earlier, during their tour of Italy. The young Gaul recognized the unforgettable physique, handsome face, and cultured manners of the pentathlon champion. Gisco was not alarmed by the recognition, but it startled Cirta. Gisco knew that there was no reason for Romans to connect him, a Greek, with their Carthaginian enemy, and he also knew that Romans were not aware that Hannibal had already crossed the Alps.

Gisco had learned to speak the language of the Gauls fluently, and he carried on a long, friendly conversation with the young warrior and his friends. Indirect questioning of the Gauls allowed Gisco to confirm that Roman legions were still using tactics he and Cirta had studied earlier. They had obtained detailed military documents that explained, for Roman commanders, official procedures and tactics used by Roman legions. Gisco had been instructing Carthaginian officers in this military doctrine for many months, as it was a basis for all Roman military maneuvers in combat, seldom violated by disciplined Romans. It was also the basic foundation from which Hannibal had planned his tactics for fighting the legions and around which he had organized his army.

The young Gaul and his comrades spoke derogatorily of the Roman army. They had become disillusioned by the way they were being treated by Roman military personnel. Many Cisalpine Gauls had joined the Roman army for the promised pay, food, clothing, and adventure, but they found that Romans discriminated against them and treated them as inferiors. They were paid only half as much as Roman citizen-soldiers for the same work and risk, and they were not trusted nor given much responsibility. Gauls felt like outcasts, their morale was low, and they resented Roman overbearing presence in their homeland.

When he thought he could do it safely, Gisco gave the Gaul and his friends silver, then told them that Hannibal was in the Padus (Po) valley with a large force of soldiers to fight Romans and free lands of the Gauls from Roman occupation. He told them that Hannibal would treat Gauls as equals, he would provide better pay, better food, and they would be fighting to free their homes from the Roman scourge if they joined him. Gisco asked them to tell their fellow Cisalpine Gauls about this, and that all who came to join Hannibal would be given welcomes and rewards in silver.

Gisco learned from conversations with Roman officers in Placentia that the patrician consul, Publius Cornelius Scipio, had arrived from Pisae (Pisa) to take command of legions that were stationed there. As Gisco was preparing to leave the fort, messengers arrived in Placentia with news that Hannibal had crossed the Alps and that he was already in the valley of the Padus. Scipio was shocked by this information, as he hadn't expected Hannibal to be able to cross the Alps until next year, if at all. He had just announced this belief to his staff of officers shortly before the alarming news arrived. Gisco decided to delay his departure from the fort when he heard Scipio assembling a large force to march north against Hannibal. Scipio decided not to delay until reinforcements could arrive to help him, because his messengers had reported that the Carthaginian army was depleted and weak as a result of its climb over the Alps. Gisco heard Scipio announce to his troops at the assembly that he was confident his Romans could easily defeat the ragged Carthaginian army because it had run from battle with him at the Rhone river a couple of months earlier. He also told his troops that agents reported that Hannibal's army had lost two-thirds of its original size as a consequence of the ordeal of climbing the Alps. He told his men that the few Carthaginian fighting forces able to survive the trip were now emaciated and unfit for fighting.

Gisco and his companion left Placentia and returned to Hannibal's camp with a report of their experiences. Hannibal was worried that Scipio was on his way to fight them so soon, before the Carthaginian army had fully recovered. His great commander told Gisco that the Boii and Insubres had not sent forces to join him as promised. When a few emissaries from these two tribes had visited Hannibal's camp a few days ago, as a follow-up from Hannibal's recent visit with them and before Gisco had returned from his trip, the Gauls were visibly annoyed by its reduced size and by its filthy, disorganized, feeble appearance. Hannibal told Gisco that they had no confidence in the fighting ability of the Carthaginian army and they would not make a definite commitment of troops to help Hannibal fight the tough Roman legions. Furthermore, Hannibal was seriously concerned about the low morale of his soldiers; they were becoming indifferent about fighting Romans. The great Carthaginian commander decided to do something quickly about that problem.

Hannibal designed a cunning spectacle to stimulate his troops out of their lethargy and present them with the harsh realities of their present situation. It was a typical example of Hannibal's genius for communicating with his soldiers, and it reached their minds better than words could. He gathered his soldiers and formed them into a huge circle. Then he placed some chained Gallic prisoners, whom he had captured in the recent fighting with the Taurinis, into the center of the circle where they were clearly visible to all the soldiers. He told the prisoners, in a loud voice so that all could hear, that he wanted volunteers from the prisoners to fight single battles, one prisoner against one other prisoner. Each pair of volunteers must fight with swords and shields that Hannibal would provide them, and they must continue fighting until one of them kills the other. He said that the victor of each combat would be freed, given a horse, and allowed to keep his sword and shield as a prize. Furthermore, he said, those prisoners who do not volunteer for the contest will be sold as slaves on the slave market, the normal fate of prisoners of war. As Hannibal expected, every prisoner enthusiastically volunteered to fight to the death, so that lots had to be drawn to see who the lucky pair of combatants would be that was allowed to fight. Hannibal limited the number of pairs to four. All prisoners were willing to face death rather than remain as slaves. Winners of the lottery were wild with excitement at their good fortune, and they drew wild congratulations from the remaining prisoners. Each of the ensuing, courageous contests drew the admiration of all watching, Carthaginians as well as prisoners. The dead losers were as valiant as the victors, and they received the tumultuous applause and praise of all the spectators.

After two pairs had fought to a decision, the games were discontinued and Hannibal rewarded those lottery winners, that were to fight, with their freedom. Then Hannibal called his men to come in closer to him in the center of the circle so that he could address them. He told his men to carefully reflect on what they had just seen, of men fighting to the death for their freedom, and of the glory and spoils won by the victors. He told them that the situation of the prisoners was similar to their own, present predicament. The path home for them was now closed by snow, there was no escape by sea, and Roman legions were on their way to fight them. Thus their situation was now one where they had to fight to retain their freedom, be taken as slaves, or be killed by Roman legions who were on their way to fight them. He told his men that the spoils of victory, the fabulous wealth of Rome, would make them rich men. It would bring them fame and glory throughout the lands as they freed forever their homes and homes of others from ravages of Roman conquest. For those reasons, he said, there is only one choice we have: fight and win, or die. To lose and live is a fate worse than death, as it means a life of slavery in Roman hands.

Hannibal's scrubby-looking soldiers clearly saw the point. "Victory or death" became their motto. With renewed purpose, they summoned up an amazing reserve of vigor. They washed, shaved, re-sharpened their weapons, and reconciled themselves to either conquering the Romans or die trying. Hannibal's brilliant allegory worked much better than words could have to motivate his men.

Chapter 4

FIRST ROMAN ENCOUNTERS: TICINUS AND TREBBIA (November, 218 to May, 217 B.C.)

Hannibal shared his secret thoughts with Gisco about his reluctance to engage the tough Roman legions, for the first time, with his depleted, tired army. He needed more time for his soldiers and animals to recuperate, and he had hoped to have masses of allied soldiers joining his army for its first encounter with them. Now, he realized they had no choice because Scipio was on his way to fight, and there was no going back. The brilliant Carthaginian general had already made a personal inspection of the terrain ahead, on horseback, and he knew where the terrain was most suitable for the tactics he intended to use against the Roman legions. He decided to move his army out so that the first battle would take place on the plains of the Padus (Po) Valley, where he could use his fast-moving cavalry to its best advantage against the ponderous legions.

He figured that his infantry was no match for the Roman's, but his cavalry outnumbered its Roman counterpart. Regardless of its weakened condition, Hannibal believed, his Numidian and Celtiberian horse-troops should be able to outfight the smaller, less-capable Roman horsemen. It was in cavalry, he figured, that he was superior to the oncoming Roman forces. He had no intention to fight the tough legionnaire foot-soldiers in hand-to-hand fighting, their most formidable strength, while his own infantry was still in a weakened condition.

Gisco told Hannibal and his chief of intelligence, Carthalo, about his promise to Gallic soldiers serving in the Roman army. Hannibal would give them money and respect if they would defect from the Romans. He also told the two about the Gauls' low morale, resulting from Roman discrimination against them. Hannibal was elated. He was also happy to learn from Gisco that Scipio was overconfident, an emotion that the crafty Carthaginian liked to exploit in combat.

The Roman problem, concerning morale of Gauls serving in the Roman army, reminded Hannibal of the growing problem of morale within his own multinational, polyglot army. To make matters worse, some of his soldiers were slaves with an owner-slave relationship. In combat, all had to share in the same risks, and all should receive similar rewards. Hannibal had been sensing a growing discontent within his army, so he decided to do something about it before he had the same problem that the Romans were experiencing.

He called a meeting of all officers and announced that henceforth soldiers of all nations of his army would have the same privileges as Carthaginians. He told them that all slaves who were accompanying their masters would have their freedom, and their masters were to be compensated in silver for their market value. After the meeting, officers passed this information to all of their men, and there was great jubilation. Morale of the soldiers was raised considerably. Carthaginians, who were a small minority in the army, recognized the need for the policy, and they accepted the new decree by their beloved commander. Later, Hannibal promised all his men that they would be given land in the country of their choice - Spain or Africa - as soon as they defeated the Roman army. He said that they could have silver in lieu of land if they chose. He also promised his men that they would be free to leave his army and return to their homes after Rome was defeated. At a meeting of his officers, Hannibal told them of Gisco's confirmation that Roman legions were still using the battle doctrine that they had been studying for many months under Gisco's guidance. He reiterated the fact that the strength of the Roman army was in their rigid, disciplined battle formation, the manipular legion, a formation of infantry marching in ranks that varied from 400 to 900 across per legion; if there were more than one legion, the width of the formation would be that much more. There would be up to nine ranks deep, behind this broad front, as they advanced menacingly like marionettes with shields and spears ready. Only token cavalry was used, compared to that of the Carthaginian army. Legionnaires were trained never to break formation, flee, or pursue the enemy, whatever the situation, unless ordered to do so. Hannibal told his officers that he did not intend to use his weakened infantry against the superior strength of legionnaires. He intended to make maximum use of the maneuverability of his superior cavalry, and he would only use his foot soldiers as decoys. The smaller Roman cavalry was used for purposes of scouting, protecting flanks of the infantry in combat, and pursuing routed armies. The Roman military doctrine did not use cavalry as an offensive weapon, as Hannibal had planned to use his cavalry. Roman horses were slower than the Numidians' horses, and Roman horse-soldiers were not as highly trained as Hannibal's Numidians or Celtiberians. Hannibal's entire army contained highly

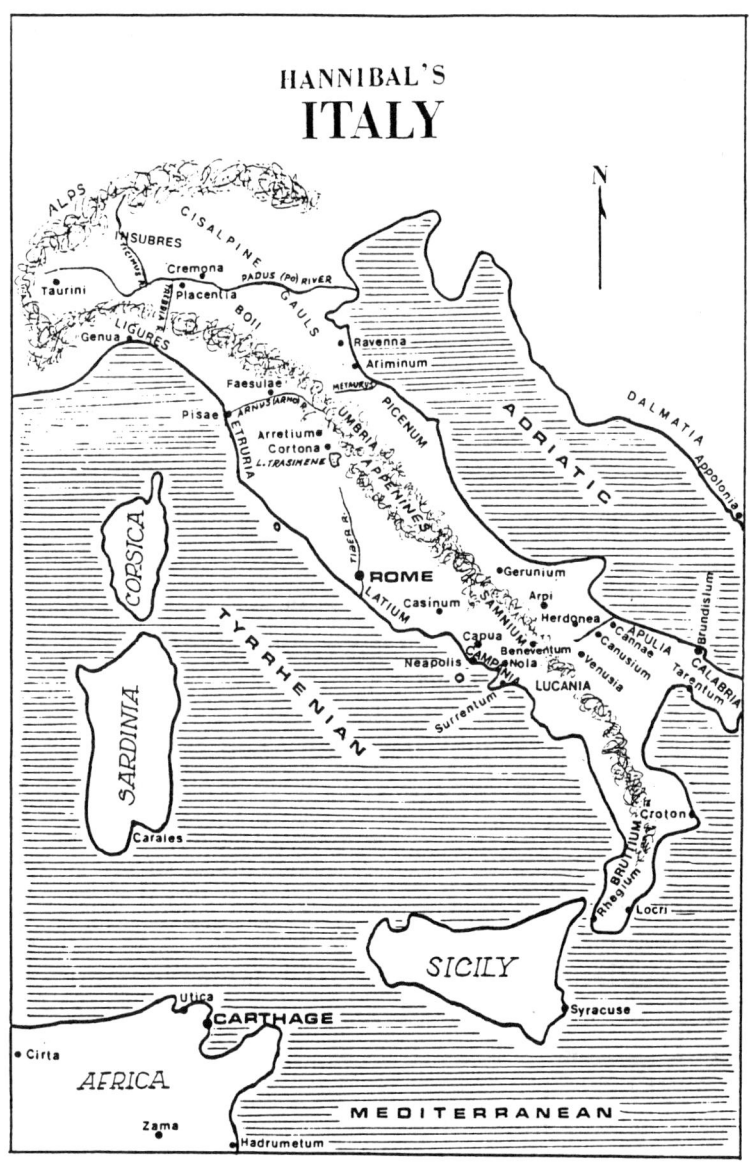

trained, hardened, professional soldiers who had years of combat experience together under his command. After a long planning session, and thorough indoctrination of his troops on tactics they would use in the first battle, the small, weak army marched east to the open plain on the north side of the Padus. Hannibal sent 500 Numidian cavalry, led by the cunning Maharbal, to scout ahead as a steady rain fell. Maharbal pillaged all Roman colonial farms and villages along the way, while sparing those of the Gauls.

The next day Maharbal returned to report that a large Roman force was building a bridge across the Ticinus River, north of the Padus and to the east of Hannibal's position. The marching Carthaginian army came within sight of Scipio's legions near the Ticinus the next day. Both of the enemy columns stopped as they met on the plains of the Insubres nation. The disciplined Roman soldiers immediately formed a huge, intimidating combat formation with efficient, military precision, all commands being given by trumpet, soldiers moving like marionettes. Hannibal's troops expected exactly what they saw, but the sight was awesome and frightening as they viewed it for the first time.

Scipio positioned his line of skirmishing spearmen and his Gallic cavalry in front of his formation, with the remainder of his cavalry protecting his flanks, right and left. The Consul and his fasces, the bronze-bound rods and ax, symbol of his authority hanging on a pole overhead near him, were located in the cavalry in front of his legions. Mechanically, the menacing, precise formation of legionnaires moved steadily toward the apparently unorganized, amorphous mass of emaciated, polyglot foot-soldiers that was the Carthaginian army facing them.

Hannibal had purposely situated his infantry in a huge bunch as a decoy, as though they were bait for a trap, to entice the overconfident Romans. He had no intention of letting them fight hand-to-hand with enemy infantry. Hannibal saw that his 6,000 horse soldiers outnumbered the Roman cavalry by a margin of more than three-to-one, as he had expected. With Gisco and Cirta at his side, he planned to lead the Celtiberian bridled cavalry, with its strong, stocky horses, shields and swords fixed, out to meet Scipio's vanguard cavalry. He ordered Maharbal to lead the fast moving Numidian cavalry, with its javelins, to attack Roman cavalry on Scipio's flanks. Numidians would attack the Romans, launch a cloud of javelins while still out of range of the Italian weapons, then run to regroup for another attack.

Gisco and Hannibal had discussed their planned tactics at great length. While the infantry stayed behind, the Celtiberian horsemen would ride at full gallop toward the Consul's fasces pole as a target, with the intent of attacking the Consul. Hannibal, Gisco, and Cirta rode in the lead of this group. The Spanish cavalry picked up full speed as they charged the fasces, and the Roman spearmen, who were on foot and out in Scipio's front, panicked at the horrifying sight of thousands of horses charging at them. Fearful of being trampled, they hastily retreated to the rear of the Consul's guarding cavalry, which was originally positioned behind the spearmen. The terrified spearmen fled to the rear without discharging their first salvo of spears at the charging Spaniards.

There was a tumultuous clash as the two cavalries collided. Momentum favored the Spaniards who were moving rapidly on their stocky Iberian horses, and their force bowled over the frightened, vastly-outnumbered, Gallic horsemen who were only moving slowly. A thunderous cacophony was created by clanking of swords and shields, thuds of bodies and horses colliding, and screams of pain and war shouts. Momentum of Hannibal's horses carried them into the Consul's mounted bodyguards before slowing, as Hannibal had planned. They fought their way to the Consul with awesome ferocity as they slashed arms and heads of the enemy, knocking many off their mounts. Many of the outnumbered Gallic horsemen, intimidated by what they saw and less disciplined than Roman troops, fled, hastily moving out of the way of the unstoppable Celtiberians. In their retreat, the Gauls clashed and tangled with their own spearmen behind them. Cirta was the first to reach Scipio, and he severely slashed the Roman commander's arms and neck before the Consul plunged from his horse to the ground. The Consul was further injured by hoofs of horses that trampled him in the melee.

While Hannibal and his Celtiberians were crushing the vanguard of the legions, Maharbal's Numidians were crushing the outnumbered and out-skilled Roman cavalry in the wings of the Roman infantry. The wings collapsed under the pressure and all Roman horsemen fled over the plains. Next, Maharbal's cavalry sped around, rapidly to the rear of the helpless infantry, and started sending clouds of javelins into its rear, killing many.

Soon, remnants of Scipio's cavalry, vanguard and flanks, broke and scattered over the countryside. That left its unprotected Roman infantry at the mercy of the hit-and-run tactics of Numidian javelin-throwers who remained safely out of range of the stationary Roman soldiers. Numidians could launch their javelins while at full gallop on their horses. This added momentum, provided by swiftly moving horses, gave their javelins much added range over those launched by the stationary Roman soldiers. Demoralized by what they saw, surviving Roman officers ordered trumpets to signal a retreat. A small group of loyal guards, bravely led by Scipio's young son, fought its way to the severely wounded Consul and carried him away to safety. Remaining Romans retreated to their previous camp near the Ticinus in tight, defensive formation, while constantly being harassed by the deadly Numidians. That night, under cover of darkness, Roman survivors crossed the rivers Ticinus and Padus and destroyed the bridges behind them so Hannibal could not pursue. The badly beaten troops settled in at their fort in Placentia. Hannibal took 600 prisoners in mop-up operations behind retreating Romans.

Visiting emissaries from the Boii and Insubres nations had watched the entire skirmish from a safe distance, on a rise of terrain where they had a good view. Hannibal's infantry had orders not to attack, but they watched the scene with glee. The unprecedented spectacle of Roman legions commanded by a consul and fleeing from an enemy made a great impression on the visiting agents of Hannibal's potential allies. Previously, they had serious doubts about the fighting ability of Hannibal's motley army. Their former low opinion of the depleted army changed to one of great admiration and respect. Hannibal's army had very few casualties, and the encounter gave it a great uplift in morale and much confidence in its ability to fight the vaunted Roman legions. It also provided further confirmation that the legions were still using tactics which Gisco had been instructing to Carthaginian officers.

The Roman debacle encouraged 2,000 Gauls serving with the Roman army to kill their officers by decapitation, flee with 200 valuable horses, and join Hannibal's army to take advantage of Gisco's offer to them. Hannibal gave them a warm welcome, a reward of silver, some warm food, and wine. He made a speech to them in their own language and requested that they return to their homes, recruit fellow countrymen, then return to join his army. He told them he would pay them well, feed them well, treat them well, and that they would gain fame and fortune by helping him evict forever the hated Romans from their tribal territories. He promised them land after Rome had been defeated. The amount of land would be determined by the importance of their contribution to the fight. He promised them that Carthage wanted none of their tribal territories, and that his army would leave Italy soon after defeating Rome.

Carthalo, Hannibal's chief of intelligence, selected a few of the more intelligent Gauls of those who had defected from the Romans to form the nucleus of a spy ring he wanted to establish within the enemy camp. He instructed them to return to their units under cover to provide Carthaginians with a source of information about activities at Placentia. All were promised rich rewards, and they were also asked to urge more of their Gallic comrades to defect.

Most of the 600 prisoners captured in the Ticinus skirmish were not citizens of Rome. Most were Italians from territories conquered by Roman legions, and they were subsequently recruited into the Roman army as allies of the regular citizen-army. The captives had expected to spend the rest of their lives as slaves, the normal fate of prisoners of war. Hannibal unexpectedly treated them with great dignity and respect, fed them warm meals, and sent them to their scattered homes. He wanted them to spread information throughout Italy about Hannibal's fairness and mercy toward prisoners who were not citizens of Rome. He told the prisoners that he had come to Italy to fight Romans, not Italians, and to give Italians back their cities and lands, giving them freedom from their oppressor. He said their interests and his were the same.

Hannibal hoped to alienate people in Italian territories from their allegiance to Rome, and to foment revolt in Italian territories that were dissatisfied with Roman rule. He also hoped that this would encourage non-citizen soldiers of the Roman army to defect. Hannibal also believed that this policy would facilitate recruitment of much-needed troops in small villages as he marched through Italy. These were the first of many prisoners that Hannibal would release in such a manner. Roman citizen-soldiers were treated much more harshly: they were put in chains and kept as prisoners to be used for trading purposes; or they were sold to slave traders that followed the armies when a battle was expected.

The first dividend from Carthalo's spy ring inside the fort at Placentia was received by late December. Agents reported that the second consul, Tiberius Sempronius Longus, had been diverted from his previous orders, to attack Carthage in Africa, and that the Roman Senate had ordered him and his legions to reinforce Scipio's army at Placentia. Sempronius had arrived with his legions to make the small fort very crowded. The Senate, and all of Rome were alarmed that Hannibal was now in Italy. Scipio was confined to his bed with wounds received at the Ticinus when his co-consul arrived. Scipio was in no condition, physically or emotionally, to return to the battlefield.

The new consul Sempronius, on the other hand, was ambitious and naively overconfident about engaging Hannibal's army. The combined armies at Placentia were now 40,000 troops: 16,000 Roman-citizen infantry; 20,000 allied infantry; and 4,000 cavalry. Sempronius, the politician eager to make a name for himself in Rome before the annual Senate elections in January, was anxious to attack the ragged Carthaginians. The Senate was scheduled to elect two new consuls to head the armies for the next year, and he wanted to be re-elected.

Scipio, who had learned from personal experience about fighting Hannibal, strongly cautioned Sempronius against rushing into combat with the cunning Carthaginian. He recommended that they wait until spring when weather would be better. Scipio also wanted Sempronius to familiarize himself with the troops and terrain before committing to combat. He told Sempronius that he had never seen such massive, mobile, expertly trained, aggressive cavalry as he had seen fighting against him at the Tacinus encounter. He said that he was amazed to see how accurate the cavalry was at launching its weapons while in full gallop.

The overconfident Sempronius dismissed Scipio's admonition as an emotional exaggeration, influenced by his recent defeat and by his severe wounds. Furthermore, he didn't think that Scipio was as good a commander as himself, which he believed accounted for much of the wounded man's caution. However, they were co-consuls according to the Senate's edict, thus Sempronius needed Scipio's approval before he could attack Hannibal. The situation greatly displeased and frustrated Sempronius. The only way he could override Scipio's objections was to find extenuating circumstances that could be used as justification to act against the Senate's edict. Sempronius thought it ridiculous that such a large Roman force should be intimidated by such a small force of weakened, undisciplined barbarians.

All of this information was brought to Hannibal by two astute spies, and they were paid well for their efforts. It was now past the winter solstice, and rain was gradually turning to sleet, with an occasional snow flurry. The small fort at Placentia was becoming overcrowded by the combined armies of the two consuls, and its streets became a muddy morass. The consuls decided to move out of the fort a short distance, up the east side of the Trebbia River to higher ground where they also had more space. They fortified their new camp on defensible ground.

While this was going on, Hannibal's forces had crossed the Padus River and made camp on the other side of the Trebbia, the west side, less than ten miles away from the Romans. They began forging land and plundering crops of Roman colonists in the area, but they were careful not to harm Gallic farms. Local tribes, after seeing the success of the Carthaginians against Roman legions, seeing that they paid in silver, began supplying them with many of their needs. Many Cisalpine Gauls joined Hannibal's forces. Hannibal captured some rich Roman military grain storage depots, much to the chagrin of Sempronius, causing him to become more impatient to do something about the plundering of Roman property.

When the next report from agents in Placentia reached Hannibal, it included the statement that Sempronius was agitated and frustrated because the Carthaginian army was freely foraging the land everywhere around the Roman camp, unopposed. The great Carthaginian general decided to use this information to his military advantage in the next battle. The cunning Hannibal was expert at exploiting personal weaknesses of his adversaries, the reason he always sought information about his opponents' personalities and foibles. He knew that Sempronius was overconfident and anxious to attack him in battle and that he would attack if he were given enough excuse to override objections of his bedridden co-consul. He decided to provoke Sempronius into a trap. He also knew that the ambitious Consul was not familiar with the terrain on the west side of the Trebbia because he had not yet been there.

Hannibal began making elaborate preparations for an ambush many days before he intended to spring it. As a first step, while he was making other preparations, he instructed his cagey Numidian cavalry to avoid combat with Romans when challenged by them during foraging activities; instead, he told them to flee when they saw Italians, as they had done previously along the Rhone. This tactic was to reinforce Sempronius's belief that Numidians were inferior to his Roman soldiers and that they were afraid of Romans. It encouraged his overconfidence.

The tactic worked, and after a few incidents where parties of Numidians met newly arrived cavalry troops belonging to Sempronius, Sempronius was delighted to hear that Numidians ran away from their challenge for combat. It made him more anxious to attack. Hannibal was preparing to use his fast Numidian horses as bait to lure the impatient Roman commander into an ambush.

Hannibal and Gisco rode their horses around the terrain for days, studying it for a suitable battlefield site, with the knowledge that the overzealous Consul had never seen it. Hannibal finally selected an area that was on high ground, above a quagmire below, through which he planned to lure Sempronius. It was about six miles away from the Roman camp, and across the cold Trebbia. Hannibal planned to force the Roman troops to wade through the icy waters breast-high to cross the Trebbia. Next, they had to march through the muddy quagmire along the water's bank to reach the battleground that would be waiting above them. The crafty general had his men build a shallow trench along the high ground with an earthen parapet along it to shield his troops from enemy missiles.

Next, a half-mile down the slope toward the area from which he expected legions of Sempronius to be marching uphill, water-soaked from crossing the Trebbia, he located a suitable ravine off to one side. He estimated that the ravine could conceal 2,000 of his soldiers from the enemy, as Romans marched by it to engage his army on the hilltop above. He brought his capable young brother, Mago, to the site to inspect the ravine, and he showed him where he planned to hide 1,000 cavalry and 1,000 infantry on the day of the battle. He planned to have Mago's troops emerge from hiding on a prearranged signal, after the Roman legions had marched unknowingly past the position, and after they had become preoccupied with Hannibal's forces on the hilltop above. That evening, Hannibal had Mago and the leader of the Iberian cavalry hand-pick 100 of the most courageous horsemen and 100 of the best fighting infantrymen. Each of these men were told to hand-pick nine more like themselves, making up the total of 2,000 to be under Mago's command and concealed in the ravine.

All preparations were complete in a few days. The shrewd Hannibal chose to start his campaign a few minutes after midnight on a cold, rain-and-sleet night.

The Trebbia, normally a small mountain stream, was swelled by steady rains so that the soldiers would have to wade breast-high to cross it. Hannibal handpicked 500 of his Numidian cavalry known for their swiftness and endurance to lure the Romans to the selected site by using their usual hit-and-run tactics. They were instructed to attack guardposts of the Roman camp with javelins and harass the camp itself during the early morning hours. All were promised unusual rewards for their efforts, although these were not necessary because the men were very enthusiastic about going without rewards.

Consul Sempronius was wakened by the noise of the sudden assault, and he excitedly dispatched his entire cavalry of 4,000 horses to pursue the 500 African raiders. Glad to have reason to override objections of his co-consul, he sent 6,000 of his infantry to immediately follow his cavalry, while he assembled the remainder of the entire army.

After launching their attack with devastating effectiveness, the 500 Numidians sped off, but they were careful not to go so fast that the pursuing Roman horsemen would lose sight of them. While fleeing, they suddenly turned around and launched a flight of javelins into the lead group of pursuers, momentarily slowing those following. African horses were much faster and more nimble, and they easily outpaced the plodding Italians.

Sempronius was so eager for battle that he hastily formed his army to march in the darkness of early morning, in the cold rain and sleet, without allowing time for his troops to have breakfast. He ordered his soldiers to dress in full battle gear, which provided little protection from the bitter weather. As Hannibal had planned, the route they had to take in pursuit of the Numidians required them to march six miles through soggy ground, cross the flooded Trebbia breast-deep in icy water, then march through more marshy ground to reach the rise where Carthaginians and their allies were waiting, securely ensconced in the trench on favorable high ground. Hannibal's army was now swollen to 38,000 because the Cisalpine Gauls had sent many troops. Ten elephants were all that remained.

All the time that Romans were struggling without sleep or breakfast to march through the wet weather for six miles, Hannibal allowed his army to finish a good night's rest, then warm themselves in leisure at campfires, eat a hearty breakfast, and wear warm cloaks made of animal skins over their battle dress to protect themselves from the bitter cold. Hannibal had his men anoint their bodies with oil earlier as further protection from the cold. His men rested in place as they waited for the Roman army to come to them.

As dawn broke the Roman cavalry crossed the Trebbia in hot pursuit of the Numidians. They climbed up the slope to see the massed Carthaginian army waiting for them. They did not see Mago's group hidden in the ravine. They had expended many of their missiles during their chase of the Africans, so they decided to rest and wait for the Roman army to catch up with them. When the Consul arrived, scrambling out of the icy water, he and his army were wet, thoroughly chilled, hungry, and tired. They could hardly hold their weapons in their freezing hands. Sempronius regrouped his army as it emerged from the water. He had brought his entire four legions: 16,000 Roman legionnaires; 20,000 allied infantry; and the 4,000 cavalry that were waiting for him. Ahead, a mile up the slope, they saw Hannibal's men protected by the trench and parapet. Sleet pummeled their faces as they marched up the slope to commence the battle. Balearic slingers were posted in front of the trench. Hannibal's cavalry had grown to 10,000 with the addition of allied Gauls, and they were evenly divided on each side of the trench, as were the elephants. Soon the unsuspecting legions marched in perfect formation past the ravine concealing Mago's troops and into range of the Balearic slingers' long-range missiles. Slingers were able to bombard the approaching legions long before Romans could retaliate uphill with their own short-range weapons. When the legions moved closer, slingers moved to the sides where they concentrated their fire on the tired Roman cavalry. Soon, huge clouds of javelins rained on the weary Italians as they continued their climb up the rise, still unable to reach Carthaginians with their own missiles.

Horses in the cavalry of Sempronius were not accustomed to the sight and scent of elephants, and they bolted wildly as they were attacked by the mammoth beasts. Many of the terrified horses were completely out of control and they gyrated into one another in their panic to escape. Clouds of flying missiles were raining on the hapless Roman horses and riders. Those that continued to live were outnumbered more than two-to-one, and they were completely routed, dispersing as they fled for the river.

Hannibal gave the signal for Mago's detachment to enter the fray, attacking the Italian infantry from its rear. Denuded of its cavalry, remaining legions were completely encircled. Mago caught them by complete surprise, as they were already totally absorbed with more than they could handle with Hannibal's troops in front of them. Hannibal's slingers and javelin throwers sent clouds of missiles down on them, and elephants began to attack the infantry. Soon, the Carthaginian cavalry returned from the rout of its Roman counterpart and started to cut the defenseless legions apart. Shaken by the onslaught, confused, and completely demoralized, Roman officers gave the order for trumpets to signal retreat. Only a few legionnaires were able to bravely fight their way through Mago's troops to reach the river. Only 10,000 of the Consul's original 40,000 soldiers were able to return to their camp across the Trebbia, and of those missing, more than half were slain. The remainder were either left wounded on the battlefield, captured, or had defected. Many had been slain by Numidians as they tried to cross the Trebbia.

Hannibal's losses were heavy, but most of the losses were his Gallic allies. Very few of Hannibal's African and Spanish troops, the most difficult soldiers to replace, were lost. Sleet turned to a chilling, torrential rain, so Hannibal did not order his army to pursue the Romans across the river. He knew his troops were cold and tired, and the weather was turning worse. Hannibal had his wounded attended to and dead buried. Then after mopping up the Italian stragglers and salvaging the armor and jewelry from corpses, Hannibal allowed his elated army to return to its warm camp. They had won another decisive victory over the vaunted Roman legions, completely destroying four consular legions.

As in the past, Hannibal allowed all captured soldiers who were not citizens of Rome to return to their homes, and he treated them with kindness and a hot meal. He also made his usual speech, telling the captives that he had come to Italy to fight Romans in their behalf, to free their homes from the Romans scourge. All Roman citizen-soldiers were put in chains and held for sale to slave traders. A few of the high-ranking officers were held to be ransomed later.

Sempronius did not disclose the extent of his catastrophic defeat in his reports to the Roman Senate when he returned to Rome to be there for the January elections. He tried to cover up the debacle by reporting merely that he was prevented from achieving victory by the bad weather. He didn't provide many more details. However, returning soldiers, vendors, and others who had witnessed the conflict gradually disclosed the astonishing facts to the Roman population. The news electrified Roman citizenry. Four legions of two consuls were destroyed by the amazing Hannibal and his elephants.

The elephants had an enormous psychological affect on the Roman populace, far more than would have been justified by the actual contribution elephants had made to the battle. Although only ten elephants were available for the battle by this time, the part that elephants played was greatly exaggerated in stories repeated by citizens. Just the thought of them fed the wildest imaginations. Inhabitants of Rome and other cities in the Roman confederation of states expected the invincible Hannibal, his elephants, and his ragged hordes to be at their city gates in a few days. The thought terrorized them.

Sempronius was not reelected; the Senate elected two new consuls in January. Gnaeus Servilius Geminus, an aristocrat, was elected by the Senate, and Gaius Flaminius, a plebeian, was elected by the popular party. Neither of the two new consuls was known to be a capable military commander. In a panic, Rome began war preparations, and new armies were hastily recruited in the city. New military grain storage depots were established at two strategic locations, Ariminum and Arretium, where armies were to be sent in hopes that they would intercept Hannibal before he reached Rome. The efficient Carthaginian spy network reported this information to Hannibal.

If there was any remaining doubt in the minds of Cisalpine Gauls about Hannibal's fighting ability, it was dispelled at Trebbia. The Carthaginian commander was treated as a savior by the Gauls and was shown great hospitality in the area. Hannibal's troops rested under roofs during January and February, the first complete rest since leaving Spain. The time was used recruiting and training more allied Gauls.

Hannibal salvaged a considerable amount of armor from the defeated Roman soldiers. He was able to equip his own men better and provide equipment for new recruits. Hannibal was able to improve his tactics for use in future conflicts as a result of his observations of tactics used by both the Romans and his own troops during the recent conflicts. Gauls of the region helped him gather provisions for the next campaigns. Hannibal told Gisco, "When you're a winner, even those who hate you will hold to you; if you are defeated, even your friends will leave you."

As partial proof of his statement, the Boii and Insubres brought their forces to join the Carthaginians. In addition, many of the soldiers Hannibal had released earlier to return to their homes began returning with many friends as recruits to swell his forces. Chieftains of many tribes of the Padus Valley, wearing heavy gold jewelry, came to join the African campaign against their common enemy, Rome. Hannibal promised them that neither he nor Carthage desired territory from their lands and that he would leave their lands as soon as the Roman army was defeated. The new allies were impressed by the fasces of Consul Sempronius, captured in the battle, and it became a symbol of power for Hannibal's army. If there was a secret weapon that Hannibal had used against his enemy other than his unique use of overwhelming numbers of horse-mounted troops to encircle the Roman legions, it was the superior swords used by his soldiers. This superiority became apparent to Hannibal, as well as to Romans, during their first two encounters. The Iberian "falcata" sword and the double-edged, slashing-swords used by the Celt-Iberians were far better than swords used by the Roman army.

These weapons were already very good before Gisco improved their metallurgy by applying knowledge he gained from his studies at Alexandria. Gisco's improvements made them so strong and sharp that they could cut everything the swordsmen struck in battle, including bronze armor. The swords could cut through bronze armor - helmets, shields, greaves, breast plates - down to the bone without losing their razor-sharp edge. Gisco had shown forgers how to obtain exceptionally pure Spanish iron, cast it into the desired shape of swords they wanted, then reheat them to high temperatures over charcoal by using bellows and hammer them to temper the edges. Heating the swords over charcoal at high temperatures caused a small portion of carbon from the charcoal to coat the swords with much tougher iron (a mild form of steel). During campaigns in Spain, Hannibal was so impressed by the performance of the swords that he ordered them for all his soldiers. Though each tribe had its own sword shapes, they all were tempered the same way. Infantry as well as cavalry were equipped with these super-swords. In the battle at Trebbia, most Spanish troops were not wearing as much defensive armor as the Romans, but the Spanish sword fighting verged on the acrobatic. This excellent, athletic swordsmanship, coupled with the use of superior swords, made Spanish swordsmen far superior to their enemies. This became apparent to all at Trebbia.

Another factor that impressed Hannibal during the last two battles was the organization of the Roman legions. He noted the effectiveness of the Roman manipular formations he faced in combat. The manipular formation was an improvement over the phalanx, where the infantry merely lined abreast in close, deep ranks and files. The phalanx formation was unsatisfactory for use in broken, rough terrain. Although Hannibal and his officers were schooled in what to expect from the Roman legions, they were impressed by the efficient way legionnaires performed while using it in the recent encounter. Hannibal decided to adopt a similar formation to improve performance of his infantry.

The maniple, a tactical unit in which each soldier had a square yard upon which to stand, separated from his next soldier by an additional yard, gave the individual legionnaire much more freedom to use his weapons. It also dispersed the soldiers so that they were not such tightly-grouped targets for enemy missiles. In Roman legions, the first two waves of infantry (1200 *hastati*, who were the front line troops, and 1200 *principes* who were in the second line, but consisting of soldiers more in their prime) were made up of thirty maniples, each maniple composed of forty-men wide in the formation, and three-men deep (two "centuries" of sixty-men each). Formation of the third wave (*triari*) usually contained 600 experienced veterans, and its maniples were usually six-men wide and ten-men deep (two "centuries" of thirty men each). In front of the line of maniples were 1200 lightly armed skirmishers (*velites,* the youngest and poorest soldiers) in a straight-line vanguard. When the maniples lined up in formation, a space of one maniple was allowed between each, but the waves of maniples were arranged in a checkerboard fashion so that following waves of maniples lined up in the empty spaces left by the line of maniples in front of them. The 300 horses in each legion's cavalry normally lined up with 150 horsemen (*equites*) on each flank of the infantry. Hannibal particularly liked the way the cavalry was organized into ten squadrons of thirty horses each. Organized this way, the normal Roman citizen-soldier legion was composed of 4,200 infantry and 300 cavalry. (Each consular army consisted of two Roman and two allied legions, about 18,000 to 20,000 soldiers.) Hannibal decided to organize his army in a similar fashion to improve his command and control of the army.

By the Ides of March, 217 B.C., the warlike spirit of the Cisalpine Gauls made them impatient, thirsting for rich spoils they expected to take from Romans. Hannibal's hosts were unhappy with the fact that Carthaginians were eating all of the food stores in the area. Hannibal didn't want to outstay his welcome, so he decided to move his army south to forage on Roman soil and win more victories. Hannibal had been told that the easiest route south to Rome was one that skirted the rugged mountains (Apennines), traveling on their eastern edge until he came to the easiest pass to cross, one that would take him through Arretium (Arrezo). He knew this was the route Romans would expect him to take because the only alternative routes were known to be too difficult to bring an army through. They did not know the mind of the great Carthaginian, a master of deception. Hannibal decided to take the most unexpected route, one that was more directly south (through Collina), even though it meant crossing the rugged mountains on a most difficult pass, a task almost as formidable as crossing the Alps.

While Hannibal was moving south, the new Roman consul, Servilius, was sent to Ariminum (near Rimini) with two legions expecting to meet Hannibal's forces as they moved along the eastern edge of the mountains on their way to the easiest pass. The other consul, Flaminius, was sent to Arretium with two legions, expecting to trap Hannibal between two consular armies as he passed through the easiest crossing. Hannibal did not do what his enemy thought he would do.

Hannibal had to pay a high personal price for taking the route he chose. By selecting one of the shortest, but most difficult passes over the mountains, he was required to march his army over a high, rugged mountain pass (from near Bologna to Pistoia, using Passo Collina), which thoroughly chilled his soldiers and killed many animals. As they descended from the summit, they landed in a swampy quagmire created by run-off from melting snows, and for forty miles (between Pisoia and Fiesole) the low lands were flooded.

Hannibal pushed his men for three days and four nights through the swampy area without stopping on dry ground to get a night's rest because there was no dry ground. In many places the army marched chin-deep in foul water, and all elephants died from the cold except one tall Indian elephant called Surus. Many pack animals perished. During the march through the swamp, Hannibal confided to Gisco that he was suffering from severe head pains. It alarmed

Gisco and he immediately called his friend, the physician Synhalus, to treat their stubborn commander. The physician recommended that they get Hannibal to dry ground immediately so they could treat him for a dangerous head infection. Hannibal refused, insisting that there was no time to waste and that it was necessary to continue their course through the inundated valley. As a last resort, Gisco convinced his obstinate commander that he should ride the one remaining elephant, Surus, to keep him above the swampy water. Gisco and Synhalus wrapped him in warm clothing and put him on the elephant, but the infection became worse. Before he recovered, the infection had damaged nerves of one eye, causing him permanent loss of sight in it.

Finally, after the long, arduous trek through the marsh they came upon the beautiful, dry valley of Faesulae (Fiesole), one of the richest in Italy. For the first time in many days, surviving animals found green grass, and troops could build fires and sleep on dry ground. Hannibal didn't allow the army to rest too long, and they soon continued their march southeast, passing ancient Etruscan ruins of Etruria until they reached a great river (Arno). It was here that Carthalo made contact with two spies he had sent out earlier; they had been posing as merchants of imported goods, using clothes and equipment that Carthaginians had captured. They reported that two Roman legions were waiting for Hannibal at the Roman fort of Arretium (near Arezzo), forty miles to the south.

Again, Hannibal found himself in a situation where his army was in a weakened condition from the ordeal of climbing over the cold mountains and the debilitating march through wetlands. He decided he would not attempt to fight Flaminius in the hills near Arretium where his superior cavalry could not be an advantage. He decided to bypass Flaminius by keeping to the valley.

Spies reported that Flaminius had sent an emergency message to the other consul, Servilius, reporting the information that Hannibal had come a different route than expected and that he was presently in the valley near Arretium. Flaminius had requested Servilius to speed his army down the Flaminium Way (which Flaminius had built), so that they could trap the Carthaginian between their two consular armies. The Flaminian Way would bring Servilius south of Hannibal's position, in the direction the Carthaginian army was headed. Flaminius told his co-consul that he would follow behind Hannibal's army as it marched south. With Servilius in Hannibal's front, the Carthaginian would be between their two armies.

When Hannibal received this information, he requested that his agents provide him with details about personal characteristics of both Roman Consuls. While he was traveling south through the swampy area, he couldn't receive reports about these commanders from his other agents, and the great Carthaginian was vitally concerned about them. Such details were always important factors that Hannibal used in his planning. Agents reported that they had details about the plebeian consul, Flaminius, but that they would have to provide details on Servilius later. They reported that Flaminius had little military ability, although he had easily, and ruthlessly, conquered a much weaker, outnumbered Insubres army in a battle years earlier. That Roman victory kept the Insubres nation subdued until Hannibal contacted it, and it gave Flaminius an unjustified, inflated opinion of his military ability to command an army in combat.

The army commanded by Flaminius had ravaged and raped the Insubres' homeland, so Hannibal realized that his allies, the Insubres, would have a strong desire for revenge. Agents reported that the Consul's main weaknesses were overconfidence, impatience, and his habit of failing to secure flanks of his army along the route of its march. Flaminius was so impatient and confident that he did not use scouting forces to secure his flanks as other commanders were in the habit of doing. He only sent scouts out to the front of his marching path. Hannibal immediately began thinking about how he could use this information to trap Flaminius.

Chapter 5

LAKE TRASIMENE TO CAMP AT GERUNIUM
(June, 217 B.C. to July, 216 B.C.)

As Gisco observed Hannibal the next few days, he noticed that the Carthaginian was unusually preoccupied and quiet. When Gisco made a comment to his commander about it, Hannibal told him that he was trying to develop a plan to fight Consul Flaminius on terms that would be favorable to Carthaginians. He explained that he didn't want to commit his weakened army to a head-on battle against the Consul, but he knew that he had to fight him soon because Servilius was on his way. The two Consuls were planning to trap his army between their armies, and it would be much better if the Carthaginian army fought the Roman armies one at a time, rather than all at once, as the Romans were planning.

Hannibal needed a satisfactory plan to ambush Roman legions of Flaminius long before Servilius arrived with his army. Intelligence reports indicated that Flaminius had 40,000 soldiers at Arretium. Hannibal knew he couldn't afford to lose many of his hard-core veterans, the African and Spanish troops, in a battle with Flaminius because it would be many months, if ever, before he could get replacements for them. Such replacements, if they were to come, would not be as tough and well trained as those veterans he had handpicked to make the trip to Italy. Furthermore, he had grown attached to them, they were very loyal to him, and he didn't want to see them harmed if it could be avoided.

The less disciplined, warlike Gauls were easier to replace, but they were no match for the veterans he brought from Spain. The backbone of his army was made up of the disciplined veterans who had been with him many years and had been through that training crucible in Spain, the training ground for the Italian campaign. Thus, a victory over Flaminius would be a Pyrrhic victory if many of his valuable, hard-core veterans were lost. He would win the victory, but he would lose the war because he would not have a strong enough army remaining to fight the next 40,000 Romans that were coming soon with Consul Servilius. Hannibal and Gisco were well aware of a similar mistake which the Greek king, Pyrrhus, had made in battling the Roman army about sixty years earlier.

The alternative of safely running away from battle was never a serious consideration for the confident, audacious Hannibal. Furthermore, the warlike spirit of his Gallic allies, particularly that of the Insubres who had a strong desire for revenge against Flaminius, was making them anxious for battle. He was planning to fight the Consuls one at a time, but time was drawing near for him to decide upon a plan because Sempronius might arrive soon. Gisco and Cirta accompanied Hannibal as they hastily scouted the terrain around them for a suitable site. Finally, they discovered an ideal one, and as usual, Hannibal rapidly began to make elaborate preparations. He developed a plan that put the factors of terrain, weather, time of day, surprise, and ambush all to his advantage. Hannibal was counting on the known weaknesses of Flaminius to be the trigger of his plan.

The ambush site Hannibal had selected was on a road that ran east and west along the north edge of Lake Trasimene, only a few miles southeast of the place his army was bivouacked in the valley near Cortona. The four-mile stretch of road he selected ran through a long, narrow pass at its entrance that was enclosed on both sides by a line of small hills. At the east end of the east-west road was a steep promontory that ran out into the water. It provided an obstacle to the road because it contained sheer slopes that were more difficult to climb.

Between the two ends of the four-mile stretch, the road ran along a line of hills on its north side, which had promontories of varying lengths that ran toward the water on the south, and the south side of the road was bordered by water of the lake most of the way. Some of the promontories, because they jutted out close to the water's edge, caused the road to be very narrow at some points of that stretch of road, while ravines between the promontories allowed the road to be wide at other points.

Gisco noted that a heavy, low-hanging fog had formed each of the two mornings that they had visited the site, and it had obscured the road. The heavy mist cleared by late morning, each time they were there, as the sun rose higher, heating up the atmosphere. It had burned the fog away by noon every day.

As soon as Hannibal and Gisco, in consultation with other trusted officers, had worked out all details of the plan for an ambush of the Consul's army along the planned site, the Carthaginian magician started actions that would lure Flaminius out of his fort in the hills long before the Consul had intended. He knew that Flaminius was remaining in his safe fort, reluctant to leave, until he had determined that Sempronius was in place to close the trap on Hannibal.

To lure Flaminius to follow the Carthaginian army to the ambuscade earlier, he expected to make use of the Consul's personal foibles. Because there was not much hope of getting local inhabitants of Etruria to revolt, as they appeared to be remaining loyal to Rome, Hannibal sent his cavalry up and down the rich valley near Cortona looting and burning all villages. Some of this activity was near the Roman fort, Arretium. As expected, the impatient and overconfident Flaminius could take no more of the humiliation of having Carthaginian troops devastate Roman land outside his doorstep while he did nothing. He exploded with rage and decided not to wait for Servilius to arrive. He marched his entire army, 40,000 strong, after Hannibal as fast as he could muster his troops.

Hannibal was in the valley near Cortona when his scouts told him that Flaminius was coming after him. They reported that he was only twenty miles behind. It was late evening and Gisco noted that a heavy mist was starting to form on the lake, indicating there would be a heavy fog again in the morning. Weather was expected to be perfect for the planned ambush.

As darkness began to fall, Hannibal marched his troops through the pass on the west end of the road, making it look to any Roman scouts as though he were fleeing the Roman army. When he was certain he was not being watched by Roman scouts, after his rear guard had signaled it was all clear, he deployed his soldiers in the hills along the four-mile stretch according the prearranged plan. All troops had been thoroughly briefed well in advance about details of the plan, and each man knew what his job was to be, as well as how his part fitted into the overall strategy. Hannibal and Gisco took African and Spanish infantry to cover the escape route at the east end of the road, positioning themselves on the high ground of the promontory over which the road climbed.

At the entrance to the planned battlefield, on both sides of the narrow pass, concealed on higher ground, Gallic cavalry were placed on the north side, and slingers and pikemen were hidden on the south side. Between the two ends of the road, light infantry was dispersed in the hills overlooking the road below. The road became so narrow in some places that a marching army had to string itself out in very thin lines to pass, causing the rest of the army to be bunched up waiting its turn to pass. Hannibal planned to have heavier concentrations of his troops at these choke points.

That night, Flaminius camped a short distance north of the lake. Impatient to catch Hannibal, he marched his army at first light on 21 June, 217 B.C. When he reached the lake at seven o'clock in the morning, a heavy mist had obscured the terrain on all sides. His army followed fresh tracks that Hannibal's army had made, tracks that the wily Hannibal had instructed a special division of soldiers to provide by traveling a few miles ahead of the Roman army early that morning. Roman soldiers couldn't see more than ten yards in any direction, as they slowly made their way through the thick mist by following Carthaginian tracks.

True to his habits, as reported earlier by spies, Flaminius did not take the precaution of having scouts investigate his flanks as he marched his entire army into the four-mile stretch of road. The overconfident Flaminius believed Hannibal was fleeing from combat with him. His soldiers were not prepared for combat

BATTLE
OF
LAKE TRASIMENE

217 B.C.

and carried their war equipment slung on their spears and hung on belts. They were able to march faster and more comfortably this way. The well disciplined Roman soldiers believed there would be ample time to prepare for combat and make their formations when their vanguard legion signaled they had caught up with the Carthaginians, whom they believed to be twenty miles ahead. The Roman soldiers were all in good humor, as survivors later reported, and they were anxious to fight the soft-touch Insubres whom the Consul had easily defeated years earlier.

The overoptimistic Flaminius now hoped to catch up with the Carthaginian army and win a victory before Servilius could come to share the credit with him. If he were to march for a day and a half along the road he was on, he would reach the Flaminian Way along which Servilius would be marching to join him. Flaminius had sent a vanguard legion ahead of the main body of his stretched-out army as an early warning device to tell him when he had finally caught up with Hannibal's army. That legion was following the fresh tracks of the division of Carthaginians that Hannibal put in front of them as bait. Slave traders were following the Romans at a distance with empty carts and iron chains, expecting to buy Carthaginians as slaves, and other spoils they expected the vaunted Romans to capture in the coming battle.

Carthaginians, up on a higher elevation, were surprised to find themselves above the low-hanging fog bank which was only twenty yards deep. As Hannibal and Gisco had planned, they could see each other across the hills, but they couldn't see legionnaires marching below them. They could only hear the clank and clatter of marching soldiers below. After Hannibal learned that the last Italian soldier had entered the narrow pathway through the entrance to the four-mile long ambuscade, he gave the visual signal to his men, most of whom he could see deployed laterally across the higher elevations, to descend upon the defenseless marching legions below. War cries were not made, so as not to alert the unsuspecting Roman army.

Roman soldiers soon began to hear thuds of missiles striking bodies, clanking of swords, and moans and groans of their wounded compatriots coming through the fog from all directions. They didn't know where the attack was taking place nor where the enemy could come from, until they themselves where suddenly overwhelmed by an avalanche of Carthaginian soldiers. Unbeknown to Romans, the exit ahead was now blocked by Spanish and African divisions, and cavalry and pikemen now blocked a Roman retreat through the entrance to the battlefield. Between, Romans were hit from all sides at once, front, rear, and flanks where there was no water.

They were cut down while still in marching formation, and most were killed while wondering what to do. The result was panic, terror, and disorganization of the normally disciplined legions, ending with their massive slaughter. Some soldiers ran wildly out into the lake in an attempt to escape death, but they were later cut down by Carthaginian cavalry which rode its horses out into the water after them when the mist had cleared sufficiently.

Insubres attacked Flaminius and his guard with an animal ferocity seldom seen as they sought revenge for the Consul's rape of their homeland. Agile Spaniards, well-trained for this type of fighting as a result of many years of similar fighting in Spain, cut a huge swath through the unsuspecting line of marching soldiers before the helpless soldiers knew what was happening to them. Baleareans rained clouds of their missiles through the fog down on the defenseless column below. The slingers had accurately measured the range of the road from their positions earlier so they knew how to hit their target through the fog.

Gisco accompanied Hannibal and the other soldiers guarding the exit as they descended down the hill to meet the oncoming Romans in the fog, before they were able to rise above the obscured area. Hannibal's men had full armor and weapons ready, and they were in a battle formation best able to surprise the Roman vanguard. They succeeded in surprising the marching legion before it was able to put on its armor, and many did not have their shields available before they were struck down. Somehow, the Roman vanguard of 6,000 men got lost in the fog, and it marched up the hillside unmolested, past the Carthaginians guarding the exit.

By ten o'clock in the morning, almost three hours after the initial attack, there was no more fighting along the road, and the sun began to burn off the fog covering the battlefield. The advance Roman legion of 6,000 soldiers that Flaminius had sent ahead climbed above the mist, and as the fog began to disappear, the soldiers turned around to view the lakeside behind them. To their astonishment, they could only see Carthaginians alive; the rest of the Roman army, the other 34,000 soldiers that were supposed to be behind them, had disappeared.

Maharbal's Numidian cavalry caught up with this Roman vanguard a little later, surrounded them, and the entire 6,000 surrendered after Maharbal promised they would be released if they surrendered their weapons. When Hannibal heard about Maharbal's promise to them, all of whom were Roman citizen-soldiers, he was irate. He had a heated argument with Maharbal and told him he should have known about his policy for treating citizens of Rome with hostility. Hannibal countermanded Maharbal's promise, and all of the prisoners were put in chains to be sold to the Greek slave-traders that had expected to be buying Carthaginian slaves from Romans. Hannibal remained true to his vow.

Of the 40,000 soldiers in the Consul's army, 15,000 were eventually taken prisoner. Most of the remaining 25,000 were killed, but a few succeeded in fleeing over the hills in the fog returning to Rome with the gruesome story of the disaster. Hannibal's army had lost 1,500 killed and wounded, mostly Gauls. Hannibal released all noncitizen soldiers after treating them well and giving his standard speech about coming to Italy to free their homelands from the Roman tyrant.

Hannibal, Gisco, and Cirta rode over the battlefield that afternoon to inspect results of the massacre. Bodies and armaments were strewn everywhere on the bloodstained road and its vicinity. It was an appalling sight, even to the seasoned veterans of many battles. They looked for the body of Flaminius, but it couldn't be found. Insubres had probably stripped his body of all accoutrements, including his fasces, and then discarded the body. There were many Silver Eagles of legions and standards of maniples strewn around, and there was much booty to sell to Greek traders who had been following the Roman Army. Hannibal ordered that dead Carthaginian soldiers be picked out of the heaps of mangled bodies and be properly buried. Thirty of the highest ranking Romans were buried.

That evening Hannibal and Gisco went to Hannibal's shrine-tent and thanked the gods for their success. Priests provided ritual cakes and sacrificial wine for the ceremony. Afterward, the great Carthaginian called a meeting of his officers to discuss their next move. Many officers, confident as a result of their recent great victories, advised their great commander to proceed directly to the gates of Rome. Gauls, particularly, were anxious to go straight to the Roman Capital, but Hannibal told them that the soldiers and animals had not fully recovered from their debilitating trip which took them over the cold pass and through the swampy morass. He told them they needed a secure place to recuperate, and most officers agreed.

Finally, it was decided to head east to a region near the Adriatic coast which was rich in agriculture where there was ample grass for the animals. This meant they had to cross over the mountains (Apennines) again, with the long wagon-train that was now carrying the war equipment and other supplies they had captured from Roman legions. However, this time they intended to follow prepared roads that took them along a much easier route. They knew that legions of Consul Sempronius were still on their way to attack them, traveling along the Flaminian Way. Hannibal kept his scouts out, well ahead, to keep a lookout for the vanguard of Sempronius, as Carthaginians used the easier Flaminian Way to cross the mountains.

Three days after the battle at Trasimene, while Hannibal's army was marching east of the junction of the Flaminian Way and the original road he was taking south, his scouts accidentally met 4,000 cavalrymen of Consul Servilius, an advance party of the army coming from Ariminum (near Rimini) to join Flaminius. Hannibal dispatched Maharbal with his huge cavalry, still close to 10,000 strong, to intercept them. Maharbal's force killed half of the enemy horsemen on its first attack, and it eventually captured the remaining 2,000. This provided Hannibal with many additional horses and much new armament. Maharbal's losses were minimal, because his men could throw their javelins accurately with their horses at full gallop, and they stayed out of range of Roman missiles.

Hannibal marched eastward through Umbria, headed for territory that bordered the Adriatic (Roman territory of Picenum), an agricultural area with villages that promised rich provisions for his soldiers while his army recuperated.

Carthaginian agents in Rome later reported to Hannibal that the news of another catastrophic defeat of a consular army had shocked Rome, and the news was announced to the citizenry at a public assembly. The citizens were told that the entire army of Flaminius had disappeared, and that a total of 40,000 soldiers were lost to the barbaric hordes of Hannibal. Then, only three days after it heard the news of the disaster at Trasimene, the city learned of the loss of the entire cavalry of Servilius. Hannibal had outmaneuvered four Roman consuls, Scipio, Sempronius, Flaminius, and Servilius, in succession. The inability of these armies to stop Hannibal struck renewed terror in the citizenry of the Roman capital, and it prompted the Senate to take drastic measures. Romans were expecting Carthaginians at their gates within days.

In an unprecedented move, a Roman dictator was named in a popular election, and he was given absolute powers. The newly elected dictator was the elderly Quintus Fabius, a very patient and gifted leader with strong determination. He later became known as "The Maximus" (The Greatest), but he had much to do, and he had to survive many pitfalls before he was to earn that title. Fabius attributed much of the failure of Flaminius to a lack of proper consultation with the gods, and one of the dictator's first moves was to order a sacrifice of 300 oxen to the god, Jupiter, among other sacrifices and religious measures. He ordered a scorched-earth policy: all crops in Hannibal's marching path were to be destroyed and all livestock were to be moved out of his way before he arrived. Unfortunately, no one knew where Hannibal would march, not even Hannibal.

Fabius also initiated new, emergency conscription and training of soldiers to increase the size of the army, then he took to the field to pursue Hannibal as a hands-on military commander. He left Rome with two newly formed legions, and he fired Servilius and took command of his legions. This gave Fabius four Roman legions as well as legions of allies. Servilius was demoted and sent to command soldiers on war vessels (marines) guarding the coast of Italy. As a deputy for Fabius, the Assembly elected a "Master of the Horse," Marcus Minucius Rufus.

While all of this Roman activity was in progress, Hannibal continued his march eastward. He soon discovered he couldn't get citizens in districts of the Roman confederation to defect from Rome as he passed through them. None would provide his army with recruits. Hannibal decided to implement a scorched-earth policy of his own in those areas that remained loyal to Rome. He allowed his soldiers to loot and burn the landscape on their way east. The Carthaginian commander believed that he could possibly weaken Roman resistance, weaken its economy, and weaken its will to fight by reducing its food supply. Furthermore, the scorched-earth policy was a message to fear Hannibal more, for districts that remained loyal to Rome solely because they feared Roman reprisal if they were to defect to the Carthaginians. It was intended to convince districts that were on the borderline of deciding whether or not they should join Hannibal's cause. Resources of food that he couldn't use for his army, he burned or otherwise destroyed.

One small, fortified settlement he encountered along the way, Spoletium, gave his army an unexpected, strong resistance to its attack. It caused an inordinate number of losses to his troops, and it made Hannibal think of the irreplaceable losses he would suffer if he tried to storm the strongly fortified walls of Rome, with its much more formidable defenses inside. Rather than try to fight Roman soldiers in their fortified positions, he began to think that his best strategy was to lure the legions out of Rome, to battle them on his own terms. That way, maybe, he could get Rome to sue for a truce or surrender. This policy dumbfounded citizens of Rome, who were expecting him to be at their gates soon. It also dismayed a few of Hannibal's officers, especially the Gauls and Maharbal, who wanted to attack Rome without delay. They couldn't understand the strategy Hannibal had adopted out of necessity.

Carthaginians reached the coast, in the southern part of the Roman territory of Picenum, by the first of July. The army didn't receive opposition from Roman legions because his previous victories had intimidated them into being very cautious. Hannibal spent much of the summer of 217 B.C. resting his troops and animals in a rich territory where he was master. The terrain was flat enough to allow his huge cavalry to answer any challenge that may have come from the dictator's legions, but none came. He refitted his army, and he had his soldiers discard their worn and tattered garments in exchange for the best of the newly acquired clothing and armor captured from Roman legions. Many Gauls soon began to look like legionnaires, wearing the same clothes and armor. Roman swords were inferior to those produced under Gisco's supervision in Spain; those Roman swords his Gallic allies didn't need were sold to Greek traders for cash.

Condition of the animals was gradually restored to full strength, and Hannibal and Gisco spent much of the time available reorganizing and training the army, improving combat formations, based on what they had learned from recent experience. They adopted many techniques that they had observed Romans using, believing they would improve their own performance. The heavy cavalry was given heavier protective armor, and it was trained to adhere to organized units consisting of 500 and 150 horses for better control. The most important strength of Hannibal's Spanish and African army was in its long experience with combat and its thorough training together, as a unit, for many years. Most of their Roman adversaries were raw recruits, in comparison, who had only limited experience in combat and limited training together. Roman organizations had been formed for only one year at a time. Hannibal had already destroyed a large portion of the few veterans that Rome had available to its armies.

Hannibal sent messengers to Carthage by fast galley with a full report of the victories. This encouraged the elated government in Africa to provide "full support" for war efforts in Spain and Italy, but the government was not made up of many people who were conversant with military needs and strategies. The Barca faction (a political "party") in the

Carthaginian Senate's Privy Council that had fully supported Hannibal and his father before him, was strongly opposed by the Hanno faction that had historically opposed the Barcas. The Hanno faction didn't appreciate the long-run implications of the Roman expansionism in the Mediterranean area and what it meant to their centuries-old dominance of trade on the Mediterranean Sea. Hannos were more concerned about current trade and current costly expenditures for the military forces than they were the long-run security of their trading economy.

Carthage was a nation of traders that relied, primarily, on hired mercenaries to do its fighting; it had few military soldiers. The Carthaginian government's concept of "full support" was not of the same degree of support that the Roman Senate believed was necessary, with Hannibal at its doorstep. The Hanno faction succeeded in watering down, or otherwise subverting, the "full support" that the visionary Barca faction usually envisioned. Regardless of the obstacles, the Barcas succeeded in sending a convoy of 70 warships past the Roman naval blockade, from Carthage to Pisae (Pisa), to provide logistic support for Hannibal's army, but Hannibal had already marched farther south than expected when the fleet had arrived. He was at Lake Trasimene when the convoy arrived at Pisae, so the fleet had to turn around to avoid the strong Roman navy.

While he was near the Adriatic, Hannibal took the opportunity to send emissaries across the water to King Philip of Macedonia who had recently resisted Roman occupation of his lands. Hannibal believed that the king would be an ally in the Carthaginian campaign against Roman tyranny. The ruler of Macedonia was impressed by Hannibal's victories, and he soon sent envoys to Hannibal with instructions to work out an agreement. The envoys arrived in Hannibal's camp during the fall, 217 B.C.

Hannibal had sent his young brother, Mago, to Spain earlier, to solicit troops and silver from his brother Hasdrubal who was left in command of Spanish forces during Hannibal's absence. Mago returned from Spain with news of the war on the Iberian peninsula and some money, but no troops. He reported that the Roman brothers, Publius and Gnaeus Scipio, had reached northern Spain with their legions, above the Ebro, and tough Spanish tribes of the north were fighting them. This meant Hannibal's line of communication by land, over the Pyranees to New Carthage, was cut off, so Hasdrubal could not send him troop reinforcements for a while.

Hannibal's camp in southern Picenum became fetid after a while. He was using up food resources in the area quickly, so he began a series of frequent moves southward into Apulia, staying along the Adriatic coast. Dictator Fabius arrived with his four legions, but he did not attack. Hannibal devastated the eastern slopes of the Appenines along his way south, in a deliberate attempt to antagonize the dictator, hoping it would lure him to combat. Hannibal and Gisco planned many elaborate ambushes for the trailing Roman legions, but the patient and cautious dictator could not be provoked to fight. Instead, he had his army closely follow the Carthaginian army. The strategy of Fabius was to delay any decisive battle for a while, until his legions could regain the confidence lost in the recent demoralizing defeats and allow time for his newly recruited troops to become more seasoned.

In the meantime, Fabius wanted to wear down

Hannibal's army by attrition. He intended to attack small Carthaginian foraging parties, and he was willing to sustain small losses of his troops as long as he made Hannibal lose some of his valuable soldiers. The dictator's numbers were greater than Hannibal's, so he could afford to trade the African army on a basis of two-for-one for an indefinite time, hoping to deplete its small numbers. New Roman forces were continually recruited and trained to replace legionnaires lost, but Hannibal was having a difficult time finding replacements for his losses. Hannibal was only able to recruit some poor, starving peasants as he ventured farther south in Italy, but he was not successful in getting the major defections among Rome's confederation of districts he was hoping to get to augment his small forces. Hannibal and Gisco had planned that many would defect from the Roman confederation, but territories south of the Padus River remained loyal to Rome for the most part, or they were indifferent.

Thus, Hannibal was beginning to think that his best alternate strategy was to continue a scorched-earth policy in an attempt to weaken Rome by destroying its food supply. He hoped that this would eventually cause Rome to sue for peace, or as a minimum, it would buy time until he could obtain sufficient reinforcements from Spain or Carthage in large enough numbers that would allow him to sack the city of Rome in a direct attack.

The dictator was continually fearful of another of Hannibal's traps, and he issued a strong warning to his army that it must avoid battle where Hannibal could use his superior cavalry on flatlands. As a result of this policy, the dictator's army was kept safely in hills, on high ground where cavalry could not be used effectively, or in fortified cities, as he continued to track Carthaginian movements in valleys below. Most fortified cities were on mountain tops. Romans continued to raid small foraging parties that Hannibal sent out, but no matter how hard the Carthaginian tried, Hannibal could not lure Fabius into a decisive battle. Carthaginians pillaged villages and burned landscapes in valleys below while the vast, frustrated, army of four legions watched from hilltops.

The dictator's soldiers were becoming dissatisfied with this policy of do nothing. His elected deputy, Marcus Minucius known as "Master of the Horse," began to openly criticize the dictator's policy which required the huge army to be spectators to the vandalization of Roman lands for months. The dictator had nothing planned that would change the status-quo. Most tribunes and centurions of the army were opposed to this policy, and they nicknamed the dictator, "the Delayer." Their frustration gradually made them more open about their opposition to the policy.

Fabius ignored their protests and patiently adhered to his strategy of waiting. Indeed, he tightened his control over the soldiers by ordering restrictions on their normal foraging parties that required many to leave camp. Fabius said that he didn't want to have his soldiers wandering out of camp because he wanted to keep a strong, defensible formation in camp. Instead of foraging, he arranged to have ample supplies brought in to supply the army from its rear. This prison-like environment added to the troops' frustration, because many were now deprived of the enjoyable relief of riding around the countrside for forage they formerly had available to them.

Fabius remained very cautious, and he required that all areas ahead of his army be thoroughly scouted before he would move it from dug-in positions of one camp to a new one, as he followed the Carthaginians' movements. Spurred by the agitation and open criticism of the deputy, Minucius, near mutiny broke out in the army as it appeared, increasingly, to the soldiers that the dictator was abandoning the Italian countryside to the hated Carthaginians, for use as Hannibal's army wanted. The soldiers didn't have the doubt about their ability to defeat Hannibal that the dictator had. Hannibal's informants kept him apprised of this rift in the Dictator's army, and he did all he could do to nurture it by openly taunting the Romans with his actions.

One of the better battle sites that Hannibal had carefully selected, and had attempted to lure Fabius into unsuccessfully during the midsummer of 217 B.C., was one on the Aufidus River, near Cannae (west of Barletta on the Ofanto River). Hannibal's planning indicated that this was an ideal site, and he had plans that would put odds in favor of a decisive Carthaginian victory. Unfortunately, after many attempts to lure the dictator to the site, Hannibal was unable to break the dictator's strong determination to avoid a decisive battle. Roman officers were enraged, further, by the Delayer's refusal to accept Hannibal's latest challenge to fight. Hannibal noted the eagerness of Roman officers to fall into this trap, and he filed the information away in his memory for future reference.

Hannibal marched his army through the Samnium district, staying to the valleys where he could use his superior cavalry on flatlands. He devastated the land and captured villages, in a deliberate attempt to aggravate the frustration of the Roman army and further reduce the food supply of the city of Rome. As the fall season came upon them, the citizenry of Rome became increasingly disgruntled by the tactics of "The Delayer." Food shortages were starting to be felt, severely, in markets of Rome.

From the Samnium area, the motley Carthaginian army marched to Campania, which contained some of the most fertile and beautiful lands of Italy, as well as some of its richest cities. Hannibal had his army enter the plains of Capua (north of Naples) through a narrow pass that was an ideal place for Fabius to attack him, as his Roman officers were quick to point out to The Delayer. Fabius refused to take advantage of the opportunity, much to the irritation of his men. Hannibal pitched camp on the north side of the Volturnus (Volturno) River, on plains where his strong cavalry offered security from The Delayer's army. Hannibal continued his unopposed pillaging and burning of the whole plains, making a spectacle of Roman cowardice for all to see, as four legions and their allies watched. He collected vast amounts of rich booty and supplies for the winter, and there was much more richness in the plains than he could either use or destroy. By late autumn, it was time to find secure winter quarters in the east where his army could enjoy its newfound riches. Hannibal also believed that he was too vulnerable to attack in the plains of Capua, since there were only a few exits, all of them with treacherous, narrow passes through which he must escape if it were to become necessary.

To reach the east, he decided to return through the same narrow pass he had used earlier to enter the plains. He knew that route provided an excellent opportunity for Fabius to trap the Carthaginian army, so he was very cautious. Hannibal sent an advance scouting party to reconnoiter the pass before he sent his entire army to move through it. The egress road went through a valley that gradually narrowed to a steep inclined ravine leading to the summit. The dictator had positioned 4,000 of his troops at the exit of the pass, at its summit, to block the Carthaginian egress. Fabius dug his remaining troops and himself into a fortified camp on the high ground of the slopes that overlooked the entrance to the narrow ravine below. Hannibal's scouts soon discovered the Roman forces blocking egress from the pass at its summit, and they saw the dictator's army ensconced on hilltops of its entrance. In a skirmish following this discovery, Numidian scouts lost 800 men and Romans lost only 200 because of terrain adverse to the Numidian style of fighting.

For a while, it appeared Hannibal's army would be trapped in the area for the winter, but the grand master was determined to leave the plains. At a conference of his officers to discuss alternatives for breaking out of this predicament, Gisco reminded Hannibal of a tactic that Spanish troops had used in 228 B.C., in the battle (Illici) where Hannibal's father was killed. After much discussion, the commander decided to use the same procedure on Romans that night.

Gisco quickly recruited Spaniards known to have used the technique, and he used this small nucleus as teachers to rapidly instruct a select group of 2,000 Celtiberian soldiers in use of the method. The Celtiberians were hand-selected because they were experienced night-fighters in mountains. The Celtiberians were rapidly taught how to attach bundles of kindling to horns of oxen, which would be used as torches that night. While this instruction was taking place, thousands of other soldiers gathered the necessary kindling and dry brush which would be used as material for the torches.

When darkness fell and Romans could not see them, 2,000 oxen with kindling attached to their horns were herded up the steep side of the narrow ravine, past the dictator's troops high above them on the ridges of the pass. By midnight, all oxen were in position on the hillside of the ravine, above the road and near its high exit at the summit, with kindling ready to light. When Hannibal gave the signal, all torches were put aflame at the same time, and Celtiberian cattle-drivers stampeded the 2,000 oxen up the ravine on its steep side, headed for the high side of the narrow pass. The beasts became crazed by the fires and they stampeded wildly up the pass. Stampeding hoofs, terrifying bellowing of animals, and war cries of the 2,000 Celtiberian night-fighters suddenly broke the silence of the night, resulting in a thunderous reverberation that echoed throughout the ravine in the black of the night.

The 4,000 Italians guarding the summit were awakened from their sleep by the tumult to see 4,000 torches coming at them at high speed, with some running in directions that made it appear that there was an attempt to surround them. The thunderous, mystifying sound accompanying the torches made it all the more fearful and confusing to the Roman guards. Fearful of being surrounded, they panicked and ran, each man for himself, in the direction of the least number of torches. They vacated the exit at the top of the pass. The 2,000 Celtiberian night-fighters followed the animals, secured the exit at the summit, and killed Roman stragglers.

Fabius and his soldiers watched the mystifying spectacle below them from their hilltop positions.

When his officers pleaded with him to give the order to pursue what they believed to be soldiers carrying torches and scrambling over the pass in the darkness, the cautious Fabius refused because he was fearful of another one of Hannibal's traps. He didn't know what was happening in the black of the night, with the perplexing sounds and torches below him. The entire Carthaginian column, loaded heavily with rich spoils, moved through the pass and over the summit long before dawn. After his army was through the narrow defile, Hannibal sent some of his soldiers back to help the Celtiberians to safely rejoin his main force. The army was then able to travel without opposition, eastward along the Via Latina to a permanent winter camp in Apulia near the town of Gerunium (approximately 35 miles northwest of Foggia on the river Fortore).

Hannibal's escape, and the refusal of Fabius to attack the Carthaginian army when he had it hemmed-in, further inflamed the ire of the dictator's soldiers. The story reached Rome and it stirred further resentment against The Delayer. Food supplies were becoming sparse in Italy because of Hannibal's scorched-earth policy, and citizens were complaining about the inaction of Fabius, which allowed Hannibal to pillage freely. Furthermore, angry protests from landowners and plebeians, who were suffering from hunger, began to demand why patricians in the Senate refused to take action to stop Hannibal, especially since they were the ones responsible for declaring war against Carthage.

To make matters worse for Fabius, Hannibal had brilliantly ordered his troops to avoid harming property owned by Fabius as they came upon it, while all property around the dictator's was destroyed. This did not escape the notice of the Roman public, and many accused Fabius of making some kind of agreement with Hannibal whereby the dictator would not attack him if the Carthaginian didn't attack his lands. Although it wasn't true, many Romans believed it just as Hannibal had cunningly planned. The dictator's political enemies widely publicized the idea, to add to the growing public sentiment that was already overwhelmingly against Fabius. Fabius was recalled to Rome by the Senate after being a dictator for only six months. Fabius left his deputy, Minucius, Master of the Horse (his main critic for not attacking Hannibal), in temporary command of the four legions and their allies. He gave Minucius strict orders not to attack Hannibal and to be cautious while he was around the strong Carthaginian cavalry.

Hannibal's efficient network of informants kept him abreast of the growing dissatisfaction that existed in Rome and in its army, and he continued to take actions that would exacerbate the situation. When the ambitious Minucius, now in command of the army, followed the Carthaginians to the eastern coast of Italy, the wily African commander decided to deceive the overeager Minucius. Hannibal used a foil he had used many times, most recently against Sempronius at Trebbia. That is, when Minucius had his forces attack Hannibal's foraging parties, the Carthaginians were ordered to retreat without fighting, to give the Roman Master of the Horse the impression that Africans were afraid of his troops. Soon after this policy was adopted, Carthaginians deserted an outpost that they had held on high ground when Minucius made a fierce attack against it. The Roman commander was led to believe that he had gained a "glorious victory," and he reported it to Rome as such. The Roman populace, which hadn't heard good news for such a long time, automatically deduced that as soon as Fabius was out of the way, victory by attacking Hannibal was possible.

This publicized success of Minucius caused the Roman Senate to recall him to Rome to reward him for his brilliant generalship. He was elected "co-dictator" to Fabius by the Assembly, and it was ratified by the Senate. This was a political maneuver against Fabius, as much as a reward for Minucius, to dilute the power of Fabius in response to the overwhelming popular sentiment against the dictator.

Minucius, in the glow of his new popularity, demanded that he and Fabius each be given command of their own, separate halves of the army, each with complete freedom of action, rather than be given joint-command in the combined army, as was the custom. This arrangement was approved, and the co-dictators went out into the field separately to follow Hannibal, each taking command of his separate army. They made separate camps near Hannibal's. Minucius now had an inflated sense of power and ability, much of it due to Hannibal's cunning. Fabius was still his old careful self, avoiding combat with the dangerous Carthaginian. Fabius made his camp on high ground where Hannibal's superior cavalry could not be used to advantage, while Minucius made his camp on lower ground, nearer Hannibal's camp.

Aware of differences in temperaments of the two co-dictators, Hannibal set a trap for the impetuous Minucius. The night before he intended to spring the trap, when he knew he was not being observed by Romans, Hannibal concealed 5,000 fast Numidian cavalry in a sunken ravine out of sight of both Roman camps. The next day, he ordered the rest of his cavalry to seize a hill halfway between the two co-dictators' camps, not far from his hidden cavalry. The hill occupied by the Carthaginian cavalry threatened free communications between the two Roman camps. The hill was seized so suddenly and swiftly that Minucius was enticed to attack the African cavalry occupying the hill without taking the elementary precaution of scouting the terrain in advance of his attack. Minucius naively launched his troops against the hill, little by little, until his entire army was in position for Hannibal to spring his trap.

At the appropriate time, Hannibal's forces completely surrounded his army. Carthaginians started to annihilate the entire army commanded by Minucius, using the same encirclement tactic that they had used at the Battle of Trebbia. Hannibal's soldiers inflicted a horrible toll in dead and wounded on the trapped troops of Minucius, and Carthaginians would have completely destroyed the army if it was not for the late intervention of Fabius. The cautious Fabius had carefully watched the battle from a distance on his high ground, and after waiting a considerable time, he decided to come to the aid of his co-dictator. As soon as Hannibal saw that the advantage was lost and that he couldn't do more damage without incurring great losses to his own troops, he ordered his soldiers to return to their base camp.

Minucius was so shocked by his experience that he decided to return what was left of his army to a combined command under Fabius. There was a reunion and reconciliation of the two co-dictators, and Minucius made himself subservient to Fabius. As their natural terms of office began to expire near the end of the year, the two companion dictators had not succeeded in obtaining a decisive victory over Hannibal. New elections were scheduled for January to determine who would command the army for the next year.

By law, one consul was to be a plebeian and the other a patrician. Hannibal's scorched-earth policy was causing a severe shortage of food in Italy, and there were many new protests from the public. There was a general call for action to override the Fabian do-nothing policy and to stop Hannibal.

The Senate dissolved the dictatorship in January. Two consuls were elected to do something to stop the Carthaginians, in response to dissatisfaction of the public with the ineffective Roman military policy. A young, impetuous, plebeian consul, Gaius Terentius Varro, a butcher's son who had no military ability, was elected because he was a rising politician, a very effective speaker, and a crowd pleaser who had led the plebeian protests against The Delayer's do-nothing policy. Varro said that if he were in command of the army, he would attack Hannibal without delay.

A more intelligent, levelheaded, elderly patrician consul, Lucius Aemilius Paullus, was elected a little later by the Senate to share command with Varro. The two consuls were directed to share command of the army, equally, in the traditional fashion. Friends warned the new consul, Aemilius, that his co-consul, Varro, would prove to be a greater enemy to him than Hannibal.

Chapter 6

BATTLE OF CANNAE
(August 1-5, 216 B.C.)

Through the winter, 217-216 B.C., and early spring the two opposing armies stood camped next to each other with little action, only minor skirmishes. Hannibal was resting his troops and animals for his next battle. He, Gisco, and other trusted officers worked through the winter in the headquarters pavilion tent making improvements in organization, tactics, and communications, profiting from all the experience they had gained from what they had seen in the battles with Roman legions. They also discussed tactics they intended to use in their next battle, one that they knew would come soon. They spent much time drilling their troops in the use of new, more efficient procedures that Hannibal planned to use.

All officers knew that the major strengths of their army were its experience, toughness, discipline, and intense training. Most of the soldiers in the Roman legions were like raw recruits when compared with the professional, experienced, soldiers in Hannibal's army. Hannibal was a demanding taskmaster when it came to the detailed preparation for battle. Most of his core soldiers, those who had followed him for many years in Spain before coming to Italy, readily accepted Hannibal's rigid discipline. They rapidly indoctrinated new recruits into their system. The enthusiasm and hard work of seasoned old-timers soon rubbed off on new recruits. Each man knew exactly what he was expected to do in each phase of the battles Hannibal planned. Each had complete faith that, based upon past experience of many battles, Hannibal had a winning plan for him to execute, no matter what the odds against his army appeared to be as it entered the combat.

Improvements in organization and tactics continued to occupy much of the army's time. Many soldiers began to look like Roman legionnaires as they scrapped their old combat attire for armor they had taken from Romans in past victories.

Soon, food stocks became low and their next move was being discussed. A few officers wanted the army to return to the security and abundance of Cisalpine Gaul to continue its rest, but the many other officers who had wanted to attack Rome as soon as possible did not want to backtrack so much. Furthermore, Hannibal wanted to provoke the legions that were following him into a decisive battle if possible, to take advantage of the two new consuls' mandate from the Roman public to attack him soon. As a last resort, if he were unable to lure the Roman commanders to a battle, he wanted to conquer more cities of southern Italy.

Finally, Hannibal accepted Gisco's suggestion that they go to the ruined stone village of Cannae, which contained a military grain storage depot with food provisions gathered from the neighborhood of Canusium (modern Canosa). Cannae was the potential battle site Hannibal and Gisco had reconnoitered the previous summer, and it was near a treeless, open plain where Hannibal's superior cavalry could be used to its full advantage. The two collaborators had developed a detailed scenario for destroying the reluctant

Fabius in a decisive battle at the site. Unfortunately, Fabius would not take the bait Hannibal offered him. By taking the military grain storage depot at Cannae, they believed they would be accomplishing two objectives: it would re-supply their army with needed food; and it would further provoke the ire of the Roman army near an ideal battle site. This movement could possibly cause the impatient Roman army to be enticed to battle, finally. Most Roman citizenry had clamored for its army to have a showdown battle with Hannibal in repudiation of The Delayer's policy of inaction. To add fuel to the fire of Roman emotion, Hannibal had the Carthaginian army raid all farms of Roman citizens along his marching route to Cannae while the Roman army watched from a safe distance, taking no action against it.

Hannibal's attempts to get Roman provinces south of the Padus to defect from Rome had not been successful up to that time. There wasn't a single province that would dare to leave the Roman confederation. The districts remained loyal to the Roman confederation because they were either indifferent or they were afraid of reprisals against them by strong Roman legions if they revolted. The districts were not convinced, as yet, that Hannibal could protect them from Roman reprisal if they were to join him, or they may have believed that barbarian Carthaginian domination would be a worse fate than Roman domination. In most cities, the lower classes who had less to lose and were suffering most from food shortages resulting from Hannibal's scorched-earth policy, were the most vulnerable to defection. Most of the senators and most aristocrats stood to lose most to Hannibal's plunder if he were victorious. They were the strongest opponents of defection in the cities outside of Rome.

Hannibal had earlier ruled out attacking the city of Rome because of its heavy fortifications until he could get sufficient reinforcements from Spain or Africa. Thus, he concluded that his best interim strategy was to defeat the large Roman army that was following him in another decisive battle. Such a victory should be enough to convince some Roman districts, those that were on the borderline of deciding whether or not to join him, that Rome's military power had become so weak it was safe to defect.

In addition to the psychological advantage of achieving another decisive victory over Rome's military forces, there was a strong possibility that the Carthaginian scorched-earth policy could finally convince Rome that it should sue for peace. His scorched-earth tactics were beginning to be felt severely in Rome, according to reports of his agents. As Hannibal saw it, victory could come without the costly storming of the fortified walls of Rome where his superior cavalry could not be used advantageously.

In reaction to the public outcry for action, a repudiation of the Fabian policy, the Senate decided to raise the largest army it had ever assembled. Under the joint command of consuls G. Terentius Varro and L. Aemilius Paullus, the new army would consist of 80,000 foot and 6,000 cavalry soldiers. Recruitment and training of the new soldiers for the huge army occupied the first half of 216 B.C. Almost two-thirds of the new army was made up of new, poorly trained recruits. Almost every household in Rome had a family member or relative caught up in the patriotic fervor to join the great crusade against Hannibal. More than eighty senators resigned their positions to join the army in the patriotic wave that swept the city. Thousands of plebeians eagerly joined the army's march against Hannibal, some out of patriotic zeal, but many because they hoped to win great spoils and Carthaginian slaves in the expected glorious defeat of Hannibal. Each of the eight Roman legions were expanded to 5,000 infantry and 300 cavalry, for a total of 40,000 foot soldiers and 2,400 horsemen in the all-citizen army. Roman allies provided another 40,000 infantry and 3,600 cavalry to make a gigantic total of 86,000 men in all.

In June, when the new additions to the army left Rome to join the legions already tracking Hannibal, co-consul Varro told the Peoples' Assembly, which was responsible for electing him, that the war would be over on the day he first saw the Carthaginian army. He assured his troops that they could not fail this time - reflecting an overconfident attitude similar to that of the ill-fated Sempronius at Trebbia. The other consul, Paullus, assured the troops more cautiously that there was no reason for Hannibal to defeat the great Roman army that they now had.

When it was reported to him, confident Hannibal was enthusiastic about the news. It meant he would finally get the decisive battle he had been planning for a long time, on his selected battlefield. The battle was shaping up to be one of hardened, well-trained, professional soldiers, with many years of combat experience, the Carthaginians, against a Roman army, two-thirds of which were raw recruits with no combat experience, commanded by two conflicting co-consuls. One consul was an impetuous amateur and the other an elderly, levelheaded but reluctant, part-time soldier who had to be coaxed to take the job. Varro, the butcher's son, had little military capability, was elected on the basis of his oratorical and political skills, and was overly confident. He was recklessly anxious to launch his troops into combat against Hannibal, the professional military genius. Aemilius Paullus, the other co-consul, had more military experience, but he was growing old and, wisely, he was very cautious about engaging Hannibal in combat. Aemilius Paullus was beginning to believe the warning that his friends had given him, that Varro would be a greater enemy than Hannibal.

The two co-consuls decided to continue the tradition of rotating command of the army on alternate days. Each would command the army for a day and then yield his command to the other consul on the following day. When Hannibal took the grain-storage depot at Cannae, it turned out to be the last humiliation that Rome could bear, as Hannibal and his lieutenant, Gisco, had hoped that it would be. The two consuls were told by Rome to attack Hannibal near Cannae. This would mean that the fight would be in an area that was a more suitable battlefield for Hannibal's superior cavalry, and it was a less suitable one for the main strength of the Roman army, its infantry.

It was during the command of Paullus that his army came within sight of Carthaginian forces, and he cautiously dug in his army five miles away from Hannibal, on the opposite bank of the Aufidus River. Paullus established a smaller camp with one-third of his army on the right bank to protect his foraging parties that had to go to that side of the river. Hannibal was on the right bank. Paullus camped the main part of his army on the left bank of the river that flowed into the Adriatic Sea five miles away.

Paullus expressed his grave concern that the battle area consisted of flat, treeless lands, which favored Hannibal's superior cavalry, and he urged caution. He urged Varro to help him try to lure the Carthaginian army away to a more favorable site before they engaged Hannibal's troops. Varro disagreed with Paullus, insisting that they should fight Hannibal without delay. The next day when it was his turn to command, under strong protest from Paullus, he moved the Roman army so that it was almost in direct contact with the Carthaginians, but on the opposite side of the river. There, he dug in the army for the night. Seeing this movement toward him, Hannibal moved his army across the river so that it was on the left bank, the same side of the river and very near where Romans had established their fortified camp. The two armies were now very close.

The next day was Paullus's turn to command, and he was terrified by the position into which Varro had maneuvered the army. Hannibal formed his army in battle formation very near the Roman camp, signaling to the Romans that Carthaginians were ready to fight. The Carthaginian army waited in this position for all to see for a considerable length of time. However, the cautious Aemilius Paullus would not move his army out of its dug in position. He made the comment to Varro that their present position was not a satisfactory one for either fighting or retreating. Hannibal was too battle wise to attack the Italians when they were in their fortified camp. After a long time, when he saw that Paullus would not come out of his camp to accept the Carthaginian challenge, Hannibal had his army disband its combat formation and return to his entrenched camp across the river, on the right bank, for the night.

Hannibal knew that Roman soldiers were anxious for battle, and that this display of cowardice by Paullus would further frustrate them. Hannibal also knew that the next day would be Varro's turn to command,

and that the reckless leader, egged on by the veterans of his army who had served under Fabius and who had been held back for such a long time by The Delayer, would probably fight on Hannibal's preferred ground, the right bank. The new Roman recruits, including many ex-senators, had come a long way to defeat Hannibal, only to see him humiliate them again when Paullus failed to accept his challenge for battle. They were anxious to put an end to Hannibal's pillaging of their countryside. The fact that their numbers were far greater than the number of soldiers in the Carthaginian army - 86,000 Romans against Hannibal's 50,000 - made them very confident of victory.

Regular Roman dispatches were rushed (by special messengers) from the eastern front to the eagerly waiting Senate, then the news was announced to crowds that were eagerly waiting in Rome's Forum. Everyone in the waiting crowd had family members or relatives at the front. The first dispatches contained good news: Hannibal was forced to abandon his camp on the left bank and was forced to cross the river to the right bank. Another dispatch stated that a raid by Hannibal's Numidian cavalry came up to the edge of the Roman camp, but it had been successfully repulsed by the great Roman army of co-consuls Varro and Aemilius Paullus. Romans were in hot pursuit of the enemy (a tactic similar to the hit-and-run tactic that Hannibal had his Numidians use to provoke Romans at Trebbia).

The actual facts were that Hannibal had called upon his wily Numidian cavalry, again, to play upon the emotions of Varro and his soldiers who, agents had reported, had become so anxious for battle that it was difficult for centurions to control them. Hannibal was planning to use these emotions to his advantage in the battle he expected soon. The dispatch to Rome had actually referred to an attack the Numidian cavalry had made on a Roman foraging party while it was obtaining water from the river for the army. Numidians had arrogantly carried the attack right up to the outpost of the Roman encampment, and they had launched javelins at the sentries in full view of the rest of the Roman army. This insult to the legionnaires added to their frenzy for battle. Varro, particularly, was enraged. He was determined not to wait for the Carthaginians to come to him. He ordered his army to prepare to move across the river early the next morning, when he would be in command. He ignored the strong objections of Paullus.

Soon after sunrise the next morning, August 3, 216 B.C., the Roman army crossed the river to the right bank. Varro had marshaled almost all of his available troops, including most of those that had garrisoned the mini-camp protecting Roman foraging parties. Only small garrisons were left at their prepared camp on the left bank to guard the supplies left behind. His army was almost 86,000 strong, and he drew them up in a battle configuration the soldiers had never used before. The spaces between maniples were reduced, and the maniples themselves were formed so that the depth of each maniple was several times greater than its width. Each maniple, which normally contained ten rows deep of twelve soldiers abreast was changed so that there were twenty rows deep with only six soldiers abreast. Varro had ordered his legions to form this unusually deep and narrow formation, expecting that they could crush the center of Hannibal's infantry line before Hannibal's superior cavalry could become decisive against his weaker cavalry. Varro's eight legions would normally have stretched almost three miles across, end to end. This new formation now stretched only a mile across. Roman infantry was not used to marching in that battle order, and the close formation crowded the maniples so closely that they didn't have much room to maneuver their weapons.

Hannibal was quick to take advantage of his opponent's formation. He anticipated what Varro was planning to do, and the wily Carthaginian magician planned to use Varro's tactics against him. Hannibal was elated when he saw Varro's legions crammed together so tightly. Originally, Hannibal had lined his infantry in a straight line, orienting it so that it was in a northwest-southeast line. This position put the strong morning summer west wind at his back so that the huge clouds of dust to be created by the feet of his maneuvering army on the dry earth would be blown into the eyes of the Romans as they charged his position. This position was such that the rising sun would not shine directly into his soldiers' eyes, as it would be off at an angle. His army had an uphill advantage over the Italians, who would be climbing up a slight grade to reach his army.

Hannibal had instructed his infantry to change its originally straight, line-abreast formation to one that had a bulge in its center. That is, he had the center of his line move forward, creating a convex-shaped bulge at its center, and he had the infantry at the flanks of the center remain behind the center bulge. Hannibal positioned his tough Spanish infantry with Celts alongside them in the center bulge, with his strong African infantry on the flanks. These were the new tactics that Hannibal had his army trained to perfect during their winter encampment. Each man knew exactly what he was supposed to do. The center of his infantry line was instructed to give ground slowly, so that the convex-shaped bulge would gradually retreat in an orderly fashion until it became a concave-shaped depression in the Carthaginian infantry line. The flanks of strong African infantry were instructed to hold their positions so that the Roman infantry would be drawn into the center, as if by a funnel. Africans, who were stronger fighters than most Romans, were instructed to force the advancing Roman infantry in toward the center of the Carthaginian line as the center of the line gradually retreated under controlled conditions. The heavily armed Africans - they were wearing the best of the captured Roman armor - were instructed to gradually move behind the Roman legions until they had the Italians nearly encircled.

Varro positioned his 2,400 Roman-citizen cavalry, which included the newly enlisted aristocratic "Roman Knights," under the command of aristocrat, Paullus, on the right flank of the Roman line - which was Hannibal's left flank, near the water. There was not much room for the cavalry to maneuver on this flank because there was not much room between the line of infantry and the water. Hannibal positioned 8,000 Celtiberian, Gallic, and Carthaginian cavalry, under command of Hanno the son of Bomilcar, on his left flank below the ruins of Cannae, to face them. The ruins would limit the Romans' ability to encircle Hannibal's army because of the position he had selected. Cavalry could not effectively climb the heights of the stone ruins, a maneuver that would be required by the Roman cavalry to encircle the Carthaginian infantry. The Spaniards, with their stocky, strong Iberian horses and their double-edged, razor-sharp, pointed Iberian swords were well suited for close-in, hand-to-hand fighting and they needed little room to maneuver. The

Celt cavalry was vicious at close-in fighting with its razor-sharp, double-edged swords. Hannibal was planning to have these cavalrymen quickly rout the smaller Roman cavalry, which they outnumbered more than three to one, then circle behind the Roman army to attack Varro's allied cavalry from its rear while Varro's horsemen were still defending against the Numidian cavalry it was facing in its front. Hannibal put his swift, agile 2,000 Numidian horses on his right flank to face the front of the 3,600 Roman allied cavalry. Varro had placed himself in the allied cavalry. Hannibal planned to have the Numidians, under the command of the capable Maharbal, hold their own by using their usual hit-and-run tactics until the Spanish and Gallic cavalry had routed their opponents, encircled the Roman army, and attacked Varro's cavalry from behind.

Hannibal placed a line of Balearic slingers and some of his most expert javelin-throwers, 8,000 combined total, in front of the bowed line of infantrymen. These formed a screen which hid the exact nature of the Carthaginian army's crescent configuration, because the Italians were approaching from a lower elevation that made it difficult for them to see over the heads this first line of skirmishers. The skirmishers, who were expert slingers and javelin throwers, would be able to pummel the approaching legions with their lead balls and javelins long before the Italians were within range of using their own weapons, in retaliation. This was possible because the hand-selected Carthaginian skirmishers had longer-range throwing ability, and they were throwing slightly downhill. Thus, a great toll was expected to be taken in lives and morale from the approaching Romans long before they could retaliate with their own missiles. Romans had not developed air-missiles to such a high level of proficiency as Hannibal's army, thanks to Gisco's wise advice and training. They planned to pull to the Carthaginian flanks as soon as the Roman line reached their position, then they were to direct their missiles at suitable targets from that position.

Hannibal, Gisco, and key officers were positioned on a knoll behind the central bulge of their infantry where they could view the entire battleground. The center was a crucial and difficult part of the plan to control. They had developed an elaborate system of pre-planned communications to help them orchestrate their complex battle plan from that position, once the battle had begun. They knew that once the combat had commenced, the noise, dust, and confusion would make communications difficult. Every element knew in advance to watch for the required signal and act appropriately when the signal was given. They had to rely heavily on visual signals, but Gisco, Cirta, and others were to help with the signal network by personally conveying messages as couriers if necessary. The system was designed to coordinate and control the activities of their many different units in the confusion of battle.

Varro had no such plan for controlling the progress of his army once the battle had begun. Varro was off to one side of his army, in the allied cavalry, and Paullus was off to the other side of the Roman line in the citizen-cavalry. Minucius, now with a reputation as an experienced Hannibal fighter, was put in command of the center of the Roman infantry. Control of the progress of their troops, once fighting commenced, was divided among the three. Furthermore, all the officers and most of the men had been with

Hannibal for many years, while most of the Roman officers and men were together for the first time. Roman commanders and their troops were strangers to one another, for the most part. There was a huge gap in the experience level of the personnel of the two armies.

Hannibal, Gisco, and key officers were standing beside their horses on a knoll with the wind blowing at their backs, viewing the proceedings. The strong breeze from their backs rippled their bright red capes, their helmet plumes, and the long manes of their horses, as they stood on a rise of the plain that allowed them to observe the entire, awesome sight of the gigantic Roman army. The legions were mechanically forming their straight lines with great precision, keeping standards of cohorts properly aligned. Unusual for Romans, their formation stretched more than a mile end-to-end in front of them, sixty rows deep. The Roman infantry in front of Hannibal and his officers outnumbered their own infantry by more than two to one.

Gisco shook his head and commented, "It is amazing to see so many soldiers in one place." Hannibal, having sensed the growing tension and apprehension in his officers because of the menacing spectacle before them, responded to Gisco's remark by saying with a broad smile, in a loud voice so that all could hear, "I'll tell you something even more amazing."All officers looked at one another, trying to figure out what their great commander meant. They were surprised to see their commander smile during such a serious, tense moment. When he spoke, all listened and paid attention. After a pause, one of the officers finally asked Hannibal what was more amazing. Hannibal replied with a smile, "They don't have, in all that vast army, a miracle man named 'Gisco,' like we have." All of the officers looked at one another and laughed at Hannibal's lighthearted comment during such a tense moment. It broke the tension. Hannibal had complete confidence in the ability of his well-drilled army to execute his ingenious plan, and his relaxed demeanor exuded his confidence.

 The well-drilled Carthaginian army executed the plan precisely as Hannibal intended it to happen, and it has since become a classic model for military officers to study. It is regarded as one of the most brilliant military plans in history. Hannibal had selected a part of the terrain to position his army upon that was not only a slight uphill climb for the Roman army, but there was also a slight depression in the earth that made a V-shaped ravine at his army's back. He placed his African heavy infantrymen, positioned on the flanks of his army, on the top of the slight rise at the mouth of the V-shaped ravine. The apex of the V was at his army's back directly behind the bulging center of his infantry. Thus, as the Roman army attacked his center and pushed his troops back up the ravine, the African soldiers on the raised ground had the advantage of fighting down on the Roman infantry, to funnel the Italians into the mouth of the V. As the already compressed formation of legionnaires pushed their way up the ravine toward the apex of the V, they became more crammed and compressed by the planned actions of Hannibal's troops, helped along by the shape of the terrain.

 As soon as the Roman trumpets sounded the order to attack, the entire 86,000 Roman army let out a tumultuous war-cry that almost shattered the ears of the Carthaginians. Their intent was to frighten their enemy, but the hardened Carthaginian army remained

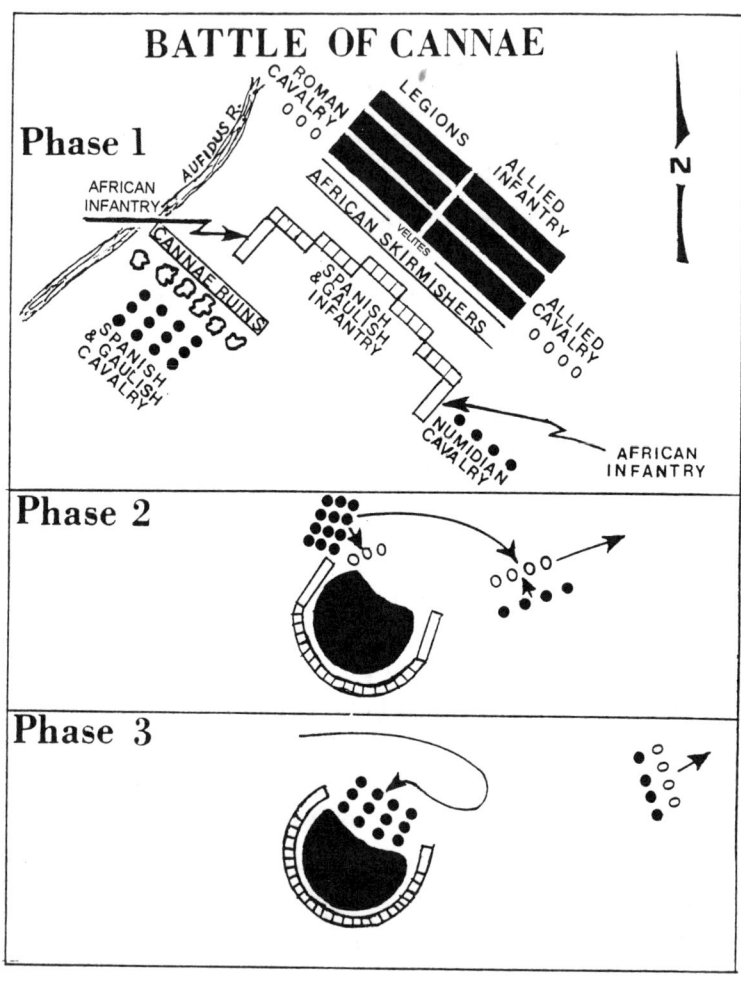

silent as it waited in a professional, confident manner for the initial contact. The Carthaginian soldiers were nervous, but their confidence in Hannibal's plan gave them the inner strength to overcome their nervousness. Hannibal's men were seasoned against such intimidation. They concentrated on executing their master plan for the defeat of the Roman army, which Hannibal and his officers had convinced them would be successful.

The massive Roman army slowly advanced toward the Carthaginian lines waiting for them. Centurions had a difficult time restraining the confident, eager Roman troops because they had been looking toward this showdown with Hannibal's army for a long time.

In the lead of the Roman army was a thin line of velites who were going to throw their four-foot-long darts with iron heads, but they were throwing into the wind and slightly uphill while Carthaginians were throwing with wind at their backs and downhill. Carthaginians were more powerful and accurate throwers. Balearic slingers, who were more accurate with their slings than most archers were with their arrows, pummeled the advancing enemy long before the Romans were within range of the velites' darts. Velites could throw their darts less than twenty-five yards into the wind, uphill, on that day.

Behind the velites came the Roman soldiers carrying their rectangular, convex-shaped shields, four-feet long and two-feet wide, in their left hands, while wearing helmets, breast plates, and greaves for protective armor. Roman weapons were the "pilium," a five-and-a-half-foot dart with an iron tip used for throwing or thrusting. Each legionnaire carried a "gladius," which was a twenty-two inch double-edged, pointed sword normally used for thrusting rather than slashing. The

Roman swords were no match for the razor-sharp, hardened swords used by most of Hannibal's men.

Hannibal's men wore the best armor selected from the captured Roman equipment, and many of them looked like Romans. Most Gauls, whose religion made them believe it was a catastrophe to die with clothes on their bodies, went naked from the waist up.

The Romans advanced through the clouds of Balearic missiles that were thrown at them, then they came into range of the Carthaginian javelins before they could launch their own weapons. As they marched forward toward the Carthaginians, Romans were finding it more difficult to see the standards that they were supposed to line upon because of the huge, warm clouds of dust that were being whipped into their faces by the hot wind.

Hannibal's men did not stand to fight to the death, but they gradually backed up in a feigned retreat according to plan, giving ground slowly to the eagerly charging Italians, as they backpedaled to higher ground behind them. It took powerful physical strength and courageous effort by the Spanish and Gallic troops to keep the line from caving in too fast under the tremendous pressure, as they backed up in a controlled manner. The center of the line became outnumbered by a factor of four to one as the legionnaires converged on the center of Hannibal's line. In their zeal, thinking they were routing the Carthaginian army, they ignored their original battle formations and the standards which they were supposed to line upon and advanced up the ravine. To the observer, it appeared that the Roman army was being sucked into the ravine by a gigantic vacuum. As Hannibal's convex line gradually changed its shape to a concave line, it caused a great bulge in the center of the Roman line. African heavy infantry at the wings of the crescent, on slightly higher ground at the sides of the V-shaped depression, held their positions by fierce fighting, forcing Romans down into the ravine, compacting the soldiers together. Their superior size, armor, sharp swords, and fighting ability allowed them to keep control as planned.

As the center of Hannibal's army backed up, legionnaires mistook it to mean that they were overwhelming the greatly outnumbered Carthaginians, and they began to let out loud victory shouts. Deceived by the backpedaling, they became more confident and they recklessly rushed forward, no longer caring about their formation. They were unaware of where they were headed in the huge clouds of dust. Though the Romans didn't care about their formation, Hannibal's infantry knew exactly what their formation was becoming. All soldiers were getting thirsty and tired from the dust and heat.

At the proper moment, Hannibal had an assistant throw a lighted torch to a stack of dry wood as a signal for Hanno's cavalry to charge the Roman-citizen cavalry commanded by Paullus. Two miles away, Hanno easily saw the dense smoke from the fire. Hanno's horses were planned to be Hannibal's main offensive striking force. Hannibal had gambled on placing the largest share of his horses under Hanno, hoping Maharbal's Numidians on the other end of the line could neutralize Varro's cavalry, which outnumbered them. Numidians were expected to hold their line until Hanno could quickly rout the cavalry of Paullus, then come to their assistance.

Hanno's 8,000 tough cavalry rode at a gallop, head-on into the 2,400 Roman horses of Paullus in a huge cloud of dust. Paullus and his horses were swept against the nearest, already crowded legion of foot soldiers. Though they fought their losing battle with courage, the Roman cavalry, outnumbered by a factor of almost four to one by Hanno's cavalry, was crushed by the first massive attack. Aemilius Paullus, who was struck to the ground with a mortal wound during the first momentous clash, gave his order for survivors of his cavalry to dismount and form a protective flank for the legion. Adding to the confusion, riderless horses bolted wildly into the lines of Roman infantry. When the Roman cavalry was quickly defeated, Hanno's cavalry circled around the back of the Roman infantry to attack Varro's cavalry from its behind, as planned. When Varro saw Hanno's onslaught, he fled for his life, leaving the battle scene with an escort of seventy horses. Before long, Varro's horsemen who had remained behind to fight were either killed or wounded.

As they continued to advance, legionnaires became more compressed, crushing into one another as they approached the apex of the V. According to Hannibal's plans, his army soon surrounded the Roman army on three sides. They were herding it into the center of the ravine as though they were putting the Italian army into a huge corral. Legionnaires began crushing one another like stampeding cattle, and they were becoming confused and panicky like caged animals. When he saw that Varro's cavalry was routed, Hanno ordered his cavalry to abandon the chase of Varro's surviving horses, leaving that to the fast Numidian horses. He began slashing the rear of the Roman infantry with his 8,000 horses.

Romans were now completely surrounded. The Italian soldiers became so packed together, they could not maneuver their weapons. The panicky soldiers in the rear and on the perimeter, attempting to avoid the deadly missiles and swords of the Carthaginian troops who surrounded them, began pushing one another inward with an irresistible force. The superhuman strength with which they pushed was a strength only crazed men fleeing for their lives could summon up. Romans were being crushed together like a stampeding herd of cattle, unable to move to use their weapons. Carthaginians, on the perimeter of the Romans, had full freedom to maneuver their weapons, and they used them efficiently.

Most of the few thousand brave Romans who succeeded in fighting their way out of the corral, seeking hiding places to save their lives, were tracked down by Maharbal's fast horsemen who had returned from the destruction of remnants of Varro's cavalry. Numidians were expert at hamstringing, and they slashed the backs of the fleeing Romans' legs with their razor-sharp swords as they fled. By afternoon, fighting had stopped and the eight enlarged Roman legions and their allies had been completely destroyed. Hannibal's brilliant plan, perfectly executed by his well-drilled soldiers, made it evolve into a fight that was like shooting ducks in a pond.

That evening Hannibal, Gisco, and Cirta rode their horses over the battlefield. The carnage was an appalling sight, even for the battle-hardened warriors. The great Carthaginian commander ordered a search for all of his own soldiers who were wounded, and they were brought to the physician's tents for treatment. Many Romans, covered with blood, were mercifully killed if they showed signs of life, many at their own pitiful requests.

Hannibal had his cooks prepare a huge feast with plenty of wine for everyone to celebrate the great victory. Although they were exhausted by the day's events, which started soon after sunrise and continued in the hot, dry wind with continual fighting for their lives for eight hours, they were supremely exalted by the outcome of the battle. That they had survived against such great odds added to their exaltation. They ate and drank heartily.

The next day, Hannibal ordered that bodies of Aemilius Paullus, ex-consul Servilius, and ex-dictator Minucius, all of whom were killed in the battle, be buried with their weapons and insignia. Among the dead were eighty senators, twenty-nine military tribunes, and all of the aristocratic Roman knights. Varro had left garrisons of soldiers guarding their camps, and Hannibal's men quickly captured them. The battlefield was a ghastly sight with more than 70,000 bloody, mangled bodies piled in all directions. All bodies were stripped of jewels, armor, weapons, seal-rings, and anything else of value. Roman cavalry had used solid silver trappings for their horses. These were taken by Hannibal for his treasury, which was running low on silver because shipments from Spain could not get through to him.

It was difficult to make an accurate count of the jumbled piles of mangled bodies on the battlefield, but a reasonable estimate of Roman lives lost was made by subtracting the number of known survivors, as later reported to Hannibal by agents, from the number of Romans that had entered the conflict. This indicated that more than 70,000 of the original 86,000 Italian soldiers had died in the battle. Less than 15,000 of Rome's gigantic army had survived the catastrophe. Survivors included about 4,500 prisoners taken, while 10,000 had succeeded in escaping. The lucky escapees gradually straggled into Canusium from all around the countryside. These included Consul Varro and the seventy cavalrymen with whom he had fled from the battle scene. Varro eventually took command of the survivors in Canusium. Among those who had escaped was the young Publius Scipio, son of the consul of the same name who was wounded at the Ticinus River skirmish. Young Scipio, who had bravely saved his father's life at the Ticinus, was destined to command an army much later, against Hannibal.

Hannibal lost 5,500 of his troops as killed or wounded. Only 1,500 of these troops lost were his hard-core Spaniards and Africans, while the other 4,000 soldiers lost were his mercenary Gauls. His men were physically and mentally exhausted, otherwise he would have ordered the survivors in his army to go after Varro and the other escapees at Canusium. The aggressive Maharbal pleaded with his commander to immediately march to Rome and take the city, but Hannibal knew how heavily fortified the capital was and how many more lives would be lost from his small army.

Hannibal knew that his army wasn't large enough to besiege the city of Rome, even in Rome's weakened state. The entire world now expected him to take the capital city, but the more levelheaded Hannibal hoped to wear down the Romans and compel them to sue for peace without losing more of his soldiers. As noted earlier, the great Carthaginian magician's greatest assets - massive, mobile cavalry, surprise, ambush, brilliant maneuvering of his army - were not qualities suited for a prolonged siege of a fortified city. The difficult eight-month siege of Saguntum much earlier, and the unsuccessful attempt to besiege the small fortified town of Spoletium, more recently, gave

Hannibal a healthy respect for what he could expect from a siege of Rome.

Reports from his intelligence network had educated him about the formidable defenses he would have to face at the capital city. Hannibal and Gisco had decided that they would have to augment their small number of soldiers with many more from Africa, Spain, Cisalpine Gaul, or elsewhere before they could be victorious in an attack on the city. At present, their army was not large enough. A siege would take many months, and Rome had many garrisons in forts throughout Italy and in its other provinces that could be ordered to come to the aid of the capital city during a prolonged attack.

Contrary to popular belief, particularly Roman belief, Hannibal disliked war and combat. He only fought when he believed it necessary, when he believed that odds where overwhelmingly in his favor, and when he could use his superior cavalry, surprise, maneuverability, terrain, psychology, and weather to his advantage. A siege of the city of Rome offered none of these advantages. Until now, Hannibal had relied on drawing the enemy out of fortified positions, then outmaneuvering them on an open battlefield by using his genius to put them into situations where Hannibal had overwhelming advantages. A decision was made not to go to Rome, 200 miles away, until later, if at all.

News of the catastrophe did not reach Rome until much later. It trickled in to the Forum slowly, first as rumors because almost all men at Cannae had been either slain, captured, or had fled to Canusium. Those who were not slain or captured were ashamed and reluctant to make a report from Canusium. Rome sent scouts out to get information about the battle when reports stopped coming to it from the front. Rome was shocked to learn from its scouts that there was not a trace of the army left, only mutilated bodies of tens of thousands of dead Roman soldiers. A camp could not be found. A report did not come until later, when Varro arrived to take command of those that had taken refuge at Canusium. Varro sent a report to the Senate, then he reluctantly appeared in person before the Senate to present a candid description of the debacle at Cannae. Surprisingly, he was thanked by the Senate for his service to the people. Much to his astonishment, he was also thanked by the Assembly of the People.

The citizens of Rome were now convinced that there was no army to defend them, except the garrisons of soldiers that were within their walls. They believed that Hannibal would soon be at their gates. There was loud wailing and weeping in the streets of Rome because nearly every household had a son, brother, or husband in the ill-fated army. The levelheaded Quintus Fabius, the ex-dictator, finally took complete charge of the government since most officials had been caught up in the patriotic fervor that swept the city, and had gone to Cannae as volunteers for the ill-fated army. Fabius ordered that all women be kept indoors, that lamentations were forbidden, and that silence was to be enforced in the city. Fabius the "Delayer," who would not fight Hannibal and who was a hated man until now, became the most revered leader in Rome. His hesitancy to attack the Carthaginian army and his strong advice to be cautious now appeared to be good advice to follow. He soon became known as "Maximus" (the "Greatest"). He took immediate action to raise four more legions by using slaves to fill out the ranks of the new army create to defend the city. Frantic preparations for defense of the city commenced in earnest.

Chapter 7

STALEMATE (216 - 211 B.C.)

As Rome frantically prepared for the assault from Hannibal that did not come, its leaders slowly realized that Fabius the Delayer was the one with the sound policy for coping with Hannibal's military genius. Fabius's policy recognized that the Carthaginian wizard could not be defeated on an open plain where he could use his superior cavalry to advantage, and that the Roman army must remain extremely cautious of being lured into one of his cunning ambushes. However, those policies would not prevent Hannibal from ravaging the Italian countryside as he desired. Many in Rome urged peace with Carthage, but they were in the minority. Fabius took control of remnants of the Senate to appoint a Dictator, M. Janius Pera.

Hannibal sent couriers to Carthage, Spain, and to the chieftains of the Cisalpine Gauls to announce his spectacular victory and indicated that Rome was now weak and ripe for a war-ending attack. He pleaded for more assistance from them so that he could get the resources necessary to defeat Rome while it was still reeling from its catastrophe. He sent his brother, Mago, to Carthage requesting reinforcements, silver, gold, and supplies. Mago brought interesting artifacts with him to Carthage. They were some of those taken from high ranking Romans, and he used them as impressive evidence of the magnitude of the Carthaginian victory. Mago told officials in Carthage that Hannibal had defeated six commanders and two dictators, that he had killed 200,000 soldiers, and that he had taken 50,000 prisoners. All of this was accomplished by the small army he had led over the Alps, within the two years he had been in Italy.

Hannibal had many enemies in the Carthaginian Senate who opposed giving him any reinforcements. Many were jealous of him, but most were members of the Hanno faction (party) that had been political opponents of Hannibal's father and of political supporters of the Barca family - the Barca faction. Most opponents of the Barcas were afraid of the successes of Hannibal, worrying that his victories would give him such popularity and political power that he would return to Carthage and become a dictator. Historically, Carthaginians had been distrustful of their military commanders, fearful of just such an outcome.

Additionally, the Hanno faction suffered from a lack of foresight. It could not see the long-range implications of Roman expansionism. The Hannos' main concern, since they were primarily traders, was continuing a profitable day-to-day trade. The Barcas, who were much more visionary, believed that Roman expansionism would eventually overwhelm Carthaginian trade. Rome's recent confiscation of Carthaginian trading colonies in Sicily, Sardinia, and Corsica was evidence of its expansionistic intentions. That was the main concern of the Barcas who were not only worried about the future of Carthage trade but were concerned about the very future freedom of their nation. The Hanno faction in the Senate made the argument that since Hannibal was having such success with the resources he already had, that was evidence that he did not need more.

Carthaginians, as Phoenicians, were primarily hard-nosed traders with centuries of trading experience behind them; they were not fighters. That is the primary reason that, traditionally, they had to hire mercenary troops to do most of their fighting. The Hannos did not understand Hannibal's military needs. They did not feel a sense of urgency to support Hannibal's desperate needs, with the war being fought so many miles away and across the sea. Romans felt a deep sense of urgency to support their army's needs, with the war at their doorstep. The Carthaginian Senate was making its deliberations in a safe atmosphere. The Roman Senate, on the other hand, had a great urgency to support its legions, with Hannibal in its backyard, and with survival of the Roman nation depending on its quick action.

After a leisurely, prolonged debate, Hannibal's friends prevailed in the Senate, and they voted to send him 40 elephants, 4,000 Numidian cavalry, and 500 talents of silver, to be shipped from Carthage to Italy. They also voted to send Mago to Spain to raise more troops, an additional 20,000 infantry and 4,000 cavalry, also to be sent to Hannibal. These were skimpy reinforcements considering the resources Rome had available to send against Hannibal. Carthage could easily have afforded much more with so much at stake.

At Gisco's suggestion, Hannibal decided to experiment with a new approach to his treatment of the Roman-citizen soldiers taken prisoner at Cannae. As usual, all allied soldiers who had been fighting with Romans were released and returned to their homes in the normal fashion after being treated well, given good meals, and receiving Hannibal's customary speech. Roman citizens, who would have been treated roughly, put in iron chains, and sold into slavery in accordance with past policy, were, instead, suddenly treated with dignity. They were fed well and held for ransom from the Roman Senate. Hannibal and Gisco hoped this policy would have a good influence on public opinion in Rome. Hannibal was hopeful of reaching a peace treaty with Rome to avoid more bloodshed. Another reason for this policy was that the ransom money, which was more than local slave traders were willing to pay, was sorely needed to pay the Carthaginian army in coming months. No silver shipments from Spain had been received and the money supply was getting low.

After Hannibal treated the captive Roman citizens well, he decided to send Carthalo to Rome to negotiate the ransom in exchange for the prisoners he had taken at Cannae. Carthalo could assess the fortifications during his visit, as well as arrange for the exchange of money for prisoners. Carthalo requested that Gisco accompany him because Gisco spoke the Roman language, Latin, and he had toured Rome before he joined the Carthaginian army. Gisco and Carthalo had a good rapport because they had worked together on intelligence matters many times before, and Gisco could provide his expertise during the negotiations, as well as provide an extra pair of eyes to evaluate fortifications they would see. The two wanted to see, first hand, what spies had been reporting to Carthalo. Gisco wanted to go with Carthalo incognito, wearing a wig and the costume of a slave so he would not be recognized by the Romans. He was planning to visit the city at a later date to gather more firsthand intelligence about its fortifications. Hannibal released ten citizens of Rome to go with them on the promise that they would testify about the good treatment that Hannibal was giving captured legionnaires. He made the ten pledge that they would return to his camp after they had testified before the Senate in Rome. The ten men wanted to secure the release of their comrades and readily gave their pledges to Hannibal.

As the party approached the Collina Gate in the wall of the city - a gate that Gisco had selected as one that he wanted more information about - they were met by a representative of Fabius. They were told that the Dictator would not allow them inside the city. Carthalo told the magistrate's representative about his mission and said that Hannibal was ready to exchange each captured citizen-cavalryman for 500 denarii (Roman coins weighing 18.17 grams of silver), 300 for each citizen-infantryman, and 100 for each slave. The ten legionnaires Hannibal had released to testify about the welfare of the remaining Roman citizens in his captivity were allowed to proceed into the city to testify before the Senate. Carthalo and Gisgo were told they had to leave Roman territory immediately and that the Senate's decision about the ransom would be sent to Hannibal after it had been made.

The Senate had a heated debate over the ransom issue, and it finally decided not to give Hannibal ransom, even though they sorely needed the soldiers for the defense of their city and even though the prisoner's families sorely wanted them home. Rome was using slaves as soldiers, an unprecedented move, and it was releasing inmates from the city prisons to serve in the army because of the severe shortage of manpower. However, the Senate did not want to give Hannibal ransom money for soldiers who were not willing to fight to the death. Many senators said that they did not want to honorably receive the survivors of Cannae back into the capital. The survivors were treated as cowards and traitors. Of the ten legionnaires who had given their pledge to return to Hannibal's camp after they gave their testimony, all but one returned to the camp. On hearing the Senate's decision, Hannibal sold all captured Roman-citizen solders to Greek slave traders from Delos.

The Roman Senate, instead of desiring a peace treaty, began to adopt Hannibal's hard philosophy as he had dramatized it for his troops in Turini soon after they had crossed the Alps. That is, the Senate decided there were only two practical alternative courses of action: fight and win the right to stay free; or die fighting. To live and lose would be a fate worse than death, as losers live in slavery the rest of their lives. Thus to fight to the death was the only alternative to winning. By sending a message to survivors of Cannae that they could not come home, the Senate was pronouncing its philosophy to all other soldiers. Romans, particularly the wealthy aristocrats of the Senate who made the decision, believed that a peace treaty with the barbaric Hannibal was not a consideration. The Roman propaganda machine had exaggerated Hannibal's military campaign as being one of senseless, barbaric atrocities, a view that was not entirely true. Each of Hannibal's actions had a military purpose, nothing more. His actions were less barbaric than those of Roman legions, and they were consistent with the mores of contemporary fighting armies throughout the world. Hannibal's policy of releasing non-citizens of Rome, rather than selling them as slaves, was a much more humane treatment than was customary of other armies.

In addition, the behavior of Hannibal's army in territories that did not oppose him with force, other than Roman provinces that remained loyal to Rome, was much more humane than was customary. In such regions, his policy was to pay for most supplies in silver, to allow each to remain free with its own government, and he did not place a levy on localities for soldiers for his army. He obtained recruits for his army through paid volunteers - mercenaries - as was the custom in his homeland, Carthage.

Hannibal's purpose for fighting in Italy was to free men and territories from Roman dominance, and he had no desire to obtain territory for Carthage. He usually made explicit promises about this to leaders in each friendly district as he marched through it. By doing this, he hoped to gain more allies and induce a general revolt for freedom from Rome's ruthless tyranny and voracious expansion. By doing this, Hannibal hoped to achieve his overall strategic goal: eliminate the long-range enemy of Carthaginian trade and freedom.

Like most generals who have seen bloody combat, Hannibal always hated war, in spite of the fact that he was trained for it, by necessity, his entire life. He had a deep-rooted compassion for and commitment to his troops, most of whom had been with him for many years. He regarded his troops as part of his family. Learning from his brother-in-law, Hasdrubal, he usually tried to achieve his goals through diplomacy and peaceful means whenever he could. That was a reason he gave Carthalo authority to negotiate reasonable peace terms during his aborted trip to Rome.

Information about the Senate's hot debate over the issue of ransom for Hannibal's prisoners reached Varro's 10,000 escapees in Canusium. They were made to feel like outcasts. Survivors of Cannae were no longer made to feel welcome in Rome, regardless of the severe shortage of manpower required to defend the capital city

A subdued Varro returned to Rome to make his report, leaving his survivors in Canusium. Varro was surprised to learn that Rome was glad to see him and that they forgave him. Welcomed back, he was sent to Picenum to raise a new levy of troops in the district. Varro's troops in Canusium were sent to Sicily for the duration of the war as punishment

The effect that Hannibal's great victory had on the morale of many Italian provinces was what Hannibal and Gisco had hoped it would be. A large part of southern Italy came over to the Carthaginian cause, and other peoples were gaining courage to secede from the Roman-dominated confederation. Peasants of Apulia and the Samnites made peace with Hannibal. Leaders of Capua, the second most affluent city of Italy, revolted from Rome after its emissaries were promised by Hannibal that they would keep their freedom, that he would protect the city from Roman reprisal, and that they would not be required to provide troops for the Carthaginian army. Volunteers, as mercenary soldiers, were always welcome to join his army. Hannibal's cause appealed to the masses of the people, the lower classes of the Italian population who were not among the more affluent. Opponents to the Carthaginian revolution were usually the aristocrats of the cities, and particularly Senators.

Capuans had killed all Senators in their city opposed to joining Hannibal, as well as others, including all Roman soldiers garrisoned there, when they took control of their metropolis. Capua was an older city than Rome, and there was considerable jealously and competition involved in its defection from the confederation dominated by its rival, Rome. By the end of winter, peasants from Picenum, Lucania, and Bruttium had joined Hannibal's fight for freedom. Greek towns in the south joined the fold, many recruited by Gisco's able persuasion. In response to Hannibal's plea for help, the Boii and Insubres in northern Italy defeated 25,000 soldiers, the entire Roman border army, killing its commander, G. Postumius Albinus.

Military operations had slowed after Cannae. To meet the challenge of controlling and protecting the large territory that Hannibal now dominated in southern Italy from Roman reprisal, Hannibal divided his forces into two divisions. He commanded one division with Gisco and Cirta at his side. All new recruits were assigned to his division of the army so that they could be trained with help from Gisco and Cirta. The other all-veteran division was originally commanded by his brother, Mago, before Mago was sent to plea for more troops in Carthage. Mago made his headquarters at Compsa (near Pescopagano). Hannibal left all baggage and captured material there for storage. Mago's task was to control towns that had not renounced their allegiance to Rome and to persuade them to join the Carthaginian cause. Towns in the south were the ones most recently conquered by Rome, and ones most likely to revolt. Hannibal led his division of the army through Samnium and Campania to the west. He made his headquarters on a hill called Tifata (Mount Maddaloni), outside the city walls of Capua. It was here he intended to establish his major camp for defeating Rome.

There was much more good news for the Carthaginian cause in addition to the 25,000 Roman soldiers killed by the Cisalpine Gauls to the north. During the autumn after Cannae, King Philip V of Macedonia, encouraged by Rome's weakness and Hannibal's demonstrated ability, sent emissaries to Hannibal with the purpose of forming an alliance against Rome. In addition, there was good news from Syracuse, in Sicily, where the ninety-year-old tyrannical King Hiero II, a staunch ally of Rome, was dying and about to leave his fifteen-year-old grandson, Hieronymus, to rule. Uncles of the new king told Hannibal that there was much sentiment in Syracuse to defect from Rome.

More good news was the information received from Spain. Hannibal's brother, Hasdrubal, was holding his own against the two legions commanded by the Scipio brothers, whom Rome had sent to conquer Spain. In still another area, news came that citizens of Sardinia were revolting against Rome, thus diverting more of Rome's attention from Italy. Carthaginian agents were sent there to exploit the situation.

The great Carthaginian genius had achieved considerable progress in the two years since he entered Italy with 26,000 troops. He had control of most Greek towns in southern Italy, Gauls controlled the northern part of the peninsula, Macedonia was now an ally, Rome had to fight in Sardinia, Syracuse was about to revolt, and Hasdrubal was holding his own in Spain.

The bad news was that Rome still controlled the seas with its strong navy. The Roman navy had warships superior to those of the Carthaginian navy. Rome's innovative use of large numbers of legionnaires (marines) on each of its vessels and the technological advantage it had gained by outfitting its vessels with grappling-irons and boarding-walks enabling its marines to board enemy vessels to capture them, had drastically changed the balance of power on the seas. Carthaginians, with their Phoenician heritage for sailing the seas had, at the beginning of their war with Rome, a great advantage of being superior sailors. Carthage had made no serious attempt to regain mastery of the seas from the Romans, once it was lost. The more determined Romans were focused more on military capability than their enemy, who was focused on peaceful trade.

Hannibal was not getting the full support from his government in Carthage that the Roman Senate was giving its military establishment. Furthermore, Rome had vast resources and short supply lines when compared with those of Hannibal. Hannibal's only hope for reinforcements from outside Italy were limited to those that could successfully sneak by the Roman naval blockade. His brother, Hasdrubal, couldn't bring him help from Spain by land, over the Pyranees, as long as the Scipio brothers continued to blockade the land route out of Spain.

The debacle at Cannae had only strengthened the Roman Senate's resolve and determination to fight, and it had spurred Rome to increase the size of its army and navy. In 215 B.C., the Roman Senate had authorized a total of fourteen legions, with seven of them confronting Hannibal in the south of Italy. In the meantime, while Roman military strength was building up, its army was following Fabius the Delayer's policy of cautiously watching

Hannibal and avoiding battle on open plains. Fabius planned a war of attrition against the Carthaginians as his interim policy, whereby the Roman army engaged in small skirmishes with Hannibal's foraging parties, trading casualties with Carthaginians. Fabius could replenish his army's casualties much easier than Hannibal could.

From his headquarters pavilion on Mount Tifata, on the edge of Capua outside the city walls, Hannibal enjoyed riding over the beautiful Campanian plain with his faithful companion and aide, Gisco. They could see the smoking volcano, Vesuvius, as they visited the sacred, picturesque Surrentum (Sorrento), and the small fishing village of Pom-Vesuvius (Pompeii), where they bought trinkets carved from coral and sea shells made by local inhabitants. The lush, abundant agriculture of the area included cereals, grapes, figs, other fruit trees, and vegetables. The mild weather yielded more than two crops a year, and there was ample grazing ground for the animals. It was a pleasant countryside.

Capuans were a cultured, affluent people, and they did not trust many of Hannibal's rough-hewn soldiers, particularly his recruits from the hills of Bruttium and Samnium, as well as most of the crude Gauls. These troops had a strong desire for plunder, and they became restless when they went too long without it. Hannibal had a difficult time controlling them, and they made Capuans very uneasy when they were near them. Hannibal issued strong orders to his troops, telling them to remember that they were guests of the Capuans, not conquerors, and that they must pay in hard coin from their amply stocked money belts for all food, wine, souvenirs, women, and merchandise they obtained in Capua. It was important to Hannibal that he retain the goodwill of the people as part of his overall plan to gain acceptance of his crusade against Rome. His soldiers were given strict orders to conduct themselves lawfully while in the area, and he promised severe punishment for offenders.

Gisco was more comfortable in the social life of Capua than Hannibal. The young Greek attracted many friends and admirers among the Capuan aristocrats because they all studied, discussed, and admired Greek literature, medicine, geometry, and philosophy. The highly-educated Greek marvel, Gisco, organized Greek-style intellectual symposiums among Capua's intelligentsia. Here, his wide knowledge of most subjects outclassed that of everyone else. Hannibal usually accompanied his companion. He enjoyed the meetings, and he vigorously participated in the discussions with great academic interest and competence. The military genius could match local leaders on a quid-pro-quo basis in discussions of most subjects. He amazed and profoundly impressed Capuans with his versatility, and he spoke Greek with an excellent, cultured accent. However, he did not feel as comfortable in that environment as Gisco. First of all, local inhabitants took their food and wine while reclining on divans in the Greek fashion, while conducting their discussions, but Hannibal preferred to sit on a stool, upright, during the symposiums. Capuans preferred their Falernian wine, and they only feigned to like the Carthaginian date-wine that Hannibal cherished. Neither Hannibal nor Gisco allowed themselves to become intoxicated from the wine as most Capuans were accustomed to doing. The two disciplined Carthaginian officers did not gorge themselves with food as did the local leaders at their meetings. The two warriors ate and drank sparingly and selectively. As Gisco had noted, a well-fed lion is listless and lazy, but when he is hungry, all of his senses - smell, hearing, sight, taste, touch, and general alertness - are at the peak of their performance. Gisco and Hannibal noted that their own senses responded to food and drink in much the same way as the lion's. The pressures of their situation in Italy required them to be capable of peak performance at any time, as a matter of survival. They drank and ate in moderation.

Hannibal needed a seaport near Tifata to establish communications by sea with Carthage and Spain. He attempted to take the town of Neapolis (Naples), a nearby port, but the formidable defensive walls deterred him. Hannibal had a policy of not assaulting towns that were heavily defended by war engines and walls, if he could avoid it. The cost in killed and wounded was usually too great, and he did not want to pay the price in manpower. In such situations, he would attempt to gain his objective by establishing a blockade to starve the fortress into submission, or use his considerable diplomatic powers to achieve his goals without bloodshed. Because Neapolis was a seaport and Hannibal didn't have control of the sea, a complete blockade was not possible. He withdrew his forces to the town of Nola, a few miles to the east of Neapolis, situated on the Via Latina. Although it wasn't a seaport, Hannibal selected it as a target of opportunity to test his new recruits, and to give them some seasoning.

Agents had reported that many of the proletarian inhabitants of Nola were considering revolt against Rome, but senators and other aristocrats did not want their city to defect. Senators of the town called on the Roman praetor, Claudius Marcellus, who was camped nearby at Casilinum, to come to Nola to prevent the town from defecting, when they determined that so many of its citizens were leaning toward going over to Hannibal. Marcellus was inside the city walls with his legion when the Carthaginians arrived.

Hannibal put his troops in combat formation outside the city walls, inviting Marcellus to come out and fight. His army had already blockaded the city gates. After a few days of this, when Marcellus did not accept Hannibal's invitation to come out and fight, his Carthaginian army began to grow restless. The new recruits, particularly, were not as disciplined and patient as Hannibal's veterans, and they were becoming inattentive. Marcellus noted this listless demeanor of Hannibal's new troops and decided to test them with a masterful stroke. He ordered his legionnaires to suddenly disgorge themselves from three gates of the city at the same time in a surprise attack on the unsuspecting, inattentive Carthaginians. The Roman legionnaires added greatly to the surprise and pandemonium with loud war cries as they attacked the lethargic Carthaginians. Vicious fighting ensued, with neither side gaining a distinct advantage.

Hannibal's recruits did not fight as well as he had expected, and he withdrew his army. He decided the town could not be taken without paying a high price in manpower. The significance of this skirmish between Marcellus and Hannibal was that it gained Marcellus great fame in Rome as the first and only commander that Hannibal was unable to defeat on a field of combat. The scarcity of successes for the Roman government to report against the Carthaginians to the waiting throngs in Rome's Forum caused the government to exaggerate the significance of this event. It did not deserve such attention, except that it demonstrated the willingness and ability of Marcellus to fight Hannibal where the Carthaginian master could not use his cavalry to his advantage.

Some critics have since claimed that the soft life in Capua took its toll on Hannibal's army, particularly his hardened veterans. Luxurious living with good housing, baths, servants, good food, wine, and women, they claim, undermined the toughness and willingness of his soldiers to endure severe hardships, as they had endured when they came over the Alps, marched through the swamps, and won victories against great odds at Trebbia, Trasimene, and Cannae.

It is true that after the sojourn at Capua, Hannibal's army was never the same again, and it never reached the peak of effectiveness attained at Cannae. It is a tribute to Hannibal's genius that he was able to keep such a wide mixture of races and creeds, each with its own language, united in an army and motivated to fight for so many years. There was never a major defection from his army and it continued to revere its leader, following his orders with enthusiasm and competence. Thanks to his genius, he was able to keep his small army from being obliterated by the growing hordes of Roman soldiers in the coming years. Hannibal had some spectacular successes against great odds in coming years.

A major reason why Hannibal's troops appeared to be less effective after Capua was that the Roman army became more cautious, following the doctrine of Fabius. This did not allow Hannibal so many opportunities for victories of the magnitude he achieved in his former battles, although some battles allowed him to display his mastery over the best that the Roman military establishment could offer. Hannibal couldn't lure the cautious Roman legions into an ambush as often, nor could he entice them to battles on open plains where he could use his superior cavalry to advantage as often as before. Rome was able to confine the fighting, with rare exceptions, to fortified towns and cities, or in hand-to-hand fighting on terrain where cavalry could not move freely. However, this doctrine allowed Hannibal to move freely about the countryside where there were open plains.

While Hannibal was waiting patiently to be reinforced from outside Italy and to obtain more recruits within Italy, Roman armies gradually regained their strength, thanks to the rapid rebuilding program made possible by taking large numbers of slaves into the army and releasing some prisoners to join the army. That was a major change in policy for the Roman Senate because until Hannibal arrived in Italy, only citizens with property valued at more than 11,000 asses could join the Roman legions. The strong support given to its army by the Roman Senate, and by Fabius, accounted for this swift recovery from the Cannae disaster.

Fabius and his officers soon realized that the size of the territory Hannibal had conquered was so large that it would be difficult for the small Carthaginian army to patrol effectively. Hannibal could not defend his new domain over its entirety because he could not be everywhere at once. Fabius developed a policy of moving into an area as soon as Hannibal moved out of it with his troops, and, selectively, Roman legions would regain towns that had defected to Hannibal. Legionnaires would exact horrible punishment on citizens of the defecting towns, as frightful examples for other communities that may be contemplating defection from Rome. Roman soldiers would crucify the town's citizen-leaders and its citizens would be sold into slavery, to put fear of defection into the hearts of potential defectors. Rome would then put strong garrisons in the regained towns, behind its fortified walls that Hannibal was not usually willing to attack. The sheer magnitude of the army and the resources available to Rome, compared to those that the Carthaginian Senate had made available to Hannibal, were overwhelming in the long run. Hannibal's only hope was to obtain substantial increases in the size of his army, or achieve another victory the magnitude of Cannae.

Without reinforcements for his small army, Hannibal could not guarantee towns that defected from Rome that he could protect them from Rome's dreadful reprisal. Hannibal would conquer a town or enlist it as an ally by persuading it to defect from Rome, but he could no longer protect such towns from Roman retaliation. For example, while Carthaginians were gaining many towns in southern Italy, three towns of the Hirpini - Vercellium, Viscellium, and Sicilinium - which had revolted from Rome, were retaken by legions of praetor Valerius. Leaders in these towns were crucified and 5,000 of their citizens were sold as slaves. Fabian strategy effectively neutralized Hannibal's superior military skill on the battlefield, making Rome's great numerical advantage of its army a decisive factor and checkmating the ability of Hannibal to gain more ground in southern Italy. The main weakness with this Roman policy was that it was slow to take effect, and Hannibal was allowed to roam about the countryside almost at will. No one in the Roman army was willing to challenge the great military genius in a head-on battle, such as the one at Cannae.

The first few years after Cannae, Hannibal's gains in territory in southern Italy were almost matched by his losses to Roman legions. He was gradually forced to become more defensive, holding as much of the south as his military genius could hold with his small army, while waiting to be reinforced by the soldiers from Spain, Carthage, Macedonia, and Cisalpine Gaul that he had been promised. Time was on Rome's side as it aggressively expanded its military forces. While the Roman Senate was providing maximum support to its army for its war effort, Hannibal's enemies in Carthage were blocking his government from sending him comparable support, sufficient for him to attack the city of Rome and thus end the war decisively.

Hannibal was able to take most Greek towns in Bruttium and Lucania, in the far southern part of Italy, during 215 B.C. Exceptions were the seaport towns of Rhegium in the toe of Italy's boot, which had been heavily fortified by Rome, and the town of Tarentum in the southeastern heel. The hidden seaport of Locri, also in the toe of the boot, was taken by the Carthaginian army, giving Hannibal seaborne communications with Carthage whenever ships were able to run past the Roman picket ships. At long last, the 4,000 Numidians and their horses, forty elephants, and 500 talents of silver arrived at Locri. These token forces were the ones the Barca faction was able to get approved by the Senate in Carthage earlier, over the objections of the Hannos. It was a pitiful supply compared to the resources available to his enemy and to the magnitude of the task he faced, but it was some help. (Hannibal's enemies in the Carthaginian Senate were able, later, to divert the 24,000 troops that Hannibal's brother, Mago, had been authorized to raise in Spain as reinforcement for Hannibal).

Hannibal's lieutenant and long time friend, Hanno, who had taken command of the southern division of his army when Mago was sent to Carthage to plead for more troops, did succeed in recruiting more than 10,000 Bruttians and Lucanians in the south. However, Hanno was defeated in a battle with Gracchus, who had two full legions, in a battle near Beneventum. Hanno lost most of his force of 18,000 troops in his losing battle, when he and his calvary of 1,200 African horses were almost the only survivors.

A vessel arrived from Carthage carrying devastating personal news for Hannibal. A courier told him that his wife and son had become victims of a plague that swept Carthage, and they had died horrible deaths. The news severely depressed Hannibal, and it was only one of a very few times that his friend, Gisco, saw him appear in his private quarters as vulnerable, weak, and helpless. Hannibal continued to maintain a strong, disciplined front for his men, but his most trusted officers knew that he was taking it hard. Hannibal spent many hours of the next days visiting sacred temples, making animal sacrifices, and paying tribute to the gods.

Gisco also received sad news within a few days of the woeful tidings received by Hannibal. A courier arrived from Athens with a letter from his wife, which contained the painful news that his grandfather, Archelaus, had died in August of 215 B.C. Gisco obtained Hannibal's permission to go to Athens to arrange his affairs. Hannibal asked him to visit King Philip V of Macedonia while he was across the sea, to tell the king how he could best help in the war against Rome. Hannibal also wanted Gisco to evaluate the military value of help he could expect from the king. Gisco boarded a fast commercial trading vessel destined for Athens, excited about seeing his beloved wife and son again. He knew that he would be too late for the elaborate funeral, but he intended to take care of related personal family business and make any necessary arrangements for the welfare of Tarra, Gisco II, and his mother.

His wife and son were very glad to see him, and there was an emotional reunion. Gisco was relieved to learn that his family was well-adjusted to their life in Athens and that their needs were being taken care of very well. Gisco's intelligent mother, Procne, was still in good health and the three -

Procne, Tarra, and Gisco II - were getting along happily and affluently. His young son's education was being managed very well by friends and relatives, and the boy was following in his father's footsteps. Now almost ten years old, he was progressing rapidly in his studies. His education was being carefully controlled, and arrangements were made to continue his schooling under competent supervision. The family business was flourishing, and it was being ably managed by close relatives. Plans were made to take Gisco II into the family business when he became old enough. Gisco II had been hearing spectacular stories of his father's achievements and had read the few letters Gisco was able to send home. The young son wanted to train as a soldier to join his father in the crusade against Rome. Gisco finally convinced his son that one member of the family in the Carthaginian army was sufficient and that his mother and the family business needed him at home in Athens.

After a few enjoyable weeks with his family, Gisco made a fast trip to Macedonia to talk to King Philip. The king received Gisco with great hospitality, after the Greek gave him a letter of introduction from Hannibal. Gisco emphasized the urgent need for more troops to overwhelm Rome before it could build up its military forces much more than it had already done. Gisco explained specific ways that the king could help. Under the guise of helping to improve the military capability of the Macedonian army based on lessons learned while fighting Roman legions for three years, Gisco evaluated the Macedonian troops. He learned they were very incompetent. Philip found Gisco to be very convincing, and the king was favorably influenced by the erudite Greek. He promised Gisco that he would start immediate preparations to prepare a task force to send to Italy along the lines that Gisco had suggested.

On his return to Italy, Gisco reported to Hannibal that Philip appeared to be a weak military leader and that his troops were not very tough or disciplined. Furthermore, Gisco told him that the King of Macedonia appeared to have too many diversionary interests and ambitions in areas other than Italy that could distract him too much. However, the king did promise to send a task force to Italy soon, so that would help to some unknown extent. Gisco and Hannibal noted that the mere entry of Macedonia into the war would cause Rome to divert many of its military resources from the Italian theater of operations.

While Gisco was away, Hannibal was feeling unusually lonely and depressed as a result of the loss of his wife and son. To take his mind off his sorrow, and to help shake him from his spiritual doldrums after a few weeks had passed, Hannibal's closest officers devised a scheme to introduce him to a beautiful, voluptuous, girl from Bruttium. She wasn't on the intellectual level of his deceased wife, Imilce, and Hannibal had no intention of marrying her, but she had a pleasing personality. She appeared to like Hannibal very much, and Hannibal began to spend many spare hours with her during lulls in the fighting. As his group of trusted Carthaginian officers had intended, Hannibal found her company uplifting and a welcome distraction from his troubles. The girl was a dark-eyed brunette with charming manners, and she was sincerely attracted to Hannibal who continued to be very handsome and unusually appealing to women. Although he wore a patch over one eye, his magnetic personality and unusual charisma were as charming to women as it was to the soldiers who were willing to give up their lives to follow him into battle.

By 215 B.C., Xenophanes, the Macedonian emissary sent by King Philip to form a treaty with Hannibal, had finally put a pact in writing for Hannibal to sign. Among other provisions, it provided for Philip to raise 200 ships and an army to carry out offensive operations by land and sea against Rome, in return for a Carthaginian promise to support a war against any states that may make war on Macedonia after Rome was defeated. When Xenophanes and his party left for Macedonia with the treaty to be signed by Philip, Hannibal sent emissaries with them to witness the king's final acceptance of the pact and to bring back a copy of the document. On their sea voyage to Macedonia, the party and the written documents were captured by fast Roman vessels off the Calabrian coast. The entire party was put in chains and taken to Rome where they were imprisoned. Documents of the pact were read to the Roman Senate.

The facts that Hannibal now had a new ally and the war arena was now becoming wider for the Romans, was a great concern for the Senators. Rome already had a heavy military burden, and it was heavily in debt, but the Senate decided it was necessary to increase the size of the army and navy. An additional one-hundred vessels were ordered to be built, and they were to be manned by one new legion under the command of the competent Marcus Valerius Laevinus. Valerius was given orders to patrol the Adriatic region and prevent Macedonian troops from reaching Italy. Hannibal received this information from his intelligence network within a few days of the order.

King Philip did not know what agreement had been reached, since the documents never arrived in Macedonia. By the time Hannibal was able to send a messenger to the king to explain what had happened to the document, it was late fall -- too late for the Macedonians to take military action. Support for Hannibal from Macedonia was thus delayed until the following year, too late to reach him when he needed it most. The Romans would use another year, advantageously, for their military buildup.

Hannibal was given another setback in 215. As noted earlier, his brother Mago had been sent to Spain by his Senate to raise an additional 24,000 troops to take to Italy. All of the troops were diverted from Hannibal by politicians in Carthage. Most of these troops, sorely needed for the war in Italy, were ordered to go to Sardinia rather than Italy. Sardinia was an unimportant side issue in the war against Rome, where local inhabitants had revolted against the Roman rule. These troops were sorely needed by Hannibal to defeat the main target of the war, the city of Rome. If Hannibal were to sack Rome, as the Gauls had done many years before, the war could possibly have come to an end soon. As it was, on the way to Sardinia the Carthaginian task force of sixty vessels commanded by Hasdrubal Calvus was blown into the Balearic Islands by a severe storm. Considerable time was required to refit the storm-damaged Carthaginian fleet in the islands, but the time was wisely used to recruit additional troops in the islands to strengthen the army.

Taking advantage of the extra time, Rome sent an army commanded by the competent praetor, T. Manlius Torquatus, to strengthen its garrison in Sardinia, to put down the native rebellion. The praetor's army was waiting in Sardinia before the Carthaginian forces arrived, and when the task force finally reached Sardinia, the strong Roman army was waiting for it and attacked it in strength. After a fierce fight, the entire Carthaginian army was killed or taken prisoner, lost forever to the Carthaginian cause in Italy.

More bad news for Hannibal came from Spain. The brothers Publius and Gnaeus Scipio defeated three armies of Hasdrubal in successive battles at Iliturgi and Intibili in the Baetica region of south-central Spain. Native tribes of eastern Spain defected from the Carthaginians and went over to serve Rome. This was a severe blow to Carthaginian efforts in Spain, but it was also more bad news for Hannibal's campaign in Italy because it gave decision-makers in Carthage another excuse to divert more military resources from Hannibal to Spain.

The Roman treasury was depleted by: losses suffered at Trebbia, Trasimene, and Cannae; losses suffered from Hannibal's scorched-earth policy; and the expense of increasing the size of its army and navy. The requirement to support the war in Spain, Sardinia, Macedonia, northern and southern Italy, and to maintain large garrisons in other areas, was bankrupting the treasury. Food had to be imported by Rome at great expense from foreign sources to replace that destroyed by

Hannibal. The Roman Senate had already confiscated many treasures of sacred temples to pay for the war, and it was running out of money. Taxes had already been increased to the limit.

This information did not escape the notice of Hannibal, who continued to exacerbate Rome's problem wherever he could. However, Rome's business men and private lenders came to the rescue of their country by making long-term loans to the government to meet the growing demands of war. The Roman Senate was able to deficit-spend to fight the war, thanks to the willingness of its business men and lenders to provide large loans to the government. The Carthaginian Senate was not making such sacrifices to support Hannibal's army, or to support the effort in Spain. Carthage had ample resources to do so if it desired.

During the winter, 215-214, Hannibal moved his headquarters from Capua in western Italy to Arpi (near Foggia) in the east of Italy to be closer to the Adriatic and his new ally, Macedonia. He wanted to come away from Capua because he did not want his army to consume too much of the local food supply and he did not want to wear out his welcome with the inhabitants. The Roman consul, Gracchus, had been following the Fabian policy of caution by keeping a close watch over the Carthaginians from a safe distance. He followed Hannibal to the east, and he made his camp at Luceria (Lucera). Fabius kept his army in Campania, and the Capuans believed his army was a serious threat to them.

Capuans were very nervous when the close protection of Hannibal's troops was suddenly removed because they feared brutal Roman reprisals for their defection from Rome. Capuans had a guilty conscience because they had brutally killed the Roman garrison in the city when they defected from Rome. Rome's demonstrated policy of exacting horrible retaliation against all communities that had revolted against them once they had been recaptured, caused the city leaders great concern. They appealed to Hannibal to return, and he grudgingly came back to his camp on Mount Tifata. Again, Gracchus followed, and Fabius rapidly moved his army closer to Capua. Thus Hannibal was confronted by two Roman armies. The two new consuls elected for 214 B.C. were the deliberate Fabius, and Marcus Marcellus, the only commander that Hannibal had been unable to defeat in combat. Marcellus took command of the army left by Gracchus. The Senate had authorized a total of twenty legions for the year, with ten legions in the south to face Hannibal's forces.

After returning to Tifata, Hannibal and Gisco went to examine the possibility of taking the seaport of Putioli (Puzzuoli), near Neapolis. After rejecting the idea because of its strong defenses, Hannibal wanted to visit the famous Lake Avernus, a renowned crater lake nearby. The lake was two-thirds of a mile in diameter, it was surrounded by a dense forest, and it had no birds around it because of the poisonous sulfur fumes it emitted from its surface. It was a famous tourist attraction of the area. While there, Hannibal was approached by a group of citizens from Tarentum (Taranto), a major seaport in the heel of the boot of Italy. The group included some soldiers Hannibal had freed after the battle at Cannae. They told him that the seaport could be taken with their help. Cautious of a trap, Hannibal had some of the details of their story verified by his agents before deciding to act on their suggestion. As soon as he had determined it was a valid proposal, he decided to move his army south to exploit the idea.

Hannibal did not want to leave Capua unprotected again, knowing how sensitive the leaders were to the presence of a strong Roman military force near their city. However, Hannibal wanted another seaport, and Tarentum was one of the few rich cities in southern Italy still held by Romans. To protect Capua while he took his army to Tarentum, Hannibal ordered Hanno to move his army north from Bruttium to Campania, a dangerous maneuver while two strong Roman armies were close, watching every move that Carthaginian armies made. For a short period during the switching maneuver, towns of both the northern and southern areas would be unusually vulnerable to attack by Romans. The ingenious Hannibal devised some diversionary moves that made the wary Romans believe he was moving to attack Nola again. While Romans reacted to the feint of his army toward Nola, diverting their attention away from Tifata and Capua, the Carthaginian armies rapidly switched places without interference from the legions. Romans believed they had won a victory at Nola.

While Hannibal was gone to the south, Romans were emboldened because they did not fear Hanno as much as they did the great military master, who terrified them. As soon as Hannibal was out of the area, the Roman legions began to take advantage of his absence by moving their armies. Fabius remained near Capua to keep Hanno's army in check, while Marcellus moved his army against Casilinum, a town which Hannibal had captured at an earlier date by a blockade that successfully starved the town into submission. Casilinum soon fell, and not long afterward, Arpi in the east was captured. These became additional, horrible examples for other Roman cities that were contemplating defection, as well as cities that had already defected, such as Capua.

In the meantime, favorable progress for Hannibal was taking place in the Greek settlement of Syracuse, on the east coast of Sicily. Gisco began taking trips back to Athens whenever there was a long lull in the fighting, usually during the winter months when there was little forage for animals in the countryside. He did this to see his beloved family. On one of his trips to Athens, he had a conversation with a family relative who had been working on the fortifications of the port of Syracuse, which Archimedes had designed, and which the family business was helping the great scientist to construct. Gisco's relative told him there was much opposition in Syracuse to the octogenarian king's alliance with Rome, and that the situation was getting to the point that revolt was possible. The king who ruled Syracuse, Hiero II, was a tyrant who had allied himself with Rome.

Gisco decided to make a visit to Syracuse during his voyage from Athens to rejoin the Carthaginian army in Italy. Because he was a Greek, and his family business had worked there, Gisco was able to freely discuss the political situation firsthand with associates of the family business who still resided in the Greek city-state. Because he was a Greek, he was able to sound out the local politicians of the city whenever he had the opportunity, to size-up the political situation. When he finally returned to Hannibal's camp in Italy, Gisco reported that there was a good opportunity for Carthaginians to take Syracuse when the old king died, which appeared to be very soon because the old king was not in good health. Gisco had discussed the possibility of a revolt with two uncles of the heir to the throne. The two were uncles of the old king's young grandson, Hieronymus, who was destined to become the king when the old tyrant died. Gisco told them that Hannibal would be glad to provide assistance to help the uncles encourage a decision for Syracuse to come over to the Carthaginian cause. The old king soon died and the two uncles of the new king came to Hannibal's camp to persuade Hannibal to take an active role in swaying the direction that Syracuse should take, as Gisco had suggested. The uncles told Hannibal that his recent victories against Rome had caused many in Syracuse to be swayed toward an alliance with Carthage, and that there had been much political intrigue among leaders in Syracuse while it determined which direction to take.

Delighted by the prospect, Hannibal sent two brothers that Gisco had suggested for the job, both of whom were half Greek and half Carthaginian, to be his agents in Syracuse. They were sons of a Greek refugee who had married a Carthaginian wife. The two brothers, Hippocrates and Epicydes, participated in skillful political manipulation within Syracuse politics, manipulation which included the assassination of the new king. Hannibal's two agents were then able to get themselves elected to be magistrates of the city-state in an election conducted by the Assembly of Syracuse. With the city now ruled by Hannibal's men, it then defected from Rome, and a treaty for their mutual defense was signed by Hannibal and Syracuse. Thus, Hannibal had allies in two new theaters of operation, which pressured Rome to divert some of its military forces from Italy to Macedonia and Syracuse. Hannibal could not go to the city to welcome it into the Carthaginian fold because of his busy schedule in Italy.

Soon, gains made by Hannibal's agents in Syracuse began to concern the Roman Senate. It wanted to do something about the defection of Syracuse, which was now ruled by the two men Hannibal had sent there. The Senate ordered Marcus Marcellus, the first Roman commander that Hannibal did not defeat in the field, to regain Syracuse. He was given command of a flotilla of 68 quinqueremes (warships, each with with five tiers of oars) loaded with archers, slingers, javelin throwers, and long ladders for scaling the walls defending the port, which was notoriously treacherous, because they had been designed by the great scientist and mathematician, Archimedes. These were the defenses Gisco's father and grandfather had helped Archimedes build. They became world famous after the attack by Marcellus. The spectacular, complex installation was a perfect example of applying science to the art of war, masterminded by Archimedes, one of the world's greatest scientific geniuses.

Marcellus first attempted to invade the harbor of Syracuse in daylight during 214 B.C., but his attack was repulsed by catapults that Archimedes had designed to accurately cast stones and fireballs onto ships everywhere in the harbor. The range and bearing of targets for the catapults were calculated by ingenious devices to make them very accurate. Many ships of the Roman flotilla were sunk and others were heavily damaged, as Marcellus aborted his attack.

The second attempt Marcellus made to invade the harbor was begun in the darkness of the early morning on a moonless night so that he could evade visual detection by the catapults. Marcellus believed he had successfully sneaked into the harbor with his overloaded fleet, undetected, because his crews gently moved their oars so that they would not make noise. As the ships were silently nearing a sea wall that protected the port, the wall of Achradina that they had selected as their invasion site, the silence was suddenly broken by loud, startling, and strange noises coming from behind the wall in front of them. The Roman crews of the ships were extremely nervous before the noises began, but these unexplained noises terrified them.

Unknown to the invaders, the noises were made by the rapid movement of large chains, ropes, and pulleys, which maneuvered many cantilevered cranes up from behind the walls, over the top, and out over the warships in the water. The horrified Romans helplessly watched as some of the giant cranes lowered huge grappling-irons (claws) that grasped the bows of many of the ships and hoisted their bows out of the water, standing the warships on end, thus tilting the terrified crews, marines, ladders, and war materials into the water. These claws then released the bows of the ships, making them plunge back into the sea and fill with water, causing many to capsize. At the same time this was happening, other giant cranes reached out over ships filled with panicked, helpless, watching invaders. These machines dropped huge stones and lead weights, each weighing six-hundred pounds, onto the decks of the defenseless ships, penetrating their hulls, and crushing unfortunate, screaming invaders who happened to be in the paths of the huge masses dropped on them.

The defending walls of the harbor were almost in a complete circle, on high ground, with steeply overhanging crags, making climbing difficult. Large flares were catapulted over the harbor, lighting it up as though it were daylight. Great doors in the walls of the fortress suddenly opened allowing massive numbers of projectiles from archers, slingers, and spear-throwers to rain on the helpless Romans. Small catapults positioned in these openings of the wall were used to throw clouds of iron darts onto the few surviving, terrified invaders. The attack was aborted by Marcellus, and those survivors who could fled the scene as rapidly as possible. As they departed, large catapults rained huge missiles and fireballs on them. To add insult to injury, retreating Roman troops could hear loud laughter coming from behind the defender's walls, as defenders watched the rout.

Thus, Archimedes's masterful fortifications were able to hold off land and sea attacks of Marcellus for almost three years. He was only able to succeed in conquering the city in 212 B.C. by resorting to treachery within the city walls during a festival. The brilliant scientist Archimedes, who was then seventy-five years old, was inadvertently killed by an ignorant soldier when Marcellus finally invaded the city. Marcellus and most leaders in Rome were distressed by the widely admired scientist's death, which none had desired to happen. This victory over Syracuse added greatly to the already great reputation that Marcellus enjoyed in Rome as a brilliant military general.

Hannibal's fortunes suffered another great blow in Macedonia while Marcellus was busy attacking Syracuse in the summer of 214 B.C. It was then, after a long delay that the incompetent King Philip V of Macedonia finally marshaled a force of 120 triremes (warships with three banks of oars) and, loaded with soldiers, took the small town of Oricum on the Adriatic coast (now in Albania). He did this on his way to Apollonia, thirty miles north of Oricum. He selected Apollonia as his point of departure to invade Italy, because it was opposite his planned invasion site in Italy to the west.

The alert Roman praetor, Marcus Valerius Laevinus, commander of the Roman fleet charged with guarding the Italian coast against a Macedonian invasion, learned that Philip had taken Oricum on his way to Apollonia. The praetor sailed his fleet to the area, retook Oricum, then moved up to Apollonia. His Roman legion was able to sneak past the careless guards of the lackadaisical Macedonian army at night while it was sleeping, and it easily routed Philip and his army. The naked king was unable to put on his clothes because of the surprise. Naked, he fled to his ships with many of his soldiers in disorderly array. Three-thousand of his men were killed or captured by the Roman legion. Philip sailed with his ships until the waiting fleet of Marcus Valerius suddenly confronted them at sea. The fearful Philip beached and burned his entire fleet in a panic to avoid capture by Valerius and fled back to Macedonia with the few survivors of his army. So ended any hope of support that Hannibal greatly needed from Macedonians, because Philip's army was completely disarmed and demoralized.

Hannibal moved his army to Tarentum (Taranto) after he was approached at the crater lake by citizens whom he had released at Cannae. They advised him that they could get his army into the city walls, although the town had resisted Hannibal's previous attempts to bring it into the Carthaginian fold. One reason for their new desire to have Hannibal's help to escape Rome's oppressive control was a policy of Rome that required noble families of the town to provide young men to be held as hostages in Rome to deter their families in Tarentum from rebelling against Rome. If they were to rebel, their young sons would be executed. In 212 B.C., these young hostages in Rome attempted to escape from their confinement. They tried to return to their families in the southern seaport, but eighty of them were captured on their way south. All were flogged and brutally executed by being thrown from the Tarpeian Rock on the Capitoline Heights of Rome. News of this disaster caused great anger in Tarentum, and it resulted in having its enraged citizens send the delegation that met Hannibal at the crater lake.

The two men Hannibal had released at Cannae told Hannibal they were accustomed to entering a gate in the wall of the city late at night after hunting trips. They were allowed to enter the gate because they habitually gave Roman sentries at the gate a share of the game they caught. In the middle of the night, when most of the town was sleeping, Gisco and Cirta put on hunter's clothing and then helped the regular hunters carry a huge boar and other game through the gate. Gisco and the others killed the sentries and allowed Hannibal's picked men to enter the gate. From there they went to other gates, killed the unsuspecting sentries, and then allowed Hannibal's army to enter the city. It took control of the city streets after many of the Roman garrison in the city were killed or captured. Hannibal had citizens of Tarentum mark the doors of their homes with distinctive marks so that they could be identified by his troops and thus would not be harmed by them. Then, he ordered his men to plunder the unmarked houses of the Romans. Much rich booty was taken. Hannibal promised Tarentines that he would not levy a tax on the town, that it would have self-rule, and that he would not put a garrison in it.

When the Carthaginian army took the town of Tarentum in 212 B.C., many of the Roman garrison took safe refuge in the town's fortified citadel, which overlooked the mouth of the harbor. This position gave the Roman soldiers a commanding view of the port. It also prevented Carthaginians and local citizens from using the harbor because no ships could leave without being bombarded by missiles from the citadel. All ships were confined to the harbor docks. Hannibal's army could not complete the blockade of the citadel to force the Roman soldiers to surrender because it was being supplied by sea and Hannibal didn't have a navy there to prevent it.

The miracle man, Gisco, came up with a solution to the problem which Hannibal accepted:

Tarentines were told that his army would transport their ships from their docks, overland to a point where they could be launched into the sea, thus avoiding missiles hurled by the citadel's ballista. In a few days the friendly vessels were transported overland by the army under Gisco's supervision. They were launched into the water as planned, safely out of range of the Roman ballista. The ships, now manned with soldiers, were then sailed around to establish a water blockade of the citadel to complement Hannibal's land blockade. The citadel was eventually forced to surrender in 211 B.C. This gave Hannibal another port, and it removed another unfriendly town in the south. The neighboring towns, Metapontum and Thurii, encouraged by this, also revolted against Rome.

Chapter 8

HANNIBAL MARCHES TO ROME AND HASDRUBAL MARCHES TO ITALY (211 - 206 B.C.)

Capuans were a thorn in Hannibal's side. He was continually annoyed by them because Capua, the second richest city in Italy, was so helpless at protecting itself. He felt that the city should contribute much more to its own defense against Rome. Previously, in 214 B.C., the city's leaders had first pleaded for Hannibal to return from Arpi where he was in the east to be near his Macedonian allies. City leaders wanted Hannibal to protect them from Roman legions in their neighborhood menacing them. Later, in 212 B.C., Hannibal left Capua again to go to Tarentum to take that city from the Romans. The conquest of that seaport took longer than he had expected because some Roman soldiers had taken refuge in the town's citadel. It wasn't until later, in 211, that the last Roman in Tarentum was persuaded to surrender. In 212, before the citadel in Tarentum had completely fallen, the helpless Capuans pleaded once more for Hannibal to come to their aid. Roman legions had besieged Capua, and they began destroying all harvests around the city. Roman legions blockaded all roads leading to the city, preventing food supplies from reaching it. City leaders told Hannibal they could not prevent it and that unless

Hannibal came to their assistance, citizens of Capua would starve. Hannibal didn't want to leave Tarentum until the last Roman soldier in that vital seaport had capitulated. Thus, Hannibal ordered Hanno to take his division of the Carthaginian army to the aid of Capuans. He instructed the capable Hanno to organize a protected supply line of food for the city. Hanno rushed to the vicinity of Beneventum and collected grain from the area, under the protection of his troops. When he had collected a substantial amount of food, he arranged for a day on which the leaders of Capua were to bring sufficient wagons, protected by Carthaginian troops, to pick up the food. On a day mutually agreed upon, citizens of Capua arrived with far too few wagons to carry the food. Poor planning was a characteristic weakness of leaders in Capua, and Hanno was visibly irritated by the feeble effort they made to satisfy their need during a time they were supposed to be starving from a desperate shortage of food. Hanno gruffly told the leaders about their lack of interest in sending sufficient wagons to carry the food. He told the Capuans to return on another day with sufficient wagons. When they returned, they came with 2,000 wagons, a number that was so large that it confused Hanno's military defenses. The Roman commander nearby, Quintus Fulvius Flaccus, noted the confusion and took advantage of it. During the disorder, he captured the storage depot in a fierce battle while Hanno was out with troops collecting more grain. Hanno had to flee to Bruttium, leaving Capuans without a supply of food.

Again, Capuans pleaded with Hannibal to come to their rescue. This time, Hannibal promised to come in person with his army. Hastily, he moved his army to

Capua from the south in 212 B.C., before his blockade of the citadel at Tarentum had succeeded. He left sufficient forces behind to finish the task for him in Tarentum.

When he arrived at Capua, he immediately offered battle to the two armies of Quintus Fulvius Flaccus and Appius Claudius Pulcher that were blockading Capua. The two Roman armies accepted Hannibal's invitation to battle. In the first encounter, Hannibal merely used his infantry as a decoy while his Numidian cavalry used its hit-and-run tactics to harass the enemy. The first battle was primarily a battle between mounted troops, and Romans suffered the heavier losses. While the armies were fighting the second encounter, both sides withdrew from the fight when they saw dust on the horizon of unknown reinforcements coming toward the battlefield. Each side, Roman as well as Carthaginian, thought the reinforcements were for the other side. Alarmed, both sides withdrew from the engagement and returned to their respective camps. In fact, it was learned later that the troops arriving on the scene belonged to the Roman army of Gnaeus Cornelius.

Leaders in Rome soon made the siege of Capua their top military priority. Rome's grand strategy, since it now had more than 190,000 soldiers in its legions, was to regain each major city one at a time. Hannibal's small, unreinforced army had to spread itself too thin to protect all cities and towns in the vast territory that had gone over to the Carthaginians. Capua was the largest city under Hannibal's control. Throughout history there had been considerable rivalry between Rome, the largest and most affluent city in Italy, and Capua, the second largest and next richest city. The Roman military establishment was anxious to lure Hannibal away from Capua so that it could continue its siege of the city unmolested. To pull Hannibal away from the area with Roman diversionary moves, Flaccus, moved away from Capua to Cumae on the west coast north of Neapolis. The other consul, Appius, moved to Lucania in the south. Hannibal was glad to see Roman forces leave the Capuan area and give some relief to the terrified citizens of Capua. Their food supply was temporarily restored. The great Carthaginian commander was now anxious for a substantial victory over Roman legions, and he decided to pursue Appius because that commander appeared to be an attractive target for a great victory. In his diversionary moves, Appius led Hannibal around in a circuitous route, then he returned back to Capua. While Hannibal was pursuing Appius, he accidentally ran into an Italian force of 8,000 men composed of half Roman and half allied troops. They were led by an unusual, elderly centurion. In the battle that ensued, Carthaginians destroyed the entire force, except for 1,000 that were able to escape over the hills.

Both consuls, Appius and Flaccus, soon returned to continue their siege of Capua while Hannibal was away. Siege machines were brought in and all other necessary equipment was assembled near the city. Hannibal was helpless to stop this without losing too many of his scarce troops, so he decided to attack a target of opportunity agents told him about. His intelligence network reported that the Roman praetor, Gnaeus Fulvius, had been sacking towns that had gone over to the Carthaginians in Apulia to the east. It was reported that the army led by Fulvius was becoming overconfident and that it was loaded down with plunder from its recent easy victories in the area. They said this Roman army was undisciplined as a result of its unopposed series of recent successes and as a result of its debauching excesses. Gnaeus Fulvius's troops were drunk with power, overconfident, and anxious for battle. These were characteristics that Hannibal enjoyed exploiting. Hannibal, flush from his success at destroying the 8,000-man force and anxious to inflict as much punishment on Roman forces as possible, decided to make a temporary excursion to Apulia to come to the rescue of friendly towns in the area.

The enemy praetor's camp was near Herdonea (about twenty miles south of Foggia), in the district of Apulia, when Hannibal finally caught up with him. When the unruly Roman troops learned of Hannibal's presence in the vicinity, they urged their reluctant commanders to take them to fight the hated Carthaginian army as soon as possible. After darkness, soon after his arrival in the area, Hannibal secretly surrounded the enemy camp and concealed 3,000 men in farms around the area. Hannibal gave Mago 2,000 mounted troops to block all escape roads out of the enemy camp. The next morning Hannibal formed the main part of his army in battle configuration, thus inviting the enemy to fight. He knew how anxious the rank and file Roman legionnaires were to fight him. Gnaeus Fulvius was dragged into battle by his overconfident soldiers, and he formed his army to meet Hannibal's challenge, unaware of Hannibal's concealed troops. In the battle that followed, the undisciplined Roman soldiers could not maintain their proper formations, and when Hannibal attacked, most of Fulvius's 18,000-man disorganized army was destroyed. Not more than 2,000 came out alive, while Hannibal's losses were negligible. Hannibal then went back to Tarentum, where couriers told him his blockade of the citadel was finally causing the fortress to capitulate.

While at Tarentum, Hannibal received another plea from Capuans complaining he was neglecting them, and they again begged that he return to Capua to protect them. They told him that Roman legions were completing their tight blockade of the city. The armies of Flaccus and Appius were joined at Capua by another army commanded by praetor Claudius Nero. Their three combined armies began building a fifteen-foot ditch, and a ten-foot-high rampart ten-feet wide around Capua. Fortified towers were built at strategic positions around the structure. The Carthaginian blockade of Tarentum had finally resulted in the capitulation of residual Roman forces in the citadel, so Hannibal rapidly returned to Capua. He marched to the hills behind Tifata because Roman legions now occupied his old camp on Tifata. He and Gisco surveyed the Roman blockade that was almost completely constructed, then they decided to arrange a coordinated attack on the Roman legions. They were able to get couriers inside the city walls by passing through the incomplete part of the ramparts. It was arranged that the Carthaginians would attack from outside the blockade at the same time that Capuans attacked from the inside. A fierce, bloody battle ensued, but the Roman defenses with three strong armies were able to hold the blockade. Hannibal saw that it was not a productive effort to continue the assault. Gisco's advice and Hannibal's good judgment told him that he did not want to continue the attack against three dug-in, large Roman armies. If he were to succeed in winning the battle it would be a victory similar to the one fought by King Pyhrrhus in Italy in 279 B.C. That is, he would lose so many of his soldiers in the victory battle that he could no longer continue fighting the war against the rest of the Roman army - which now vastly outnumbered his own army.

Hannibal devised a desperate plan by which he hoped to draw the Roman armies away from Capua. He was able to get a message to Capuans that told them to hold out a little longer. Without explanation, he told them that relief would soon come. For security reasons, he didn't want to risk divulging his plan to the Capuans. His plan was to feign an attack on the city of Rome, hoping that his threat to the capital city would cause one or two of the consular armies to leave Capua and come to the defense of Rome. This plan would give him a better chance of breaking the blockade of this, the largest city in the alliance supporting Carthage. Hannibal also believed that if he could take Rome by surprise, now that the city no longer expected him to attack, he might have an even chance of succeeding. In any event, his attack on the capital would divert some attention from Rome's main war target at that time, the capture of Capua.

To keep his intentions secret until the last moment possible, Hannibal left many campfires burning, many tents erected, and some troops remaining in his camp as he moved his army out after dark, headed for Rome. He marched on the Latina Way, avoiding the more populated Appian Way. He wanted to keep his approach unnoticed until he was close to the city. When he reached Mount Casinum (Mount Casino), he rested his long column of troops. Because he was now in the Roman heartland, Latium, which was populated by Roman citizens and not allies, his troops foraged and plundered the area, trampled crops, burned grain, and spread terror. Then he continued his march north to Tusculum, a town located a few miles southeast of Rome. He found the fortifications of the town too strong, and not wanting to waste time and manpower on it, he headed east to Gabii on the Via Babina, a few miles east of Rome. After camping eight miles from the city gates, he continued to move up the Anio River, burning and looting the countryside within sight of the city. Afterward, he again made camp three miles from the city gates. With smoke and flames from burning houses behind him, he took a small force of 2,000 mounted troops to reconnoiter the city fortifications. He took his small force up to the Collina Gate on the north side of the city wall to personally inspect its defenses. There was much confusion, as citizens of Rome who had been living outside the city walls fled in panic to get the safety of the city when their houses were burned. Hannibal noted that the unusually thick walls were difficult obstacles to overcome. Gisco volunteered to attempt to go inside the city to make an inspection of defenses inside the walls. Hannibal said it was a good idea and that he would like to go along wearing a disguise.

When they returned to their camp, they obtained a large cart full of produce that had been captured earlier. Gisco, Hannibal, and Cirta put on disguises as elderly farmers, intending to act as if they were bringing much needed produce to the city market. Wearing clothes taken from prisoners, wigs, and makeup, they rode their cart around to the busy Flaminia Gate on the northeast side of the city. They had no difficulty entering the gate, and they found the entire city in turmoil. The citizens were expecting an attack by Hannibal's hordes, believing that he was ready to invade their homes at any moment. Hannibal and Gisco spoke Latin well, and Cirta acted as their ignorant slave.

They were able to wander around the city unmolested as they investigated its defenses. They were able to talk to inhabitants and soldiers without interference. Hannibal had never been in the city, and he had a profound curiosity, not only of the military preparations around the fortified walls, but of the architecture and life-styles of the citizens which had been the subject of his attention since childhood. The men visited the Forum and watched the Senate which was meeting in emergency session. The Senate was also standing by the Forum to advise officials during the emergency. The three men visited the Temple of Minervae, the Circus Maximus, and they walked around the Roma Quadrata. They walked through many neighborhoods. Women were observed sweeping the temples with their hair, as was the custom during emergencies, and other women were seen weeping in the streets. Many citizens were running around the streets aimlessly, and many were crowding the shrines of the gods. Soldiers were rushing to their assigned positions around the city. Many soldiers were positioned along the Servian Wall that surrounded the city, and they discovered that proconsul Fulvius had arrived in the city with 15,000 infantry and 1,000 mounted troops to augment the existing garrison of the city.

Gisco didn't want to take the time, nor the risk, of visiting the Carthaginian intelligent agents in the city. Agents within the city had been giving regular reports to Hannibal, and there wasn't much to be gained by risking a visit with them. Among their discoveries were the thousands of new recruits that had reported for duty with the Roman army in the city just days before Hannibal had arrived with his army. Their numbers, about two new legions consisting of a total of 10,000 soldiers, when added to the soldiers in the army of Fulvius that had just arrived, and in addition to the normal garrison of the city, swelled the number of defenders within the walls to an insurmountable size for Hannibal to attack. Hannibal had the misfortune to arrive at the city at a time when the number of soldiers in the city was almost double its normal size. What Hannibal and Gisco saw convinced them that they would need a much larger army than they presently had to be able to overrun such formidable defenses. They would have to wait until they received many more reinforcements from Carthage, Spain, Cisalpine Gaul, and Macedonia.

Hannibal's plan to draw troops away from the siege of Capua almost worked, but the wise, cool-headed Fabius Maximus foiled Hannibal's plan. Fabius had long experience with Hannibal's cunning and his feigned maneuvers intended to lure Roman armies into traps. He was able to convince the Senate, after much debate, that they shouldn't recall the troops from Capua. His views were given much opposition on the Senate floor, but Fabius recognized Hannibal's moves as a mere ploy. The Senate was about to recall troops from Capua, their main military objective at the time. Fabius told the senators that he couldn't see how the Carthaginian army, which was unable to break the siege of Capua, could take Rome with its much stronger defenses. He told the senators that he recognized Hannibal's movements as a scheme to break the blockade of Capua, and his argument finally kept the Senate from sending the order that it was preparing to recall troops to Rome from the siege at Capua.

Hannibal, Gisco, and Cirta returned to their camp outside the city walls and decided that, since an attack on the city of Rome was out of serious consideration, the Carthaginian army's next move should be to continue to ravage the countryside around Rome. That action should help attract legions from Capua.

Hannibal's intelligence network from inside Rome hadn't notified him yet of the Senate's decision to leave their armies at Capua. Hannibal believed that the humiliation of seeing Carthaginian troops burning the countryside within sight of the capital city would encourage the Roman Senate to recall troops from Capua. In the following days, the Carthaginian army marched down the Tiber River, burned villages, and plundered everything within thirty miles around Rome. Smoke rose from burning towns around the city, while five legions inside the city walls watched. Only light cavalry skirmishes between Hannibal's foraging parties and Roman mounted troops took place, but no serious opposition was sent to stop Hannibal. Spoils for the Carthaginian troops were becoming burdensome and included much gold, silver, and other valuables from the villages and temples they had plundered. The spoils also included a large herd of cattle gathered from around the countryside.

When Hannibal decided that enough time had passed so that news of his attack on Rome could reach the consuls at Capua, allowing them time to abandon their blockade and come to the aid of their capital city, he headed back to Capua. He traveled on a route south that would avoid meeting the expected consular armies coming north from Capua. Unfortunately, Hannibal soon learned that the armies surrounding Capua had not moved at all, thanks to the wise advice given to the Roman Senate by Fabius. Thus, Hannibal abandoned the idea of relieving Capua, deciding that the cost would be too great for his small, irreplaceable army. He decided to continue surviving with his army, inflicting as much punishment on Roman legions and the economy of Rome as he could, until he could get the necessary military reinforcements or until Rome grew so tired of the war that it sued for peace. He marched south through Samnium, Apulia, and Lucania to Bruttium.

People of Capua soon learned, from Romans, that Hannibal had abandoned them, and the impact on their morale was devastating. They began serious consideration of surrendering their city and facing the consequences from the vengeful Romans because they were starving and there was now little hope of surviving otherwise. Surrounding towns also heard the news and became afraid for their own safety with Hannibal gone. The Roman Senate approved, and the edict was widely advertised to Capuans, that any Campanian citizens who came over to the Roman side of the conflict by an announced date would not be harmed. But Capuans were fearful that their previous crimes against Rome were too great and that they would not be pardoned. The city leaders, particularly, were afraid that it was just another Roman trick. As evidence of the seriousness with which their crimes had been taken by the Romans, the leaders argued, Rome had laid siege to their city for two years, as a prime objective of the Roman Senate, even ignoring Hannibal's forces to do it. Soon, Capuans couldn't hold out any longer because they were starving. The city council voted to send envoys to negotiate a surrender in 211 B.C. Roman legions entered Capua, and those city officials who did not commit suicide by poisoning were killed by crucifixion by Romans. Surrounding towns also surrendered and their leaders were similarly executed.

Settlement of the problem at Capua allowed three Roman consular armies to be free, to be deployed elsewhere in opposition to Carthaginians. While this was in progress, Hannibal received the good news that his brother, Hasdrubal, had killed the Scipio brothers,

Gnaeus and Publius, in Spain in the year 212 B.C. The Roman Senate realized that this cleared the way for Hasdrubal to send reinforcements by land to Italy from Spain. The Senate decided to send more troops to Spain to replace those defeated ones, to hamper Hasdrubal's ability to reinforce his brother by land. A search began for a consul to replace the deceased Scipios in Spain, but no qualified commander was willing to volunteer for what was viewed as a hopeless job in a remote part of their world.

Hannibal's successes against Rome's inexperienced consuls, from the time he had come over the Alps, had caused the Roman Senate to revise its policy for selecting men to become its consuls. Men who were primarily politicians, with limited military experience, were now turned down for consulships in favor of those men who had demonstrated military experience and ability. In 211 B.C. the young son of consul Publius Cornelius Scipio finally volunteered for the thankless job. Also called Publius Cornelius Scipio, and only twenty-five-years old, he was elected for the position because there were no other qualified applicants willing to go. The young Scipio, who would later be named Scipio Africanus, had heroically saved his father's life during Hannibal's first encounter with Roman legions at the skirmish near the Ticinus River. Young Scipio had also served with distinction at Cannae, and he was largely responsible for holding the surviving troops of Cannae together to fight again, until Varro had arrived to take command of them.

The Roman success in taking Capua, although a successful offensive action against Hannibal, had required almost three years to accomplish. It was becoming apparent to most Romans that their strategy for conducting the war was too slow and unwieldy. It was ruining the Roman economy. The basic problem in any war is to seek out and destroy the enemy's war-making capability. The Roman army was not able, after seven years of trying, to seek out and destroy Hannibal's army. If left to continue with his mobile striking force indefinitely, ravaging, harassing, and terrorizing the Italian countryside (while he waited for reinforcements), he could cause Rome to slowly bleed to death economically. The cost in manpower, finances, and the general destruction of the Roman agricultural economy was becoming an unacceptable burden, and no substantial progress had been made in defeating Carthage. However, proponents for making peace with Hannibal were in the small minority, but it was not a serious consideration in the Senate.

In Spain, before they were killed, the Scipio brothers had started what was later to be seen as an embryo new military strategy that would eventually become the basis, not only for a Roman victory over Carthage, but the basis for Rome's rapid expansion throughout the Mediterranean after the Second Punic War. The first changes in policy that made up the overall strategy for fighting Roman wars evolved in the Roman Senate. The Senate soon realized that it had blundered by allowing politicians who were novice military officers to interfere with the military strategy of Fabius, a policy that had resulted in the disaster at Cannae. The Senate made some important revisions in policy. In addition to the Senate's new policy of appointing professional soldiers as consuls to command it armies - in lieu of the old policy of appointing nonprofessional, civilian-soldiers as consuls to command it armies for one year - the Senate began changing the terms of office for its consuls. The Senate began appointing better, more experienced military commanders for more than one year.

Fabius Maximus was appointed for five years, and the Scipio brothers had become career commanders in Spain for seven years. The Scipios were only replaced because they were killed. While they were in Spain, the Scipio brothers were given a free hand to conduct the war with little interference from their Senate.

Another important change came when the Scipios began copying Hannibal's methods, and unknowingly developed a new art of war for future Roman armies. They began using more long-range planning initiatives because they were appointed for more than a year. They began using more mobility with more reliance on the use of cavalry. Furthermore, a vast departure from old policy, they began hiring mercenary troops, the first Roman armies to use mercenaries. The Scipios tied down Hasdrubal's forces, and thus prevented him from bringing reinforcements to Hannibal by land, over the Pyranees. The Scipio's successes gave Hannibal's enemies in Carthage an excuse to divert troops that were originally intended for Hannibal in Italy, to Spain, to fight the Scipios. Hannibal badly needed these troops to end the war.

Before they were killed, the Scipios conquered territory far south of the Ebro River and far west of their bases in Spain. The brothers also established diplomatic contact with Syphax, one of the native rulers in Africa, and a potential ally for Rome to fight against Carthage. They provided him a Roman officer to train his army in the use of infantry tactics, and Syphax eventually caused Carthage to divert some of its military strength to fight him. This diversion in Africa came about the time that Marcellus was attacking Carthage's ally, Syracuse, in Sicily. More troops were sent to Sicily, troops that Hannibal and Hasdrubal needed badly.

The Scipio brothers began perfecting a modified version of Hannibal's tactics. The senior brother, Publius Cornelius Scipio, had learned Hannibal's military tactics firsthand at Ticinus where he was severely wounded and saved from death by the heroic action of his son. At Trebbia, he learned how Hannibal had butchered his troops while he was confined to his bed and after warning his co-consul, Sempronius, not to attack Hannibal because of the powerful Carthaginian cavalry. Publius regularly wrote home to Italy from Spain, describing his operations and tactics. His letters were studied intently by his son, who would soon come to Spain and continue developing the new art of war for Rome. Though the new military procedures were not consciously developed, they gradually evolved as the brothers conducted their operations in Spain without interference from Rome.

The elderly Scipio brothers were killed when one of their new policies backfired on them. They had been hiring Celtiberian mercenaries to fight for them, but Hasdrubal's Carthaginian army offered Scipio's mercenaries a better deal. Carthaginians had been working with Celtiberians for many years, and they knew them well. They paid the unprincipled natives of Spain a large reward to defect from their Roman employers, just prior to the decisive battle in which the Scipio brothers were killed.

The Scipios had a significant impact on Hannibal's success in Italy because they kept Hasdrubal from sending his brother reinforcements by land to Italy. This caused Carthage to divert troops that Hannibal needed to Spain and Africa.

By now, Carthage had built a large fleet of 150 warships. The Carthaginians were not soldiers by nature, and for centuries they habitually hired mercenaries to do most of their fighting. They were primarily merchant-traders, and, in contrast to the rapid support that the Roman Senate gave its war effort, the Carthaginian Senate was very slow to support its armed forces once it had declared war. After much delay, when Carthage finally decided to began expending a significant amount of its resources in support of its war effort, Carthaginian politicians spread its forces thin to battlefields in Spain, Africa, Sardinia, and Sicily, instead of concentrating its war effort in Italy, the primary target of the war. Hannibal's political enemies, primarily the Hanno faction in the political forum of Carthage, fought bitterly against the Barca faction that supported Hannibal, whenever there was a proposal for sending military forces to Hannibal in Italy. If Hannibal had been given control of all military decisions for Carthage - to focus its power on the control center for all Roman operations, the city of Rome, and to build a powerful navy - the war may have ended quickly.

A new, Roman-Hannibal was being developed, but nobody knew about it in 211 B.C. when the twenty-five-year-old son of Publius was given command of the legions in Spain. Everyone viewed the task as a losing proposition, especially after the capable Scipio brothers had been killed in action. The Senate had hesitated to give the command to such a young man, but it had to, by default, since there were no others available. The young Scipio was elected proconsul for legions in Spain.

The young Scipio, too, had observed Hannibal's genius first-hand. He had been at Ticinus and Trebbia with his father where he watched the Carthaginian magician massacre the Roman forces. He had fought at Cannae where he had performed bravely and admirably in another massacre of Roman legions by Hannibal. Like Hannibal, to a great extent, he had grown to manhood in his formative years learning military basics. He learned to admire the military genius of Hannibal, and he studied and analyzed the successful tactics of the great military general.

Young Scipio molded his own character along much the same lines as Hannibal's. In addition, he grew up under the regime of Fabius Maximus, and he adopted many of that leader's successful ways of dealing with people. He was a decided eccentric, completely dedicated to military leadership. He had a charming personality, and he adroitly used diplomacy and applied psychology, gradually becoming more and more like Hannibal, whom he obviously admired.

Whether or not he was devoutly religious, the eccentric young officer spent many hours meditating in sacred temples, and many superstitious Romans began to ascribe supernatural powers to him, which they believed were bestowed on him by the gods. He did nothing to discourage such rumors; indeed his behavior encouraged it. Although an eccentric, in the manner of many great leaders, he was also a great communicator, talking much and constantly acquiring information by asking questions. He dressed particularly well and he wore his hair in curls, in the Greek fashion during the time that he still had plenty of hair.

When he took command in Spain, he immediately began to expand on the policies that were developed by his father and uncle, as they had expressed them in their letters home. He modified their policies with ideas that he had gained by studying Hannibal and Fabius. In 210 B.C., he made a bold, surprise attack on Spain's capital, New Carthage, while three Carthaginian armies were caught unaware. He made the attack when all three armies were more than ten days' march from their capital, never suspecting such an aggressive move, so uncharacteristic of Roman commanders of the time. The Carthaginian armies had to stand by, helplessly, while Scipio captured the rich city, using surprise tactics that Hannibal would have used. He captured great hordes of gold, silver, wheat, barley, sixty-three vessels, hundreds of war machines, and more than 10,000 male prisoners. He thus deprived Carthage of the immense wealth of war material stored in its Spanish capital. Much to the astonishment of the captives, he freed the citizens instead of making them slaves as would be expected of other Roman commanders. Slaves and artisans who were captured were made state-slaves by him. They were told that they could earn their freedom in the near future if they worked hard to provide necessary war material for his army.

Among the hostages that Carthaginians were holding in New Carthage before Scipio arrived, captured by Scipio along with other spoils, were daughters of a principal Iberian chieftain, Andobales, and their aunt who was wife of the chief's brother, Mardonius. The aunt was acting as the daughters' chaperone. They had been held hostage for money which Carthaginians were trying to get from the girl's father. When he captured them, Scipio treated them carefully and with respect, then he returned them to their father, unharmed. This diplomatic gesture impressed the Iberian chief, and many other chiefs in Spain, so much so, that many tribes came over to the Roman fold. This humane act gave Scipio a majority of Iberian tribes as his allies, and it tipped the scales of power in Spain, decidedly, in his favor.

Again, the most direct effect on Hannibal's fortunes

in Italy was a further delay in receiving help from his brother in Spain, and from Carthage. It would be three more years before Hasdrubal could cross the Alps to bring support for his brother in Italy. Scipio was blocking the route over the Pyranees.

During 210 B.C., the war in Sicily had ended, further reducing Rome's war concerns in areas other than those in Italy. More pressure could be concentrated on Hannibal. It was during this year that Sheik Syphax in Africa sent a delegation to Rome to report on his battles with Carthaginians and reaffirm his backing of Rome. Roman emissaries were then sent back to Syphax with gifts. Gifts were also sent to other African tribal chiefs in an attempt to enlist them as allies of Rome. Also during this year, the Roman Senate sent a raiding party of fifty ships to the Carthaginian coast near Utica to gather information about Carthage's preparations for war. The raiding party interrogated prisoners it had taken and learned that Carthage was assembling a large military force to send to Spain. In Spain, the force was to join more forces being gathered by Hannibal's brother, Hasdrubal, who was organizing an expeditionary force to march over the Alps. Hasdrubal had orders to join Hannibal in Italy. It appeared that Carthage was convinced, at last, that it should be helping Hannibal defeat Rome in Italy.

When consul Marcellus returned to Italy from Sicily in triumph after his great victory in 210 B.C., Rome put him to work aggressively attacking towns that had defected from Rome. Marcellus knew that Hannibal did not have sufficient numbers of soldiers to enable him to leave strong defensive garrisons in each town that had joined the Carthaginian fold, because it would cut up his small army into even smaller pieces, and leave him without a strong enough army to defend itself.

Marcellus began taking advantage of this fact, and he conquered the town of Salapia on the east coast of Italy, a few miles north of Cannae. The significance of this particular victory was that in taking this town, Marcellus killed a 500-man squadron of Hannibal's best Numidian cavalry in a battle inside the town where cavalry tactics could not be used properly. The loss of these fine horse soldiers was so great that after Salapia, Hannibal was never again superior to Roman legions in cavalry. Thus Hannibal had lost one of his most powerful military weapons against Roman legions. Marcellus then seized Samnite towns, capturing 3,000 of Hannibal's garrison troops that had been left there, as well as valuable spoils, including much wheat and barley.

Hannibal wanted to do something to slow the sacrifice of his loyal towns that were being retaken by Roman legions. It was during this time that the great Carthaginian magician learned that the Carthaginian town of Herdonea, south of Arpi, was about to surrender to the Roman proconsul, Gnaeus Fulvius, who was camped near it with his army. The Roman army was threatening the small town. It was a strange coincidence because this commander had the same name as another commander whom Hannibal had defeated two years earlier at the same town.

Leaders of the town had lost confidence in Carthage when they heard that Hannibal had abandoned Capua to Roman legions and that leaders in Capua had been horribly crucified while Hannibal was powerless to prevent it. In a forced march, traveling light, Hannibal swiftly moved to Herdonea before the enemy realized it. In a classic Hannibal-controlled battle, on a site selected by him, remnants of his Numidian cavalry outflanked the Roman legions, circled around them, then attacked the legions from their rear. He killed 13,000, including Fulvius, losing very few of his own army. Hannibal captured much booty from the Roman legions. The town was burned to the ground, and its leaders, who were attempting to defect to the Roman cause, were all executed by Hannibal as a frightful example for his other allies that may have been thinking of defecting. Thus, he was matching the Roman strategy as a counter threat to the Roman threat to the towns controlled by Carthage.

Marcellus didn't seem very concerned about this serious defeat of his countryman, Fulvius, nor was he concerned about the superior military genius that Hannibal demonstrated once again. Marcellus wrote a letter to the Roman Senate telling it that he intended to pursue Hannibal until he caught him. Indeed, he caught up with him near a small town in Lucania on level ground. He formed his legions in battle formation as a challenge to Hannibal. Marcellus knew that Hannibal preferred that type of terrain for fighting, and he was bold enough to do this because he realized that Hannibal's cavalry was not as strong as it had been before he lost his best Numidian squadron at Salapia.

Hannibal, nevertheless, accepted the challenge, and there was a fierce battle that was not decided by the time darkness came. The two armies separated at nightfall without reaching a decisive outcome. Hannibal didn't like the situation where he had been fighting. Although Marcellus was correct in believing that Hannibal preferred to fight on level ground in the past, that was no longer true. Now that he didn't have a superior cavalry, he no longer preferred such terrain and he couldn't afford to lose many of his small number of irreplaceable soldiers in a head-to-head battle. Hannibal wanted to arrange a situation where there were much greater odds in his favor before he was willing to fight. The Carthaginian wizard could not conceive a decisive victory at that battle site, so he moved his army out of the area at night. He headed northeast toward Apulia. When Marcellus formed his troops for battle the next morning, he discovered that Hannibal was gone, and he rapidly picked up his trail again. Hannibal attempted to lure Marcellus into an ambush by using remnants of his Numidian cavalry with their usual hit-and-run tactics, but the Roman was too cautious. He traveled only by day after carefully reconnoitering the path ahead and its flanks. Hannibal traveled only by night. This routine continued until Marcellus was recalled to Rome for the annual consular elections in January. The two consuls that were elected for 209 B.C. were Fabius Maximus, for the fifth time, and Quintus Fulvius Flaccus for the fourth time.

Marcellus was given command of his troops for another year as proconsul, with orders from Fabius to aggressively engage Hannibal. While Hannibal was preoccupied with Marcellus, Fabius planned to march on Tarentum to recapture the seaport. As soon as the new spring season began and there was sufficient forage in the countryside to support his animals, Marcellus had his army leave its winter camp to continue its pursuit of Hannibal. While Hannibal was distracted by Marcellus, Fabius dealt the Carthaginian cause another blow by taking Tarentum. He took the seaport by treachery. A love-sick young captain from Bruttium, who was in charge of Hannibal's garrison in the city, was in love with a woman whose brother was serving with the army of Fabius. The captain conspired with Fabius, who was outside his city's walls ready to lay siege, and allowed Roman troops to enter the city at night and take command of it.

In the meantime, Marcellus caught up with Hannibal's army near Canusium (Canosa) in Apulia, a few miles southwest of Cannae. Hannibal was trying to persuade Canusium to revolt against Rome when Marcellus arrived. Hannibal moved out, Marcellus followed, and the two armies continued the previous year's routine of Hannibal moving by night and Marcellus moving cautiously by day. Hannibal's Numidians engaged the pursuing Romans, using their hit-and-run tactics, while trying to lure Marcellus into a trap. Marcellus continued to be too alert and cautious to fall into one. Finally, Hannibal found suitable conditions on level terrain where he decided he would fight. There were two battles. In the first, Hannibal's soldiers routed Marcellus and his army, killing 2,700, while losing only a few Carthaginians. Afterward, Marcellus regrouped his surviving forces, and in the second battle, Hannibal lost 8,000 men and five elephants while Marcellus lost only 3,000 men.

Hannibal didn't want to trade such losses with Marcellus because he would soon have too few soldiers to continue fighting in Italy, even if he were to be victorious. He wanted a battle where he could win decisively, in the manner of Cannae or Trasimene, or he didn't want to fight until he could receive reinforcements for his army, which he hoped would be soon. He had learned about his brother's plan to come to Italy with a large expeditionary force. He moved his army out at night to Bruttium, but to his surprise, Marcellus did not follow. His Carthaginian army had inflicted such a devastating blow to the proconsul's army in the last two battles that Marcellus was unable to continue following. Marcellus camped at Venusia (Venosa) to allow his wounded to recover. Marcellus was elected consul in the new year's elections in 208 B.C., but by midsummer, more than a year after his last battle with Hannibal, Marcellus was being criticized because he was still encamped at Venusia while Hannibal continued to ramble freely throughout southern Italy. Evidently, Hannibal had taken much of the fighting spirit out of Marcellus and his army.

Finally, Marcellus and the other consul for the year, Titus Quinctius Crispinus, moved their armies near Hannibal's army. Hannibal did not want to fight two armies at one time unless he could arrange conditions highly favorable to him. He searched for a suitable place to trap the two consuls while his Numidians continued their usual hit-and-run tactics, utilizing their great speed and longer range weapons. There were small skirmishes between enemy foraging parties, but there were no great battles because Hannibal kept his army moving.

Finally he had a minor success. Spies told him that the two consuls had decided to take Locri, in the toe of the Italian boot, which Hannibal had been using as a seaport. Agents told him that the two consuls had ordered a part of the force that was on garrison duty at Tarentum, in the east, to march west to Locri to participate in the siege of Locri. Knowing the route that the garrisoned soldiers had to travel on, westward, to get to Locri, Hannibal sent some of his troops to lay in ambush on the road leading to Locri. The ambush worked perfectly, and Hannibal's men killed 2,000 Romans soldiers and took 1,500 prisoners. The remaining Roman troops that the two consuls were expecting to arrive in Locri fled over the countryside and returned to Tarentum.

This action caused Marcellus and Crispinus to abort their plans to take Locri, because they lost so many of the troops they required. This action saved the seaport for further use by the Carthaginians. Later, the two consuls resumed their task of following Hannibal as the Carthaginian commander continued to move around southern Italy. The two consuls dogged him wherever he went, until Hannibal finally found a site that had great possibilities for a successful ambush of the two armies. By carefully planning ahead, he arranged a situation such that when he made camp at a location near Venusia, he knew that the Romans would probably camp at an attractive site a few miles away. There was a tree-covered hill between Hannibal's camp and the campsite he expected the two Roman consuls to choose. Hannibal selected the place because he knew the consuls would eventually want to occupy the hilltop. Under cover of darkness, he sent some of his cavalry squadrons on ahead to occupy the hill before the Romans had a chance to look it over. Hannibal ordered his cavalry to conceal themselves during daylight hours without moving.

Later, as Hannibal had planned, the two consuls made their camps on the opposite side of the knoll from his camp. Soon, the two consuls decided that the hilltop near their camp should be occupied, just as Hannibal had anticipated. Marcellus and Crispinus decided to personally inspect the knoll before they ordered their men to inhabit it, and they rode up to the small hill escorted by cavalry troops. Hannibal had pre-positioned a camouflaged observer in a tree so that the Romans could not see him, but the observer could clearly see them.

As the two consuls approached the knoll, Hannibal's observer gave a prearranged signal to his hidden cavalry, and it made a surprise attack on the two consuls and their mounted escorts. The sixty-year-old Marcellus was run through with a lance and fell dead from his horse. Crispinus, with two mortal javelin wounds, was able to escape and move the consular armies to a safe camp, but he died later from his wounds. Hannibal was unable to trap the two consular armies as he wished, but he was able to kill two consuls.

Good news reached Hannibal in his camp that Etruria was wavering in its loyalty to Rome and that it might defect soon. Most of southern Italy and all of the north were aligned with Carthage. If Hannibal could receive his much needed reinforcements soon, he might be able to end the war.

The young Scipio was having great success in Spain, and a large share of the Spanish population was going over to Rome. Much of his success was due to Scipio's diplomacy, his humane treatment of the natives, his generosity, as well as his military capability. The shrinking domain commanded by Hannibal's brother, Hasdrubal, caused him to believe that if he were to remain in Spain his forces would have to retreat to remote parts of western Spain and into Gallia if they were to be secure from Scipio's growing strength. In 208 B.C., Hasdrubal decided to concentrate as many of his remaining forces as he could gather together and bring them to help his brother in Italy. He left Hasdrubal, son of Gisco, with an army of loyal Spanish troops to go to western Spain, into Lusitania, where natives still supported Carthage. He ordered Massinisa, the Numidian, to take 3,000 cavalry to roam the rest of Spain, to help allies that were still loyal to Carthage, and to raid enemy territory wherever possible. Hasdrubal ordered his young brother, Mago, to take a large supply of money to the Balearic Islands to hire more mercenaries, then take them to Italy, also to help his brother, Hannibal.

Hasdrubal took his expeditionary army across the

Pyranees and into the territory of the Gauls, carrying much gold and silver with him to hire mercenary troops there. He wanted to augment the size of his small army, and he spent the rest of the year building a larger army in southern Gallia. By spring, 207, he had built his army into a 20,000 man force, then he crossed the Alps as soon as the snow melted. Ten elephants survived the trip to Italy. His crossing of the Alps was unexpectedly rapid, much faster than Hannibal's crossing, because native tribes that had resisted Hannibal's crossing - believing that Hannibal's army was there to occupy their land - now realized that Carthaginians were merely passing through their land to fight Romans. The natives also remembered the high cost they had to pay in killed and wounded, to no avail, for resisting Hannibal's army. Hasdrubal's army reached the Padus Valley without opposition, and it was soon joined by more than 40,000 Gauls in Liguria. Thus Hasdrubal's army now had a total of 60,000 soldiers.

Again, Rome panicked at the thought that two powerful, cunning brothers were in Italy with large armies to attack them, one in the north and the other in the south. Roman military strategists became determined to do all that was possible to keep the brothers apart. The combined Carthaginian strength commanded by Hannibal's military genius would be too much for Roman legions to resist. Rome was on the thin edge between victory and defeat in the war with Carthage on Italian soil. Rome's main hope for a strong future leader, Marcellus, had been killed (and Scipio had not been acknowledged yet). Fabius was growing too old. Many Roman colonies, as well as the districts of the Roman confederation, were teetering on the verge of revolt. The newly appointed consuls for the year, Gaius Claudius Nero (the aristocratic consul) and

Marcus Livius Salinator (the plebeian consul), were not known to be particularly distinguished military commanders. The two consuls were personal enemies, but they agreed to cooperate with each other in their fight against Hannibal. The panicked Senate approved an unprecedented twenty-three legions for the field. Livius Salinator took his army north from Rome to meet Hasdrubal's army near the Metaurus (Metauro) River. Nero went south to try to slow or stop Hannibal from joining with his brother.

Hannibal received word that his brother was on his way to join him, but no communication had been established with Hasdrubal since he entered Italy. Nero followed every movement Hannibal's army made, and he attempted to impede the Carthaginian's progress. There was an indecisive battle at Grumentum (near Mt. Volturino) on a river (Agri) in Lucania. But Hannibal's main objective was to meet his brother coming from the north, so he avoided Nero as much as he could. He proceeded to Canusium, having only skirmishes with Nero on the way, and he made his camp there to await word from his brother so that arrangements for a meeting could be made. Nero followed the Carthaginian military genius, not expecting to defeat him, but to delay his progress. In this way, he hoped that Consul Livius would have enough time to defeat Hasdrubal in the north before the two brothers could link up. While Hannibal was waiting, a round object was thrown into his camp and taken to him. It was the bloody head of his brother, Hasdrubal.

Hasdrubal had dispatched a party of six horsemen to carry a letter to Hannibal, telling his brother that he would meet him in Umbria. The horsemen successfully rode through enemy pickets and traveled the entire length of Italy from Hasdrubal in the north, all the way down to Italy's southern tip, looking for Hannibal's army. When they reached the south, they began to pursue the fast-moving Hannibal, and they mistakenly took a wrong turn in the road which led to Tarentum, now controlled by Romans. A surprised Roman foraging party from Tarentum accidentally ran across the paths of Hasdrubal's messengers and captured them, including Hasdrubal's letter to Hannibal. The letter was immediately sent to Consul Nero who realized the great opportunity it gave him to join his fellow consul to trap Hasdrubal's army before Hannibal was able to learn anything about it. Romans knew where Hasdrubal would be, and they could plan to face him with the two consular armies in a surprise attack. Nero knew he had to join Livius without Hannibal knowing anything about it, otherwise the Carthaginian commander would find some way of preventing it.

Nero was not authorized to leave his assigned province, but he realized that the opportunity to strike Hasdrubal before Hannibal found out about it and joined him, could not wait. Learning from Hannibal, Nero evacuated his camp near Hannibal's during the darkness of night, leaving campfires burning, tents pitched, and enough Roman soldiers remaining to mislead Hannibal's army into believing that Nero's army was still there. Since Hannibal was waiting for word from his brother, and not interested in fighting Nero, his spy network did not pick up Nero's departure. It was one of the few times that Hannibal was caught unaware.

In a spectacular, unauthorized, forced march to northern Italy to join his fellow consul, Nero traveled more than thirty-five miles per day with his army, covering the 250 miles in seven days. In a bold stroke, he had broken a cardinal rule that no consul can leave his assigned territory without orders from Rome, thus leaving his territory unguarded. It was a daring, decisive move, but he wanted to make the move before Hannibal learned about his plans. He couldn't wait for permission from Rome. Nero knew it would be easier to defeat the Carthaginian armies one at a time, when the enemy could be outnumbered in each battle, rather than face them together, when the numbers would be more equal and the fearsome genius of Hannibal would then be added to the equation.

Hasdrubal was a very competent general, but his weary army, most of whom were undisciplined Gallic mercenaries, was faced with two disciplined, enlarged, Roman consular armies. Furthermore, Rome had sent additional troops to beef up the army of Livius because of the concern it had. The two consuls attacked Hasdrubal's army as soon as they could, worried that Hannibal would find out what was happening. Hasdrubal did not want to fight because his primary goal was to join his brother before he attempted to battle Romans. He tried to escape by following the Metaurus River, but the farther his army marched along it, the higher the banks became. He couldn't cross its steep cliffs with his army. Finally, he was trapped, and he made camp for the night, unable to find a suitable place to cross the river.

That night many of the unruly Gauls drank themselves into drunken stipors and many were either still intoxicated the next morning or had lost consciousness from their drunkenness. The Roman armies, which vastly outnumbered Hasdrubal's army, saw the situation and decided to take advantage of it quickly. Hasdrubal formed his battle lines to protect his army, but without most of the Gauls answering the call for battle. Greatly outnumbered, Hasdrubal's loyal soldiers fought a valiant, bloody, violent battle (near S. Angelo in Vado), but the heroic Hasdrubal soon saw that the fight was lost. He refused to survive his troops, and near the end, he galloped his horse into the midst of an enemy cohort with his sword flying, taking many Romans with him as he died. For Romans, Cannae had been avenged. Although it was difficult to count the numbers, about 57,000 of Hasdrubal's army, mostly mercenaries, were killed, and 5,400 were taken prisoner.

Soon after the battle, Nero returned by forced march to Apulia to resume his watch of Hannibal. It was here that Hasdrubal's carefully preserved head was tossed into Hannibal's camp. Nero had been gone from Hannibal's sight for only fourteen days during his 500-mile round trip. The head of his brother was the first sight of him that Hannibal had seen in twelve years. With a very heavy heart, not only for the death of his beloved brother, but also for the catastrophic blow to his military fortunes, Hannibal retreated to Bruttium in the remotest part of Italy. Gisco and Cirta, too, were very distressed. They had known Hasdrubal very well, and they respected him almost as much as they did Hannibal. The Greek and his companion speculated privately about what could have been accomplished with the army that Hasdrubal was bringing. By his superior generalship, Hannibal was able to continue his campaign in Italy for many more years with his shrinking army, but he knew that the odds for his success were becoming slimmer. By a simple quirk of fate - whereby the messengers from Hasdrubal took a wrong turn in the road - Hannibal's fortunes had been dealt a decisive blow.

Chapter 9

BIZARRE EVENTS BEFORE HANNIBAL ARRIVES IN AFRICA (206 - 203 B. C.)

Frustrated by a steady turn of events that were beyond his control, Hannibal had to gradually submit to pressure applied on him by the superior numbers of soldiers Rome now had. The territory under his control continually shrank from 206-203 B.C. Still, in spite of their overwhelming numbers, the Romans were unable to defeat the canny genius during this period, except in minor skirmishes. The great Carthaginian general, whose military accomplishments were openly admired by contemporary Roman and Greek writers and feared by Roman consuls, continued to hold out and harass far superior enemy forces. He had brought Rome near financial ruin, as it was borrowing heavily from civilian lenders and had raided the treasures of sacred temples to continue the war. The Roman economy was severely strained.

Gisco and Cirta discussed the strange quirks of fate that continually turned against Hannibal. Bungling Carthaginian politicians, who were primarily merchant-traders and incompetent at military matters, failed to give Hannibal the strong support that his adversaries were given by the Roman Senate. This was particularly critical during the first few years after Hannibal's astounding victories over Roman legions and before Rome had a chance to recover from the shock of Hannibal's genius. When the Carthaginian Senate (actually the Council of 100 in the Carthaginian Shofet) finally decided to give the war its strong support, years later, it continually wasted its scarce military resources by pouring them into insignificant side issues such as Sardinia, Sicily, and Spain, instead of into the decisive battlefield, Rome.

Other fateful events that worked against Hannibal's fortunes were the inability of King Philip of Macedonia to provide military support as promised; the quirk of fate that caused Hasdrubal's messengers to take the wrong turn in the road, allowing them to be captured and resulting in the loss of 60,000 much needed Carthaginian troops and elephants; and the accident that thousands of new Roman army recruits were in Rome, doubling the normal size of the city's garrison, when Hannibal considered attacking it.

Hannibal's troops were becoming homesick because many of them had been gone from their homes for more than twelve years, and Hannibal was having a difficult time preventing their desertion. On top of all this, Hannibal's allied cities began losing faith in his ability to protect them and were returning to the Roman fold. If this weren't enough, a bright young Roman was conquering Spain by adopting Hannibal's policies and methods, and he was using very enlightened diplomacy to nurture allies for Rome in Africa, particularly, as it later turned out, his actions gained the allegiance of the great leader of the Numidian cavalry, Massinisa, future king of Numidia. Numidian cavalry was a main source of Carthaginian military power, a vital part of its success up to this time. Carthage could ill-afford to have any Numidian cavalry as an enemy.

If all of this were not enough to do Hannibal in, there was a bizarre series of events that was occurring before he could reach Africa, in answer to his Senate's urgent call for him to pull out of Italy and return to save his homeland from a Roman invasion. The year 206 B.C. had seen the end of Carthaginian resistance and power in Spain, thanks to the brilliant policies of the rising military genius, the young Publius Cornelius Scipio. Young Scipio's rise to power was as meteoric as Hannibal's, and there were many other similarities between the two great generals' careers. One of these similarities was that, like Hannibal, Scipio had great odds stacked against his success by politicians in the Roman Senate, who were his enemies. They opposed his rise to power.

One of young Scipio's brilliant policies, originally initiated by his father and uncle but continued by the young general, was the policy of seeking a Roman ally in Africa to provide some distraction for their enemy, Carthage, on the African continent. The Scipio brothers had made initial contact with Sheik Syphax, ruler in western Numidia and a claimant to the throne of all Numidia. Contact was made with the sheik when the Scipio brothers learned that he had turned against eastern Numidia, home of Masinissa and ally of Carthage. Masinissa was the other claimant to the throne (the heir), as ruler of all Numidia in competition with the other contender for it, Syphax.

The Scipios had sent emissaries and gifts to the sheik to form a pact against Carthage. Syphax said he wanted Roman officers to train his army in the use of infantry because his army was then made up of an excellent cavalry, but practically no strong infantry. Syphax had admired Roman infantry successes in Spain. A pact was made and a Roman officer began training his army. When King Gala, ruler of eastern Numidia and ally of Carthage, heard of this pact, he sent an army to fight Syphax. This army was commanded by his young son, Massinisa, heir to his throne. Massinisa defeated Syphax in a great battle, killing 30,000 of his soldiers. Massinisa had much help in this battle from the Carthaginian army in Spain. After the battle, Massinisa, who was educated in Carthage, joined the Carthaginian forces in Spain and was made commander of the strong Numidian cavalry there. He was leader of the cavalry that had killed young Scipio's father and he had fought against Scipio at Ilipa in Spain.

An accidental incident helped sway Massinisa, much later, to defect from Carthage and become an ally of young Scipio. The incident gave Masinissa an insight to the humanity and compassion of the great young Scipio. The incident was also a good example of Scipio's diplomatic sensitivity. During a battle in Spain, the young nephew of Massinisa named Massiva, grandson of King Gala of Numidia, was captured by Scipio's soldiers. Massiva was far too young to go to battle, but he disobeyed his uncle's orders, stole a horse, and secretly joined the combat against Scipio's army in Spain. When captured and questioned, the young boy cried, telling Scipio his entire story. The compassionate Scipio ordered his men to treat the boy well rather than sell him as a slave with the other prisoners taken with him when he was captured, as the boy fully expected. He gave the boy a gold ring, beautiful clothes, a gold brooch, a beautiful horse with all the luxurious trappings, and sent him back to his uncle, Massinisa, under safe escort. The boy cried, overwhelmed by gratitude.

Later, in 206 B.C., Massinisa remembered the incident when Scipio defeated Carthaginian forces that were then commanded by Hasdrubal, son of Gisgo, defending western Spain. After a great battle in southwest Spain, the second battle of Baecula (on the Guadalguivir River), where the Carthaginian army was soundly defeated by young Scipio, this Hasdrubal deserted his surviving troops and fled to Africa. The battle was the decisive one that led to the expulsion of the last Carthaginian soldier from Spain. Massinisa, commander of Hasdrubal's cavalry in the battle, made the decision to defect from the Carthaginian's losing cause when he saw Hasdrubal desert.

Before he left Spain, Massinisa entered secret talks with Scipio's propraetor (second in command), telling him of his intentions. Soon afterward, Scipio made a trip to Africa, ostensibly to see Rome's ally, Syphax, Masinissa's enemy, but he arranged a secret meeting with Massinisa during his trip. Scipio didn't want Syphax to know of this meeting with his bitter enemy, Masinissa. The ambitious Massinisa was impressed by the personal charm, character, and magnetism of the great proconsul, as well as by his successful military genius. Massinisa was not adverse to joining the winning side of the conflict between Rome and Carthage. He advised Scipio that the Roman general could take Carthage by an invasion of Africa, and that he, Masinissa, would become an ally of Rome as soon as he inherited the throne. Scipio and Masinissa had an agreeable meeting; each was impressed by the other's ability, and they agreed to keep Masinissa's plans secret for the time being. If Syphax had learned of the plan, this staunch ally of Rome would probably have defected from Rome and joined the Carthaginian cause, so great was his hate for Masinissa.

Later, in 205 B.C., the ambitious Scipio resigned his position as commander in Spain and returned to

Rome to be there in time for the annual consular elections. He wanted to be elected consul for the year. All Carthaginian resistance in Spain had ended, and he was returning as a victorious and popular hero of the Roman people. He had gone to Spain to face four Carthaginian commanders and four armies when no other qualified Roman would volunteer for the task. He returned to Italy without leaving a single Carthaginian soldier in Spain.

Scipio's enemies in the Roman Senate refused to allow him an official triumphal parade through the streets of Rome for technical reasons. He was not an official magistrate. However, he brought more than seven tons of silver with him for the depleted Roman treasury, which he paraded through the streets of the city in a flamboyant manner for all of the curious citizens to see. Throngs of people turned out to see the popular general, but he was largely ignored by the aristocratic senators who feared him as a possible dictator. Because he had many enemies in the aristocratic Senate (he was an aristocrat himself), who were either jealous of him or afraid of his aggressive ideas for conducting the war, the Senate was not inclined to elect him as consul. However, he was overwhelmingly elected consul by the heaviest poll recorded during the war by the Assembly of the common people. The Senate then approved his appointment, as was the custom.

The other consul elected for the year was Publius Crassus, a powerful aristocratic politician. The election had drawn such a large crowd because everyone wanted to see their hero, Scipio, whose exploits were widely admired by the people. Throngs of people followed him to his house, then watched him go to the capitol to sacrifice one hundred oxen, which he had solemnly promised the god, Jupiter, in a temple before he left Spain. He had great appeal for the common citizens who had few successful heroes to admire.

Scipio was the only prominent person who recognized that Carthage, not Hannibal, was the real enemy of Rome, and he spoke out in the Roman Senate about it. Fabius and most of Scipio's other enemies in the Senate believed that Hannibal had to be defeated first, then Carthage could be attacked. Scipio argued that if he went to Africa and attacked Carthage, Hannibal would be recalled to Africa to defend his homeland.

After the elections, there was a prolonged, running debate in the Senate over this war policy, with the elderly Fabius leading the opposition. Finally, largely due to pressure from the common people, the Senate grudgingly approved a plan for Scipio to go to Sicily to raise an army, provided it consisted entirely of volunteers, and provided Scipio did it at his own expense, with no cost to the treasury of Rome. The Senate would not authorize conscription of soldiers for the purpose, however, he was given command of the two legions of outcasts in Sicily that had escaped from Cannae. He was authorized to launch an attack on Carthage from Sicily.

A surprising number of volunteers from all over Italy joined his army, and many communities in Italy voluntarily provided supplies to build the fleet of ships that would be needed for crossing the Mediterranean, much to the astonishment of the Senate. It was an expedition that fired the interest of the Roman people, over the objections of many senators.

Friends of Fabius continued to harass Scipio, even after he had won the Senate's approval for his expedition. Through their considerable influence, they assigned a special quaestor to Scipio's staff to carefully watch Scipio's finances. The aristocratic quaestor they appointed, M. Porcius Cato, also known as Cato "The Censor," was a strong political supporter of Fabius, and he went out of his way to discredit Scipio's efforts in his official reports back to the Senate. For example, Scipio was charged in the Senate, through information provided by Cato, with wasting money by issuing to his soldiers superfluous luxuries that were spoiling them. No mention was made of the fact that Scipio was using his own money, none of the Roman treasury money. Another charge was made in the Senate against him concerning his brilliant conquest of Hannibal's port of Locri. Without mentioning the fact that Scipio had taken the valuable port from Hannibal, he was charged in the Senate, again from information provided by Cato, with many infractions of Roman rules.

The Locri incident was a stroke of genius, and Scipio should have been lauded for it in the Senate, rather than disciplined. Scipio found a group of artisans from Locri in his prison in Sicily. Scipio agreed to release the artisans and allow them to return to Locri, with a promise from them that they would let Scipio's troops into the wall of the city at night after they returned to their home. This was done, and Scipio was able to take Hannibal's largest remaining seaport while Hannibal was nearby, with very little bloodshed. Hannibal was helpless to prevent it because it was accomplished before he found out about it. Scipio's troops were inside the walls, and Hannibal was outside, before he learned about the treacherous coup.

One of Scipio's problems arose when his magistrate, Pleminius, whom he left in command of the town when he returned to Sicily, was found to treat inhabitants of Locri in a sadistic manner. This is something Scipio would never have allowed if had known about it at the time. Pleminius also violated Roman laws by mistreating two tribunes of the Roman army. Scipio's enemies in the Senate accused him of these infractions, as well as such other minor offenses as "un-Roman behavior," because he relaxed in the evenings in sandals, wearing a Greek chiton, and he drank wine while attending Greek symposiums. No mention was made in the Senate of his brilliant recovery of Locri, except to criticize the fact that he had violated the rule against leaving his assigned province, Sicily, to go to another consul's area.

Scipio discharged Cato, spy for his political enemies, by using the pretext that it was a necessary reduction of expenses. He said that he could not afford a full-time quaestor in his army, since it was Cato who charged Scipio with being extravagant and wasteful of money.

Scipio's enemies in the Senate sent a commission to Sicily to investigate the charges brought against him, with power to remove him from office. By the time the commission arrived in Sicily, Scipio had completed preparations for his invasion of Africa and he was about to make his invasion force have a rehearsal of the invasion. He put on such an efficient, brilliant, formal display for the commission when it witnessed his full-dress rehearsal for the invasion of Africa that the group returned to Rome with nothing but praise for him. The commission was particularly impressed when it learned that Scipio had recruited and trained the expeditionary force at practically no expense to the Senate.

In spring, 204 B.C., Publius Scipio left Sicily with forty warships convoying 400 transport vessels, carrying 30,000 men for the invasion of Africa. The invasion force landed unopposed near Utica, the oldest Phoenician city on the north African coast. This aggressive action, to invade the Carthaginian homeland, was reminiscent of Hannibal's invasion of Rome's homeland fourteen years before.

After Hannibal had lost Locri by treachery in 204 B.C., he was gradually forced into a smaller and smaller piece of real estate that he could control. Town after town was taken from him by Roman armies, and he didn't have the forces to prevent it. Many towns, seeing that Hannibal was now almost powerless against much larger Roman military strength, surrendered to Roman authority. Hannibal's veterans had been away from home for fourteen or more years by now. They were much older, and those who had survived had collected numerous battle scars. It was becoming more difficult to keep his soldiers motivated. However, his reputation was such that Roman commanders still feared him, and none had the courage to challenge him in a decisive showdown in battle. He continued to hold his shrinking army together as he settled near the little harbor of Croton, located in the ball of the boot of Italy, in 203 B.C.

Hannibal knew of Scipio's expedition to Africa, and knowing the disposition of the Carthaginian Senate, he anticipated his recall to Africa. Scipio had publicly announced that a purpose of his invasion of Africa was to cause Carthage to recall Hannibal from Italy to defend his homeland. Scipio had done exactly what Hannibal had done earlier: Hannibal had forced Rome to recall the expeditionary force it was sending to invade Carthage because of his bold invasion of Italy; now, Scipio's bold invasion of Carthage was forcing it to recall its forces from Italy.

Hannibal had learned earlier that his young brother,

Mago, who had left Spain to raise an army in the Balearic Islands during the winter 205-204 B.C., had raised a fleet of thirty warships and a large number of transport vessels. He was headed for Italy with 12,000 infantry and 2,000 cavalry soldiers.

Later, he landed at Genua (Genoa) in Liguria unopposed. Mago started recruiting Gauls and Ligurians to augment his army so that he could fight his way south to join his brother. He recruited 50,000 troops by 204 B.C., and he controlled all of northern Italy. The entire district of Etruria had become his ally. While Hannibal's domain in southern Italy was continually shrinking, Mago's territory in the north was growing in size. Mago had many pitched battles with Roman legions as he kept expanding his controlled territory in the north, while fighting his way south to meet his brother. In one pitched battle, which he lost, in the land of the Insubres, Mago was seriously wounded. He retreated with his army to Liguria, and it was there in 203 B.C. that he received a message from Carthage ordering him to return as soon as possible. He was told that his brother, Hannibal, had received similar orders.

Mago embarked his Spanish, Ligurian, and Gallic troops on his large fleet of vessels and headed for Carthage. While the fleet was passing Sardinia, a violent storm hit it and scattered its vessels. Mago died of his previous battle wounds on board his ship during the rough weather. With Mago's death, the second and last of Hannibal's brothers died. Mago's fleet was dispersed at sea, but many ships reached Carthage, and only a few were captured by Roman picket ships.

Thus, by July, 203 B.C. at Croton, Hannibal, unaware of the fate of his brother, sadly received orders to come to Carthage. The entire military strength of

Rome was unable to defeat him in Italy for fifteen years, and he was finally defeated by the indecisive, bickering, incompetent politicians in his own government. Had the Carthaginian government been as resolute in supporting him as the Roman Senate supported its legions, especially during the early years after Cannae (it had more finacial resources available to it than Rome had at the time), history books may have been written differently, and Carthage, not Rome, may have been the surviving power in the Mediterranean. Hannibal's enemies in the Carthaginian Senate (the Council of 100 in the Shofet) had tried for years to force him back to Carthage by refusing him reinforcements and money. Now, by direct words, he was ordered to return home. He was conquered in Italy, not by Romans, but by the envy and abuse he received from his political enemies in the Carthaginian Senate.

Hannibal's main enemy in the Senate (Shofet) was Hanno, leader of the anti-Barca faction, who did all he could to obstruct the most prominent living member of the Barca family, Hannibal, even after the majority of the Senate had voted to commit Carthage to war with Rome in 218 B.C. Neither Hanno nor his aristocratic, merchant-followers had the strategic view of what would happen to Carthage, their trading business, and the rest of the Mediterranean civilization if Rome were allowed to continue its aggressive expansion unchecked. Hannibal and the Barcas in the Senate did. Hanno was a leader of a political group whose basic philosophy was to appease Rome and to achieve conciliation and peace by any means.

The Barcas, founded by Hannibal's father, Hamilcar Barca, was represented by aristocrats who had a better long-range view of what would happen to Carthage. The Barca faction believed that peace with

Rome could only be made by losing much of Carthage's freedom, and that peace with Rome could only lead to Roman oppression and to the subjugation of Carthage by the warlike Romans. The Barcas could see no end to the insatiable Roman need to expand its territory, and they believed that Rome should be stopped by a strong Carthage, or Carthage would be doomed to become a dominated slave like Rome's other dominated territories.

The basic economy of Carthage relied on a lively and free trade throughout the Mediterranean, and this conflicted, more and more, with the growing Roman trade. Barcas believed that this would inevitably lead to aggression by Rome. Future events, in years to come, vindicated the Barcas' view of the situation as the correct one. Carthage had ample resources to support Hannibal, and to defeat Rome, as it proved too much later when it began to build a large fleet of warships and when it began raising large armies. There was no military genius in Carthage to cut through the political bickering and direct the war with a winning plan.

Hannibal and Gisco had spent many hours meditating and making animal sacrifices at the Temple of Juno Lacinia, an ancient Greek shrine located on a rise near Croton. Gisco had urged, and Hannibal had agreed, to carefully protect the old shrine. Before he left Italy, as was the custom, Hannibal placed a bronze memorial tablet, along with the many other memorials left by other people. This bronze memorial plaque listed all of Hannibal's victories during his fifteen years in Italy. Details listed on this tablet were later used by many Greek and Roman historians to authenticate many statistical facts about his battles.

During the summer of 203 B.C., Hannibal and his

staff of officers carefully selected the soldiers he would take to Africa. He had anticipated his recall, and he had taken many of the necessary steps prior to boarding the ships that would take his army to Carthage. He did this before he received official orders for his return. There were only enough ships to carry 12,000 soldiers, and he wanted all the soldiers to be volunteers and good fighters. Many of his soldiers elected to stay behind with the women and children who had become a regular part of his army during the final years. These soldiers would become the garrison for the port and neighboring towns, to protect them from Romans when he was gone.

The cumbersome fleet of transports carrying his army was highly vulnerable to attack by Roman picket ships, if Romans were to learn of his departure, so he took many measures to keep them from learning about his plans. He ordered the detachments of soldiers, who were to remain behind in Italy as part of the garrison, to occupy all of the heights surrounding the small, shallow, moon-shaped bay of Croton. He had them occupy all of the heights where an observer could see what was happening in the harbor. Next, he was careful to conceal all preparations for departure by doing it in small increments and doing much of it at night. Soldiers remaining behind were ordered to keep themselves highly visible to any Roman spies that might be watching, to make it appear that nothing was happening. Final loading of the vessels was done at night, and the fleet sailed away under cover of darkness. The fleet was well on its way, out of sight of land by the end of summer, before the local Roman commander learned of his departure. The fleet took a wide, circuitous route to Africa, sailing far to the east of Roman picketship and approaching Africa from the east, landing ninety miles south of Carthage, unopposed, at Hadrumetum.

There was an uncanny series of events that took place in Africa before Hannibal arrived from Italy. Gisco and Hannibal learned about them much later. Although none of the events were such that Hannibal could do anything about them had he been aware of them at the time, they accounted for an incredible and sudden degradation of Hannibal's future fortunes in the war. The events were like an unbelievable comic opera, and also explain how Carthage lost the war in Africa before Hannibal was able to arrive home to save his homeland from Scipio's army.

The series of events began in 204 B.C., before Hannibal was recalled to Africa. Scipio had arrived in Africa with his expeditionary forces near Utica. He had forty warships, 400 transports, and about 30,000 men. As Scipio was promised at their last meeting, Prince Masinissa joined his army there, but with only 200 horse soldiers instead of the massive cavalry, in the thousands, that Scipio had expected. The story of how Masinissa's massive cavalry was drastically reduced in size since their last meeting, and the story of how the other Numidian prince, Syphax, had turned against Rome and become an ally of Carthage, explains an important impact these events had on the ability of Carthage to defend itself. These events happened before Hannibal arrived to help save his homeland and were among the other unusual and bizarre incidents that had an important influence on Hannibal's fortunes.

Hasdrubal, son of Gisgo, the commander in Spain who had fled to Carthage after his defeat by Scipio, was given command of Carthaginian military forces in Africa. Agents had told Hasdrubal of Scipio's contact with Syphax, leader of Numidians in west Numidia and competitor of Prince Masinissa for the throne of all Numidia. He also knew about the promise that Syphax had given to Rome, swearing that he would be Rome's staunch ally against Carthage. To entice Syphax back into the Carthaginian fold, and to undo the fine diplomacy of the Scipios, Hasdrubal offered to give him the hand of his young, beautiful daughter, Sophonisba, in marriage. Sophonisba was not an ordinary beauty. In addition to having ravishing, voluptuous features, she was very intelligent, and very patriotic toward her homeland, Carthage. She had been carefully trained by Greek tutors, not only in music and literature, but the passionate enchantress was also trained in the ancient art of beguilement. She was unusually devoted to her father and her country, so she obeyed her father's request to marry the old man, Syphax. Hasdrubal sent her to Syphax, not only in an attempt to sway him to join Carthage as an ally, but he intended to have her keep him informed about the activities of this powerful sheik. The love-sick Syphax soon swore allegiance to Carthage as Hasdrubal had planned.

There was a serious problem with this arrangement. Sophonisba was already betrothed to the greatest enemy of Syphax, Prince Masinissa, his competitor for the throne of Numidia. Hasdrubal offered his daughter's hand to Syphax without consulting his other prospective son-in-law, Masinissa. Hasdrubal then had Masinissa hunted down for assassination, to get him out of the way as a claimant of the throne, so that his new future son-in-law, Syphax, would have clear title as ruler of all Numidia. After many hair-raising escapes and the loss of his cavalry, the harassed Masinissa finally met Scipio near Utica with only 200 horses remaining from his original massive cavalry. Scipio had expected Masinissa to bring him his former massive cavalry. Scipio was very concerned and disappointed, but the great skill and experience of Masinissa at warfare using mounted troops would soon prove to be an invaluable asset.

Syphax, now an enemy of Rome, took his force of 50,000 foot and 10,000 horse soldiers, all Numidians and Mauritanians, to join Hasdrubal's Carthaginian army now consisting of 30,000. They marched toward Utica where they intended to meet Scipio's troops. Hasdrubal sent an advance party of 4,000 Carthaginian cavalry to reconnoiter Scipio's forces. As a portent of his future usefulness to Scipio, Masinissa used his great knowledge of desert warfare and his strong leadership ability to convince Scipio that they could ambush the 4,000 Carthaginian horse soldiers that his scouts told him were coming toward Utica. Masinissa took his 200 horses, and using hit-and-run skirmish tactics on the Carthaginian flanks, enticed the 4,000 Carthaginians to follow him into an ambush where a large force of Roman cavalry was waiting, concealed behind some high ground. At the proper time, Romans attacked the unsuspecting Carthaginians and killed or captured 3,000 of them.

After this taste of battle, Scipio dug his troops in on a long, narrow promontory east of Utica for the winter, 204-203 B.C. The two armies of Hasdrubal and Syphax each made separate camps nearby to keep close watch on the Roman army and to protect Utica from an attack by Scipio. Both, Hasdrubal and Syphax, had their camps constructed with reeds, wood, and thatched-roof huts for the winter. The wily Masinissa sent spies disguised as peace negotiators, servants, and attendants to infiltrate both of their camps.

One night in 203 B.C., after the African troops were sleeping soundly and their vigil had been relaxed because Scipio had treacherously sent mock-agents as peace envoys to disarm their guard, Masinissa's spies set fire to the highly flammable huts in both camps. The fires were set in a coordinated effort and many of the sleeping soldiers and animals were killed by the raging fire that resulted. Survivors of the fires who awoke in time to escape from the flames, unarmed, were killed by Scipio's troops who were waiting to slaughter them in the confusion and darkness of the night. About 40,000 were killed and another 5,000 were taken prisoner. Both commanders, Hasdrubal and Syphax, escaped, but only 2,000 of their infantry and 500 cavalry were able to get away, leaving most of their equipment behind.

Within a month, the decimated Carthaginian forces, now reinforced by 4,000 Celtiberians who had unexpectedly arrived from Spain, returned to dig in at the Great Plains which were west of Carthage. They waited there for Scipio's next move while they trained in preparation for the expected battle. Hasdrubal was still in command. Hasdrubal's daughter, Sophonisba, convinced the uncertain Syphax that he should continue to support Carthage, and they all began emergency recruitment programs to fill out their depleted armies. They were able to recruit a combined total of 30,000 soldiers, but only a small, inexperienced cavalry.

Publius Scipio decided to strike the Carthaginian army while it was still weak, and before Hannibal and Mago could arrive from Italy with their armies to join the fray. Roman scouts reported that Hasdrubal and Syphax were collecting new forces and training them at Great Plains, so the Roman commander moved his army southwest to meet them. After a few days of probing skirmishes, the two opposing armies formed battle configurations opposite one another on the Great Plains. Publius had strong, disciplined Numidian and Roman cavalry that he had been training in tactics he had watched Hannibal use at Cannae. Hasdrubal's depleted cavalry consisted of untrained and inexperienced Numidian peasants that Syphax could recruit in a hurry, and the few remnants of his original cavalry that had survived the two disasters, Masinissa's ambush and the night fire disaster. Scipio's infantry was well disciplined and well trained compared to the Numidian peasants and the new, untrained recruits that Carthaginians were able to obtain on short notice. The 4,000 Celtiberians that had arrived from Spain were hard, trained mercenaries, the best foot-soldiers now available to Hasdrubal.

Using a variation of tactics that Hannibal used at Cannae, Scipio had his two cavalries attack their Carthaginian counterparts. They quickly routed the two cavalries on Hasdrubal's flanks, encircled his infantry, then attacked the Carthaginian army from all sides at once. They eventually annihilated the entire African infantry, like shooting ducks in a pond, just as Hannibal did at Cannae. Hasdrubal had his raw recruits in his front infantry ranks, and they quickly crumbled under the onslaught of Scipio's disciplined legionnaires. The 4,000 tough, proud Celtiberians that Hasdrubal had positioned in the rear ranks of his infantry fought gallantly, choosing to die with sword in hand rather than be taken prisoner and thus forced to live a life in slavery. Syphax and a few of his horse troops fled to Cirta, capital of Numidia. Hasdrubal was also able to escape to Carthage with a few of his cavalry.

Scipio had two great lieutenants, Masinissa, and

Laelius, whom he quickly dispatched to follow the fleeing Numidian cavalry of Syphax back to Cirta. Masinissa's fleet cavalry advanced into Numidia, followed by the fast-moving cohorts of Laelius to back him up. They conquered Cirta and captured Syphax. Masinissa also captured his former betrothed, Sophonisba. Masinissa married her and spent many days with his enchantress in an intensive honeymoon.

Afterward, Masinissa returned to Utica where he was reprimanded by Scipio for his marriage to his enemy's daughter. The Roman commander warned him of the danger of mixing emotion with business, and he reminded him that Sophonisba was a Roman prisoner who must be sent to Rome. He told Masinissa that he should not risk losing everything he had gained for the sake of a woman. Scipio had promised, previously, to make him King of Numidia.

In sadness, the young prince returned to his bride with a cup of hemlock. He told her that she had two choices: she could die as his wife by taking the hemlock, or live and be sent as a slave to Rome. She had hated Romans all of her life and feared the treatment she would receives from them, so she drank the hemlock and died in Masinissa's arms. As a reward, Scipio proclaimed him the King of Numidia, as promised, and gave him a gold crown, ivory scepter, a chariot of state, embroidered robe, and a rich tunic. It cheered up the new king. The captive Syphax was sent to Rome with other prisoners of war.

This was the bleak military situation that faced Hannibal, who was about to return to Africa. However, the political antics taking place in Carthage were even more bizarre than the military antics. Carthage was in turmoil, expecting Scipio to invade the city at any time. Frantic preparations for a siege began. It was at this time, in 203 B.C., that Carthage sent ships to recall Hannibal and Mago, its last remaining hope for defending the country. When Scipio's army had arrived in Africa, it put the Carthaginian Senate in a state of panic. In the hectic political discussions that followed, four courses of action for the government to take were identified: (1) start peace negotiations with the Romans; (2) prepare for a siege; (3) recall Hannibal and Mago to defend Carthage; and (4) attack the Roman fleet supporting Scipio's army. All four courses of action were adopted, to be pursued independently of one another, though simultaneously, each under the direction of separate officials. No provision was made to coordinate their separate activities.

The Carthaginian Senate ordered the naval attack on the Roman fleet supporting Scipio's army, incredibly, at the same time peace negotiators were sent to Scipio's camp to arrange for peace. Before the Carthaginian peace envoys arrived in his camp, Scipio began moving his army south toward Tunis, nearer Carthage only fifteen miles away, to make preparations for a Roman siege of Carthage. While Scipio was having his army dig in at Tunis, he saw a large Carthaginian fleet of warships headed north toward his other camp near Utica where his own fleet of ships was moored. What he saw was the Punic navy sailing north to attack his fleet as the Carthaginian Senate had ordered.

At the same time, peace negotiators were coming to Scipio's camp to arrange a peace settlement. Before the peace envoys could arrive in his camp, Scipio rapidly marched his troops back north to his old camp, arriving before the Carthaginian fleet arrived. He made a floating rampart of his transport ships by tying them together in front of his warships, as a buffer to protect them because his warships were unprepared for battle. This made his warships inaccessible to the enemy warships. When the Carthaginian navy finally arrived and attacked the Roman fleet, it was only able to cut away and capture a few of the transports, none of the warships. Scipio's warships were thus saved by his quick action, but Scipio was back in his original camp near Utica, further away from Carthage.

At that time in 203 B.C., Carthaginian peace envoys finally reached Scipio's camp. They humbly bowed to the earth with great apologies and contrition, explaining that their entire war against Rome was solely Hannibal's fault, and that he started the war without authorization from Carthage. They claimed that Carthage was an innocent victim of Hannibal's actions. (This was contrary to the facts, as it ignored that the Carthaginian Senate had declared war on Rome in front of Roman envoys in 218 B.C.)

Scipio laid down stiff peace terms for the humble Punic envoys. The terms required Carthage to withdraw from Italy, Spain, and all Mediterranean islands; surrender all of its warships except twenty; pay a war indemnity of 5,000 talents of silver; supply Rome with 500,000 units (modi) of wheat and 300,000 units of barley; and return all Roman deserters and prisoners. Scipio stated he did not have authority to officially accept peace terms, and that he would have the envoys escorted to the Roman Senate in Italy for final acceptance and the necessary signing of the peace treaty. It was agreed that an armistice in the fighting would be observed during the negotiating process. The Carthaginians gratefully accepted the terms and went to Rome, arriving soon after Hannibal and Mago had left Italy for Africa.

The Roman Senate listened to the Carthaginian's repeated claim that Hannibal, not Carthage, was responsible for the war. The senators did not believe it because they knew that their envoys in Carthage had witnessed the Carthaginian Senate's declaration of war on Rome and Carthaginians had given a strong rebuff to Roman emissaries in 218 B.C. There was considerable debate in the Roman Senate and there was general skepticism about the true intent of Carthage in seeking the peace. The senators knew that Hannibal and Mago had left Italy for Africa and suspected that the Carthaginian government was consolidating its forces in Africa to defeat Scipio's army. Senators suspected that the peace request was a ploy to give Carthaginians more time to prepare for war. The Senate decided to approve Scipio's proposed peace terms, but it gave Scipio authority to act on his own discretion if he decided to follow another course of action in the event that Carthage did not appear to be living up to the agreement.

While these negotiations were in progress, the elderly Fabius Maximus, Scipio's most powerful opponent, died. Elections were immediately held to replace him. The Senate, in the election process, did not vote to reappoint Scipio as commander in Africa. The Senate, not a strong supporter of Scipio, referred Scipio's status to the Peoples' Assembly, and he was returned as commander in Africa by an overwhelming vote of the common people, much to the dismay of many senators.

While peace envoys were still in Rome trying to get the Italian Senate to agree to the treaty terms, and the declared armistice was still in effect, a convoy of Roman ships full of supplies intended for Utica, to support Scipio, was confiscated at the direction of the Carthaginian government. The convoy, consisting of 200 transport vessels and ten escorting warships, ran into strong winds that blew most of them off their courses. Although the crews of the vessels fought the strong winds by rowing as hard as they could with their oars, most of the ships were blown ashore and scattered around the bay where Carthage was located. The event caused excitement among citizens of the town when they saw the Roman crews abandon their ships and leave their valuable cargoes on the beaches near Carthage. The Senate in Carthage hastily called a meeting at which boisterous citizens demanded that the rich spoils be confiscated from the Romans. The Senate, after a debate in which only a few of the aristocrats paid any note to the fact that seizing the Roman vessels would be a breach of the armistice, ordered that the ships and their cargoes be collected and brought to Carthage as their own.

When Scipio heard of this, he sent representatives to Carthage to protest the confiscation of his supply ships. His representatives were treated rudely and were laughed at by unruly citizens in the streets of Carthage. City officials barely rescued them from physical harm by the unruly mob of citizens in the streets. Soon afterward, the Roman envoys were told of the government's decision to confiscate the ships and their cargoes. The Peoples' Assembly, separate from the aristocratic Senate, tore up the peace treaty under the disgusted eyes of Scipio's agents. The envoys were then escorted by ship to within sight of the Roman camp, but as soon as the Carthaginian escort vessels left the envoy's Roman ship, other Carthaginian ships that happened to be in the area attacked the Roman envoy's ship. Carthaginian sailors succeeded in wrecking the Roman ships, and Scipio's agents were barely able to scramble back to their camp and report their harrowing experiences to Scipio. Scipio and his staff were irate over their treatment.

It was soon after this experience that the Carthaginian peace envoys and their Roman escorts returned from Rome to meet with Scipio. They were unaware of the supply-ship experience. They carried Rome's approval of the peace treaty to Scipio, with the Roman Senate's instructions. Scipio told the envoys that Carthage had broken the armistice. He angrily told them that their actions of contrition, and their acts of humbly prostrating themselves on the ground and apologizing for the war, had no relationship to the actual mob conditions that his Roman agents had seen during their trip to Carthage. These actions meant that Carthage had elected war and that the peace treaty was merely a ploy to gain time to consolidate defenses of Carthage and give their forces in Italy time to return to Africa. He angrily sent the Carthaginian envoys back to Carthage with no peace treaty. The common people of Carthage did not really want peace anyway, because they knew that their great hero, Hannibal, was coming. They had full confidence in him. They did not know how hopelessly the military situation had deteriorated, with their armed forces already decimated by Scipio. Even the great Hannibal could do very little with such a pitiful force against the powerful army commanded by Scipio, particularly his large, efficient cavalry.

Chapter 10

EVENTS IN AFRICA AFTER HANNIBAL ARRIVES (203 - 195 B.C.)

Hannibal landed the fleet carrying his army eighty miles south of Carthage to avoid being intercepted by Scipio's fleet which was in the north. He established his winter camp at Hadrumetum. He was returning to Carthage as an undefeated general and hero of the common people. Although he still had many enemies in the Carthaginian government, he was their only remaining hope for the defense of Carthage under the pitiful circumstances that his government had created for itself. He had the only trained, veteran soldiers available to defend his homeland.

As small as his army now was, it was the only hope Carthage had to protect it from Scipio's strong forces. The masses of common people hailed him as their savior. The Assembly of the People elected him to a position that was practically a dictator, and he immediately took charge of the few military resources that remained in Carthage. He integrated them into his meager army of 12,000 veterans he had brought from Italy, and he began, furiously, to recruit soldiers. He knew he was going to be dangerously short of cavalry because he didn't have enough ships to bring the small number of horsemen remaining in Italy when he left for Africa. He was expecting to recruit a large number of cavalrymen in Numidia to augment his troops, but as soon as he learned of the disastrous battles where Scipio had recently annihilated the entire Numidian and Carthaginian armies, he knew the cavalry would not be available as planned.

Upon hearing of Hannibal's arrival, and as soon as the spring made suitable foraging crops available for the animals, Scipio moved his four legions (23,000 infantry and 2,400 cavalry) southwest along the Bagradas Valley. Scipio was hoping to meet Masinissa' forces coming to join him from Cirta before he had to confront Hannibal. Masinissa's army had grown to 6,000 horse-soldiers and 4,000 infantry, and at Scipio's request, he was moving his army northeast to meet him. Scipio didn't want to attack Hannibal until he had the entire cavalry of 8,400 horses available because his agents told him that Hannibal would be critically short of cavalry. Roman forces would have a combined total of 35,400 men after he joined Masinissa. Romans foraged and plundered the land, the granary of Carthage, as they moved.

Scipio had received word that consul Tiberius Claudius Nero had been designated "Imperator" by his political enemies in the Roman Senate. This gave Nero a rank equal to Scipio's, and Scipio also learned that Nero was on his way to Africa with fifty warships and 100 supply transports to share his command. This made Scipio anxious to decide the war, if he could, before Nero arrived to share the glory. Scipio wanted to have full command and receive all the glory from the victory over Hannibal, which he was confident of achieving. After all, he was the one who had fought so hard to get his plan for invading Carthage approved, and this was just another way his political enemies in Rome had to dilute his glory. They were afraid of his growing power with the Roman people. Rome could have sent the supply ships without the Imperator to share his command.

Hannibal was able to obtain 2,000 crude, untrained cavalry soldiers from Tychaeus, a relative of Syphax. Ligurians and Gauls from Mago's army of northern Italy straggled into Hannibal's camp during the next few months and there was a hasty conscription of Carthaginians. King Philip of Macedonia sent 4,000 soldiers of questionable ability. A few Carthaginian cavalry soldiers were speedily assembled. Hannibal succeeded in obtaining eighty elephants, more than he ever had for one battle, but they were untrained, and new to military duties.

Recruiting took so much of the time before springtime arrived that there wasn't much time to train and coordinate the motley aggregation of men who arrived in Hannibal's camp, once they were finally assembled. Gisco, Cirta, and the rest of Hannibal's veterans did the best they could under the circumstance, but most new soldiers and animals had no military experience, and the training had to be limited to the most basic possible. A total force of 50,000 was finally collected in the Carthaginian camp, but most were poorly trained and undisciplined.

By early spring, when his scouts told him that Scipio had moved his army southwest to meet Masinissa who was coming from the Cirta, moving northeast, Hannibal decided to try to meet Scipio's army before it could join up with the Numidian forces. He knew that it would be much better to fight the two armies separately, even in the present weakened condition of his army, rather than fight after they had combined their forces. Hannibal rapidly moved his army in a direction that would cut across Scipio's line of march, hoping to intercept him before Masinissa arrived. Hannibal made camp near Zama which was southwest of Carthage, near the line Scipio was taking up the Bagradas River to meet Masinissa.

Citizens of Rome and Carthage, indeed the entire world, became excited with anticipation of the coming battle between the two greatest living commanders and the two armies of the richest countries of the world. Scipio and Hannibal were the most successful and popular military generals of the known world, and they fired the imaginations of people everywhere by their highly publicized and closely followed exploits. High stakes rested on the outcome of this momentous clash. It was probably to be the final battle to decide who would dominate the Mediterranean in the future, Rome by military power or Carthage by commercial trade. If Scipio won, Rome would rule, and if the great Hannibal won, he would be able to continue Carthage's battle against Roman domination.

Hannibal had a better picture of the military and strategic situation than any other Carthaginian. He discussed his options with Gisco at length, almost thinking out loud, but he also did this to draw out Gisco's thoughts on his view of the critical predicament in which they now found themselves. They reviewed all alternative courses of action Hannibal could take, in minute detail. They decided that the odds against their motley troops ever defeating the powerful troops of Scipio, especially with his strong cavalry, were very great. In the best case scenario, if Carthage were to win the battle at Zama, other Roman forces were on their way which they would have to defeat next. More Roman soldiers were now available from Italy. Now that Carthage no longer had the abundant resources available to it from the provinces in Spain - the manpower and silver - Hannibal could not be able to compete with Romans on the battlefield.

Hannibal decided that he should attempt to negotiate peace terms with Scipio before the coming battle. Beside avoiding much needless bloodshed, he expected to get better terms of peace from Scipio, a known humanitarian and more prone to rational negotiations, than from other commanders who would follow him. Indeed, Hannibal had a reserved respect for Scipio's military ability, based on the reports his agents gave him about the Roman commander.

Gisco and Hannibal discussed another facet of the situation, the fact that Hannibal's army had a great numerical superiority - 50,000 against 34,400. Since Scipio was unable to sec all the weaknesses in the Carthaginian army that Hannibal knew about, Hannibal may be able to finesse better terms from him before Scipio learned the facts, if he wasn't already aware of them.

Scipio played a game of finesse himself. Three of Hannibal's spies were captured by Scipio's men, and instead of executing them in the normal manner, Scipio ordered that they be shown around his camp so they could see his full strength and make a complete report back to Hannibal. Masinissa's men had already arrived in Scipio's camp, so the size of his total forces were now very impressive. When his spies returned to him, Hannibal became concerned about Scipio's huge superiority in cavalry. He and his officers quickly developed the best strategy for making the most of the bad situation.

Hannibal and his officers made a plan that would neutralize this superiority in cavalry, if their poorly trained military forces could carry it out. The plan required Hannibal's troops to defeat his own strategy of envelopment that he had used at Cannae. He expected Scipio to use the Cannae envelopment tactic against the Carthaginian army in the coming battle because it made the best use of the superior number of mounted troops. Reports that Hannibal had received from agents told him that Scipio had already started to use the encirclement tactics in Spain.

Hannibal wanted to learn more about his adversary, and he wanted to try to negotiate reasonable peace terms from a face-to-face meeting with Scipio before they resorted to bloody combat. He wanted to try talking Scipio out of the battle. He also thought that he might be able to intimidate the young Roman commander into agreeing to more favorable peace terms for Carthage. Hannibal sent messengers to the Roman camp with the official request that the two commanders have a private meeting to discuss alternatives to battle. Scipio agreed, and suspecting another Carthaginian trick, he carefully designated the time and place. The two commanders moved their armies within four miles of one another at a site that was flat so that the two generals could meet between the two opposing forces on an open plain in full view of everyone. The plain was still green from recent spring rains. Each commander rode to the center of the plain with one interpreter, and it was Gisco who rode along with Hannibal as his language interpreter. Soon, the men dismounted and approached each other on foot. Hannibal was older and taller than Scipio.

Neither great commander spoke for some moments after they met, as each observed the other with great curiosity. Since Hannibal was the one who had requested the meeting, he was the first to speak. Although he knew Latin, Hannibal elected to speak in

Greek to allow himself extra time to think while Scipio's interpreter changed the words to Latin, Scipio's native tongue, then Gisco translated his response in Latin to Greek. Hannibal began with smooth, courteous phrases and he complimented Scipio on his many glorious victories. He added that he, too, had many victories, including one over Scipio's father at Trebbia. He said it was a shame their two great countries, Rome and Carthage, ever allowed themselves to seek possessions outside their own natural boundaries. He said they should find some means of settling their differences peaceably. Hannibal said he would not have proposed peace unless he knew that it was the best alternative for both Scipio and himself. He said that his experience in warfare had taught him how fast fortunes of war could change, and that each of them knew how any one of the hundreds of vicissitudes of each battle could cause the entire outcome to turn unexpectedly in either direction.

Hannibal continued by telling Scipio that the great Roman commander had nothing to win by a bloody victory in the coming battle, and everything to lose by defeat. He said that he was willing to agree to peace terms, and personally enforce them, which stated that Carthage leave to Rome all of Sicily, Sardinia, Spain, and all the islands between Africa and Italy, in return for the withdrawal of the Roman army from Africa, and lasting peace. Furthermore, Hannibal continued, all the victories and glories that Scipio had already won, up to now, could be erased in the coming battle, the outcome of which depended upon the fickle fortunes of war. He told him that if Romans won, Scipio would not gain much more than he could have by agreeing to peace. If he lost, he would lose everything. Hannibal said that the Roman Senate would approve any terms accepted by Scipio, as was stated in the already approved instructions from Rome. Hannibal admitted there had been a lack of sincerity in his government's recent request for peace and in its failure to maintain the armistice, but now it was Hannibal who was asking for peace. He, Hannibal, would keep the peace and live up to its terms. He told Scipio that Carthage would accept terms that Hannibal approved, and he, Hannibal, the current head of the government, would enforce them.

When Hannibal had finished talking, Scipio started his statement by saying he knew the news of Hannibal's return to Carthage was what had emboldened his government to break the armistice. He continued saying that he could not reward Carthaginian politicians for their dishonesty, and that Hannibal was asking for peace terms better than those broken by them. If before Hannibal had come to Africa, he had approached Scipio with peace terms, he might have been given serious consideration. However, now that Scipio had forced him to come here to this battlefield from Italy, in spite of his reluctance, Scipio requires much more than the terms offered. Rome expected the minimum terms summarized in the previous peace treaty, as well as compensation for the ships and cargo Carthaginians took, or Hannibal and his men must be prepare to fight, Scipio continued. Scipio said that although he sympathized with Hannibal's position, he could not give Hannibal better terms than those to which his government in Rome had already agreed.

The greatest hang-up for Hannibal in the existing peace terms was the requirement to return all Roman deserters and defectors to Scipio, because many of these had been serving faithfully in his army for many years. He could not betray them. Because the two generals could not agree to peaceful terms, the dispute had to be settled by battle.

Hannibal then said that if Carthage won the coming battle, he would allow Scipio to depart Africa as soon as his peace terms, as he had just requested them, were accepted by Rome. If Scipio won, then Carthage would accept Scipio's terms. Scipio nodded in agreement with Hannibal's summary of the situation, and the two general's parted to prepare their armies for battle.

On returning to their armies, each general ordered his soldiers to return to their respective camps. In their camps, each commander made inspiring speeches to his men and ordered them to prepare for battle the next morning. Scipio adopted Hannibal's tactic of telling his men that they were in a foreign land with only two alternative courses of action: either fight and win, or fight to the death in a losing battle. To lose and live meant a life of slavery under barbarians, and thus it was worse than death.

Hannibal went from unit to unit talking to his men. He had a much more difficult time than Scipio, giving instructions, coordinating actions, and motivating his inexperienced soldiers to fight to the death. His newly organized, polyglot assortment of undisciplined and untrained soldiers all had different customs and values. Hannibal used different rewards for different groups to inspire them to fight with enthusiasm. Of course, all were given much inspiration to fight to retain their freedom, knowing if they lost the battle and were captured, they would be slaves the rest of their lives. Aside from that, Hannibal promised the Spanish retirement land in Spain and a share of the spoils. Ligurians responded to the promise of farm land in northern Italy, and Gauls hated Romans so much that they only wanted victory and a share in the spoils. Carthaginians were defending their homeland and families, and Numidians in Hannibal's army were afraid of Masinissa's revenge if he were to win. All were promised handsome pay and rewards. However, Hannibal impressed upon them that they had to win or die, as the alternative of losing and living was too horrible.

Hannibal's plan, to overcome his weakness in cavalry and the handicap of having mostly untrained infantry, involved the use of his eighty elephants in a massive charge, lined abreast, to break up the lines of the legionnaires. He hoped that the elephant charge would decimate the Roman formations and demoralize the Roman soldiers before Scipio's cavalry could route his own meager cavalry, then encircle his own infantry. His only hope was to defeat the Roman infantry before Scipio's huge number of horse-mounted troops were able to return from their rout of his own cavalry.

Hannibal had Cirta instruct his cavalry commanders about tactics they were to use as delaying tactics, to prolong the advance of the strong Roman cavalry, then lead the enemy cavalry away from the battlefield as far as possible to allow time for the elephants to do their job. It was about the only tactic he could use under such unfavorable conditions. His plan was to follow the elephant attack with launches of lines of Gauls and Ligurians in the first wave. The second wave would be composed of African and Carthaginian conscripts, all of whom were untried, untrained, and largely undisciplined. After these, his own hardened veterans he had brought from Italy would be sent against the legionnaires, whom he expected to be tired by this time. It was hoped that this hard pounding, the elephants followed by the waves of superior numbers of foot-soldiers, could cause the smaller Roman infantry to collapse before Scipio's cavalry returned from the rout of his own small cavalry. One factor, the limited supply of water, required Hannibal to depend on a quick victory. The water supply was behind Scipio's army.

The next morning, Scipio and Hannibal formed their battle lines before daybreak, facing one another. After some light skirmishing as the sun rose, Hannibal gave the signal for his elephants to begin their massive charge. Scipio had anticipated this, and he prepared for it by developing ingenious tactics recommended by the astute Masinissa who was intimately familiar with warfare using elephants. Africans had used elephants in battle for hundreds of years, and Masinissa was well acquainted with tactics that could be used against them. Scipio's plan, as recommended by Masinissa, required the first line of Roman infantry to bolt to the rear of the legionnaires' lines to safety at the first charge of the elephants. Next, Scipio instructed his maniples to form their ranks by leaving large gaps, or alleys, between them. Soldiers were instructed to channel the charging elephants into these alleys by shouting and clanking their armor to frighten them, and then legionnaires were to attack the flanks of the huge beasts as they passed by in the alleys between maniples.

When Hannibal gave the signal for his eighty elephants to attack, and the ferocious hulks came charging menacingly at the Roman lines, Roman soldiers let out a coordinated blast on all trumpets and bugles assembled near the front of their lines. In addition, all Roman soldiers let out uproarious war cries to frighten the poor beasts. Scipio's plan worked. Hannibal's poorly trained elephants, unaccustomed to war and the tumult, panicked, and some of the unruly beasts charged into their own men in the left wing of the Carthaginian line. Other elephants were able to charge as expected, and they inflicted severe damage on Roman soldiers by crushing them and tossing them around with their trunks. However, most of the great beasts were channeled into the gaps in the Roman formations, as Scipio had intended, and received the cross fire as they passed between the Roman maniples on their flanks. Most of the elephants lumbered out of the combat zone and scattered about the countryside to get away from the turmoil behind them, uncontrollable by their mahouts, never to return to the battle.

Then, the Roman first line advanced toward the Carthaginian first line, and the Gauls and Ligurians held fast at first, strengthened by archers and Balearic slingers. After a fierce battle, Hannibal's first line was broken and thrown back into his second line of Carthaginian and African conscripts. This second line found themselves fighting their own first rank of soldiers who were turning around and coming into them as they fled the Romans in panic. Heaps of bodies, dead and wounded, severed limbs, and other parts of bodies littered the battleground in slippery pools of blood. Hannibal's second line was hesitant to advance because of the confusion and the carnage before them. They finally broke their lines in the face of the tough, disciplined legionnaires, and this brought the Romans face-to-face with Hannibal's tough, fresh, well-disciplined and well-equipped veterans of Cannae in the third line. The advancing Romans, tired and severely wounded by coming through Hannibal's first two lines, now faced a different kind of army, and their fiercest fighting was about to begin.

Scipio saw this and recalled his army to regroup and rest. He ordered them to collect their weapons and pass back the wounded. Scipio's cavalry had not returned from its chase of Hannibal's horsemen over the plains, and this was also a delay to allow more time for his cavalry to return. He formed his second and third lines on the flanks of the first Roman line. This made his three long lines of soldiers overlap Hannibal's surviving line of veterans. The ensuing fight was ferocious and bitter. There was no retreating. Hannibal's veterans were clearly beginning to gain the momentum of the battle in their favor. However, just as Hannibal's veterans of the Italian campaign were starting to force the legionnaires back by their strong effort, Scipio's cavalry returned from its chase of the Carthaginian horses. Masinissa and the rest of the Roman horsemen began to attack Hannibal's veterans in the rear, and the entire tide of battle suddenly changed. It was Cannae in reverse. More than 20,000 of Hannibal's army were killed and the same number were captured that day. Romans reported losing only 1,500.

Gisco, Cirta, and a few other mounted officers gathered around Hannibal, and when they were convinced that Hannibal did all within his power to direct the fighting, they forcibly convinced him to leave the battlefield. Gisco persuaded him that he had much more work to do to prepare Carthage for the inevitable siege, and that he must now prepare the last line of defense for the city of Carthage. Gisco also reminded Hannibal about the tacit agreement he had made with Scipio at their meeting before the battle and that he should be able to work out honorable peace terms to avoid further bloodshed. Hannibal was feeling down at heart from the loss of so many of his good men, but he saw the logic in Gisco's argument. He must now work for what was best for Carthage.

Reluctantly, Hannibal departed the battlefield with the small party of eight trusted officers Gisco had organized. As they were riding to the southeast, headed for their camp at Hadrumetum ninety miles away to collect the garrison of troops left there, a squadron of Masinissa's cavalry began to pursue them. The Numidians were originally three hundred yards behind Hannibal's group when they started chasing them, but they gradually gained ground on the departing group.

A few of the fastest Numidian horses pulled out ahead of their comrades in the chase. The trail they were following soon left the plain and entered an area of small rolling hills. The trail narrowed as it climbed up an inclined ravine, and it became so narrow that only two horses could ride abreast along it. The leading Numidian horses continued to gain ground on them. Gisco signaled to Cirta and four other officers who were known to be good fighters, motioning for them to turn around to attack the Numidians coming up the hill. This would delay the Numidians enough so that Hannibal could get a safe distance away before they were able to resume the chase.

The six Carthaginians turned around and started down the trail at full gallop, two abreast, with Gisco and Cirta in the lead, to meet the oncoming Numidians head-on as they climbed up the hill. Gisco knew that he would only have to face two Numidians at a time as they came up the ravine because that was all the trail would allow. Gisco and Cirta charged recklessly into the startled Numidians, followed closely by the other four Carthaginians. There was a thunderous clash as horses, men, and armor collided. The fierceness of Gisco's sudden reversal and his savage attack down the narrow trail stunned the pursuing Numidians. Gisco and Cirta, leading the group, had the great advantage of momentum they gained by charging their mounts downhill at full gallop, as well as the element of surprise by their sudden aggressiveness. The two companions from Athens succeeded in crumbling the leading six pursuers in a massive pileup of horses and men. The first three Numidians were severely wounded by the initial wielding of weapons by Gisco and Cirta, and three others were thrown violently from their mounts as their horses piled into the horses that had been knocked to the ground by the massive collision. Two riderless horses turned and stampeded down the narrow trail, with Gisco's encouragement, into the other Numidians coming up the narrow trail. The four Carthaginian officers following Gisco and Cirta finished off the dismounted Numidians, as Gisco and Cirta climbed back on their stunned animals. They followed the riderless horses down the trail to engage the next group of Numidians that might be coming up.

Seeing what had happened to their six comrades ahead, the best fighters of their squadron, and seeing the fierceness of Gisco's and Cirta's attack, as well as the riderless horses coming downhill toward them, convinced the remainder of the Numidian squadron to flee. They decided to abandon the chase to return to the main battlefield where there was easier prey and rich spoils.

Both, Gisco and Cirta were badly wounded in the melee, but they were able to turn their mounts around and head toward their intended destination where they hoped to rejoin Hannibal. Night fell before they were able to catch up with the other group, and they decided to get a night's rest before continuing their journey in the morning. It had been a long day, since before daybreak that morning, and there had been fierce fighting at Zama before the evening's encounter in the ravine. They were all sore from their bruises and wounds, and very tired.

In the morning, when Gisco attempted to wake Cirta to continue their journey, he discovered that his beloved comrade was laying in a huge pool of blood, dead. His wounds had been more severe than anyone had suspected. Gisco sorrowfully tied the limp body of his lifelong friend to his horse and led him along the trail to meet Hannibal.

Hannibal was very saddened by the loss of Gisco's faithful and cherished companion who had been with him for more than eighteen years. He came to admire and respect his ability, and he had come to love Cirta and his distinctive limp almost as much as Gisco loved him. As harassed as he was, and as depressed as he felt about the loss of his army, Cirta was given the best burial possible under the circumstances. Gisco and Hannibal spent time making sacrifices to the gods in a sacred temple.

Hannibal sent a messenger to the Carthaginian Senate to report results of the battle at Zama. He reported the number of soldiers he had at Hadrumetum, and he told authorities in Carthage he believed he could arrange satisfactory peace terms with Scipio to avoid further fighting and to avoid the sack of Carthage. Hannibal also said that if the Senate elected to continue fighting, he would make his troops available to shore up the defenses of the city. Hannibal reported that he, personally, had no illusions about continuing the fighting with success against the strong, combined Roman and Numidian forces.

Hannibal was eagerly recalled to Carthage, and

due to his strong character, he arrived in the city with as much assurance, poise, and determination as though he had been the victor at Zama. Hannibal knew he had done all that could have been done on the battlefield with the resources he had available. He had also tried to avoid the battle entirely in his meeting with Scipio. Most common people of Carthage realized he had done the best that he could have done, and they knew he had tried to avoid bloodshed completely during his negotiations with Scipio before the fight. The common people received him in the city as their savior and only hope, and the Assembly of the People elected him as a virtual dictator. Many aristocrats in the Council of Elders (Senate) were still his enemies and blamed him for all their troubles. As commander of the army, he promptly told the Council that surrender was the only viable course of action to take, that to continue fighting would be a fruitless disaster.

The Council sent a party of thirty officials to confer with Scipio on peace terms. The party was even more humble and condescending than the party that had brought peace proposals to Scipio earlier, before the armistice was broken. Scipio, whether or not he was influenced by his meeting and tacit agreement with Hannibal before the battle at Zama, merely modified the previous terms agreed upon before Carthage broke the armistice. He added the following terms: Carthage was now required to give Rome all of its warships except ten, instead of being allowed to keep twenty as previously agreed upon; all elephants were to be given to Rome, and Carthage was not allowed to train more for war; instead of war indemnity of 5,000 talents of silver, this amount was increased to 10,000, to be paid over a period of fifty years; Carthage must give Rome 100 hostages between the ages of fourteen and thirty-one years of age as security for keeping the peace terms; the Roman ships and cargo seized by Carthage before Zama were to be returned; Carthage must agree not to wage war in the future, anywhere, without approval of Rome; and Carthage must agree to be a friend and ally of Rome.

When these terms were read to the Assembly of the People in Carthage, one die-hard participant rose before it to recommend that the peace treaty be rejected and that Carthage rearm to fight on. These words made Hannibal irate. He was exasperated by the fact that some weak politician was attempting to force continuation of the war - after all the slaughter he had seen, and with the hopelessness of the military situation as he knew it. Hannibal rapidly went from his seat in the audience up to the rostrum where the man was speaking. He roughly ejected the man from the rostrum with considerable force, to the loud cheers of the viewers. He then apologized to the Assembly for his lack of protocol, but he said that he had been away from Carthage for thirty-six years, since he was nine years old, and he was not familiar with political procedures. He then told the gathering that it was necessary to accept the treaty as the only alternative to disaster. He said that the terms offered by Scipio were much better, under the circumstances, than Carthaginians should expect. Acceptance of the peace treaty would allow Carthage to rebuild its country and regain its prosperity. Again, there was a loud cheer of approval from the audience, and the peace terms were overwhelmingly accepted by Carthage.

When the treaty was sent to Rome to be signed, there was some opposition from Scipio's political enemies and much political bickering in the Senate concerning the lenient terms that Scipio had stipulated. Scipio's enemies thought the terms too soft, and he became impatient with the contemptuous politicians who habitually opposed everything that pertained to his operations earlier (similar to the political faction in the Carthaginian Senate that habitually opposed anything that pertained to Hannibal or the Barcas). Scipio threatened to sign the treaty himself, and make it official if there was much more delay in its ratification. He said he had authority to approve it on the basis of authority given him by the Senate before Zama.

When the Senate had sent him the previous treaty, formally approved by it, Scipio was given authorization to modify its terms as he saw fit, because the Senate had suspected skullduggery by the Carthaginians. It was this authority to which Scipio referred in his threat. The peace terms were finally passed, thus the personal influence of Scipio and Hannibal resulted in the peace terms being accepted by their respective governments, just as Hannibal had suggested at their private meeting before the battle at Zama. By early 201 B.C., Hannibal saw to it that Carthage complied with all treaty responsibilities of the first year, and the last Roman soldier was withdrawn from Africa by Scipio. Hannibal then resigned as commander of the army.

Gisco was distressed by the loss of his lifelong friend, Cirta, who had been like a father to him, and by the loss of many friends at Zama. He told Hannibal he was going to take a prolonged vacation in Athens, after which he intended to return with his wife, Tarra, to live for a while in Carthage where they could be with Hannibal. Gisco had become excessively attached to the great Hannibal, after sharing so many indelible experiences with him for more than twenty years. Hannibal provided him with a fast transport vessel which quickly returned him to Athens. He found his affairs in Athens in good order and that he and his still beautiful wife continued to be very much in love. His son, now in his twenties, had grown to manhood and had married the beautiful Athenian daughter of a family business friend. Gisco was about to be made a grandfather. Tarra was interested in seeing Hannibal again, and she agreed to live in Carthage with Gisco for a short time, as long as they could return to be with their grandchild before too long. Gisco promised her that he would bring her back to Athens after a few years.

After Gisco left Carthage for Athens, Hannibal found himself in a strange country and amidst strangers. He had not been in Carthage since he was nine, and everything was new to him. Suddenly he came face-to-face with his lifelong political enemies, the Hannos (the anti-Barca faction in Carthaginian politics). They had done all they could to prevent his country from supporting him, when he believed that he could have quickly finished the war in Italy with proper support from them. These wealthy politicians were responsible for his government's slow response at meeting the demands of the war which it had proclaimed, until it was too little, too late. The Barcas blamed the Hanno faction's foot-dragging for the disastrous loss of the war. The Hanno faction blamed Hannibal and the Barcas for the war and all of their problems.

In Carthaginian history, it was the anti-Barca faction, the Hannos, all powerful aristocrats, who were most powerful in Carthaginian politics. The Hannos were originally backers of General Hanno who campaigned in Africa, to the west of Carthage, while General Hamilcar Barca, Hannibal's father, campaigned overseas in Sicily. The two generals competed in Carthaginian politics for their government's resources to support their efforts, the Hannos for Africa and the Barcas for Sicily. The fierce political competition between these factions carried over into all other matters of state.

The government in Carthage was controlled by an oligarchy of its wealthiest citizens in a Council of Elders (a "Senate" with 104 members) who served for life. Within the Council was a panel of judges elected by the Council members from among its own membership, and these judges had most power over all organs of government. These judges expected to profit from their positions in government, and there was widespread corruption and waste. The Council controlled the actions of military commanders such as Hannibal and his father. It was on this Council that the Hannos and Barcas had their fierce debates. Generals were feared, historically, by the trader-merchants as potential overthrowers of the government.

After the war in Sicily, Hannibal's father, Hamilcar, had gone to Spain where he created a virtual dictatorship for himself there, getting out from under most of the oppressive controls of the Council which opposed almost every proposed change for the better in Carthage. Over the centuries, the Council had evolved into an enormous power in the Carthaginian government, and it succeeded in strangling almost every new idea or method that was proposed for Carthage by anyone. It had become the real instrument for delaying or blocking support for Hannibal in Italy. Membership on the Council of Thirty was carefully controlled by the wealthy merchant-traders so that the government would continue a basic philosophy approved by the Council. Hannibal and the Barcas were aristocrats. Having resigned his post as commander of the army, but still recognized as first citizen of Carthage by the people, he wanted to participate in the governing of his country. By popular demand of the Assembly of the People, which still hailed him as a hero, he was given a ranking position on the Council of Thirty. This was much to the dismay of many of his political enemies who could not overcome the strong pressure to put Hannibal on the Council.

Gisco and Tarra arrived in Carthage the next year and there was a joyful reunion of the old friends. Hannibal was genuinely elated to see Gisco because he had become his close friend and confidant. But there was more to it than that. Hannibal felt that he was an outsider in Carthage, and Gisco was someone whom he genuinely liked and could trust completely. He had great confidence in Gisco's judgment.

Hannibal confided in Gisco about his anxiety over the waste and corruption in the Carthaginian government. Hannibal could not abide it, and he was used to taking quick action to correct wrongs whenever he saw them. He said that in his former army he could put things straight quickly by issuing orders and punishing the corrupt offenders. But here in Carthaginian politics, with people used to doing business in a corrupt, unjust way for hundreds of years, things were much more difficult to straighten out. First, he did not have the dictatorial power that he had in his well-disciplined army (though he seldom had to use it in the army). He told Gisco he needed his help to develop plans to reform the government, eliminate the corruption, and make it as fair in its administration as the fairness with which he had administered his army. He said he needed Gisco's great knowledge and ability to help him put things right in Carthage as quickly as possible, and to return his country to prosperity. Together, Hannibal and Gisco mapped out a plan to gather as much information as they could about the economy and the politics of Carthage to be used as a basis for their planned actions. Hannibal was used to having a constant flow of intelligence as a basis for making his decisions, and the two old friends began to establish an intelligence network that he could use to help him solve his current problems. As a member of the Council of Thirty, Hannibal had unusual powers to obtain information about the government. Hannibal and Gisco started by personally visiting all parts of the country, talking to people in all walks of life, farmers, merchants, local government officials, and requesting suggestions for improvement from all Carthaginian citizens. Gisco helped by keeping detailed records and by auditing local accounts that dealt with tax collection and expenditures of the government.

A major break for Hannibal came when Rome received the first shipment of silver as payment for the war indemnity as required by the peace treaty. The Roman Senate discovered that the silver was assayed at only three-fourths of what was required by the treaty. That is, it was one-fourth too little, having been diluted by a cheaper base metal. Carthaginian envoys in Rome who had delivered the silver were surprised and embarrassed by this fraud attempted by someone in their government. They hastily borrowed enough money on the local market to make up the shortfall. When he heard of this, Hannibal became irate, and by virtue of his position on the Council, he probed the scandal to see who was responsible for the fraud. During his investigation, an officer in the Carthaginian treasury administration refused to answer Hannibal's questions. The treasury officer misjudged the will of Hannibal, because the great veteran commander soon had the man arrested, exposed before the Assembly, and prosecuted for fraud. Further investigation revealed that the treasury official and most others responsible for the fraud were members of the anti-Barca faction, but a few were from his own Barca faction.

This fraud was only the tip of the iceberg. Information that he and Gisco had gathered pointed up numerous other such areas of corruption, and in the next few years Hannibal was responsible for making great reforms in government. Carthage soon became a prosperous country again. However, almost every reform he brought about in Carthage caused the gulf between himself and his enemies to widen further. His reforms even caused some of his fellow aristocrats and former supporters in the Barca faction to become alienated from him. Hannibal, an aristocrat, became a champion and hero of the common people, and he was responsible in the next few years for giving control of the government to the Assembly of the People, composed of the common people. He gave Carthage one of the most democratic governments in the Mediterranean area, but it cost him the enmity of most aristocrats, even many of his own Barcas.

Hannibal's next move, after the silver payment fraud exposure, was to convince the Assembly that the old government did not work properly. He told it that a change was needed. He convinced the Assembly of the People that members of the Council, who were presently irremovable, should be required to be elected annually. In a major coup against his enemies on the Council, the Assembly voted to make it so. Thus, the 104 members of the powerful Council of Elders had to become accountable to the common citizens who would elect them, and they had to be reelected every year. Hannibal had upset the ancient power structure of Carthage, whereby the aristocrats had a free hand to govern, and he had given more power to the common citizens. This further alienated him from his fellow noblemen. The chasm between himself and his fellow aristocrats became even wider as a result of many more individual situations. For example, Hannibal lived abstemiously and humbly, while his fellow noblemen, in contrast, had luxuriously furnished villas full of alabaster, silver utensils, glass-beaded curtains, luxurious cushions and mattresses, fancy wood furniture, many servants, houses filled with scent and myrrh, and wives richly dressed with pearls and expensive perfumes. They ate and drank expensive food and drink. Hannibal's austere customs, a holdover from his military training and experience, further set him apart from his luxury-loving fellow aristocrats.

Another circumstance that earned him the ire of the wealthy ruling class concerned the first shipment of silver to Rome. The Council, not Hannibal, decreed that the 16,000 pounds of silver would be raised by a tax on personal wealth. Hannibal's enemies claimed the tax was Hannibal's responsibility because he had started the war, and thus he was responsible for the war reparation payments to Rome. The members of both political factions, all aristocrats, were particularly indignant when they saw Hannibal laugh at them when he caught them complaining they had to make their tax payments. His enemies thought he was gloating. They believed he was laughing in revenge for the way they had treated his campaign during the war, particularly for their lack of support. Hannibal explained to them that he was laughing, not in revenge, but in irony because he saw them weeping at the least of their misfortunes. He said they had lost their army, navy, and most of all, the world power formerly enjoyed by Carthage. Their world power was passed to Rome, a tyrant, which would eventually be their undoing. Yet, they were only shedding tears for the insignificant part of their wealth that each of them had lost personally. Hannibal's political constituency in the government, now the common citizens, did not have to bear much tax burden because they had little wealth. Their political support for him was not diminished by the tax.

After a routine trip around his countryside, Hannibal made an astounding announcement to the Council that the tax on wealth would not be necessary to pay future installments of silver to the Romans. He said that they could be easily met from routine revenues if the graft was eliminated from the system. As Hannibal was in the habit of doing for his military campaigns, he continued to meticulously gather information about his homeland (as well as international developments from a widespread network of agents). A large share of his wealth went toward this effort. Hannibal's experience at managing the economy in Spain had given him many valuable ideas that he used to evaluate the economy of Carthage. Gisco's audit of the entire tax collection system had pointed up extensive graft, which would save considerable money. The same group that had tried to pass off inferior silver in payment to the Romans were skimming considerable funds from the tax collection system.

With these tax collection reforms, and with water

irrigation systems he was able to have built to develop new farmlands, his calculations indicated there would be sufficient revenues to easily pay off the annual silver debt. Hannibal had developed the new farmlands to provide farms for ex-soldiers in his army and restore areas that had been burned by the Romans during the war. Hannibal calculated that there was ample surplus in revenues to make annual payments to Rome and finance new government projects without the tax on wealth that the Council had ordered.

Because most of the graft was going to the aristocrats who were running the government in the past, these actions irreparably widened the chasm between himself and the noblemen. Hannibal gained overwhelming popular support from the masses of citizens, and they elected him Shofet, a virtual dictator, to push through his reforms in the government and build up his country's economy. As a result of these actions, and the fact that Carthage no longer had to support a large military force, its economy began to flourish - even with the large silver payments it had to make to Rome, and in spite of the fact that it had lost the rich silver mines in Spain.

While the Carthaginian economy was flourishing, and Carthage was becoming rich because its merchant-traders resumed trade routes to the great trading cities of the world, the economy of Rome, victors of the war, was declining. Rome became engaged in many more world conflicts which kept its citizen-soldier-farmers from tilling the land. These conflicts required the Roman people to continue to support a large military force at great expense. This burden seriously drained Rome's finances, coming as it did after the huge expense of fighting Carthaginians. It sapped Rome's prosperity. Various tribes in Spain became dissatisfied with Roman rule after Scipio left the country, and they began revolting, requiring Roman legions to put them down. As Scipio Africanus pulled his troops out of Africa, his legions were soon to fight a conflict with Macedonia. In the eastern Mediterranean, Antiochus, King of Syria, was trying to restore the kingdom of Alexander the Great with himself as ruler. King Attalus of Pergamum, a Roman ally, had requested Roman military protection from Antiochus.

Soon there was a serious blow to Hannibal's fortunes in Carthage. An officer who had been serving in Mago's army in northern Italy, and who had been badly wounded while fighting with Mago, was left behind when Mago's army sailed back to Carthage earlier. He was too weak to sail. When the officer recovered from his wounds much later, he organized and commanded a strong force of 40,000 Gauls and Ligurians, then proceeded to overrun Roman forts in northern Italy. There were heavy Roman losses, and Rome had to increase its legions in the area. The Roman Senate believed that the dreaded Hannibal, who was now running the government in Carthage, was responsible for directing this northern army. Rome told Carthage to recall this officer from northern Italy and cease directing the uprising in Cisalpine Gaul. The Carthaginian officer was a true renegade, and Carthage told Rome that it could only declare the officer an outlaw, as it had no power over him.

In Rome, Scipio spoke in favor of Hannibal on the Senate floor, saying that based on his knowledge of Hannibal and his integrity, he did not believe Hannibal would break the peace. Many in Rome were still suspicious of the intentions of Carthage while their fearsome antagonist for so many years, Hannibal, was running the country. Many in the Roman government were suspicious of the relationship that Scipio had developed with Hannibal and were critical of the fact that this perennial scourge of Rome was allowed to remain in Carthage after his defeat at Zama. Most of all, Romans were becoming jealous and wary of the growing prosperity and economic power that Carthage was developing in contrast to their own poor economy and growing financial problems. They suspected Hannibal had plans to renew his war against Rome as soon as Carthage was strong enough again. To most Romans, the name "Hannibal" struck terror in their hearts and minds, and many wanted him imprisoned or dead before they could feel safe from him.

Hannibal had no such intentions. However, his enemies in the anti-Barca party and other aristocrats who had been alienated from him by his reforms were anxious to be rid of him. They decided to exploit the situation. They secretly sent a delegation to Rome which told the Roman Senate that Hannibal was rebuilding Carthage to renew its military power to fight Rome again, in fulfillment of his lifelong sacred vow to hate Rome. They accused him of corresponding with Rome's enemies in Macedonia and with Antiochus in Syria. They also lied to the Senate, saying that Hannibal was directing the Carthaginian officer in Cisalpine Gaul. The Roman Senate decided to send a commission to Africa to investigate these accusations.

Hannibal's omniscient intelligence system kept him informed of these proceedings, and he made careful preparations to escape from Carthage before the commission arrived. He had no intention of being delivered into Roman hands by his Carthaginian enemies, to be paraded through the Roman Forum in chains as a freak for all Romans to gawk and jeer. He asked

Gisco and Tarra to escort his valuable gold and silver bullion and other personal effects to a villa he owned which was south of Hadrumetum. He asked them to arrange for a fast ship and crew to be ready for a prolonged sea voyage in the next few days. Gisco and Tarra bid a sad farewell to their longtime friend as they left Carthage, with the intention of returning to Athens after they had accomplished these last tasks for Hannibal. Gisco made arrangements for Hannibal to contact him in Athens by messenger as soon as the great Carthaginian had settled in some country. Hannibal told Gisco where it was he was headed, in strict secrecy, but he was not certain that he would be fully accepted where he wanted to go. Gisco had a prearranged, discreet contact point in Athens that was long a part of Hannibal's elaborate intelligence network, where Hannibal could safely send his messenger.

Chapter 11

EVENTS AFTER HANNIBAL FLEES AFRICA (195-182 B.C.)

The day before the Roman commission was to hold its first hearing in Carthage, in 195 B.C., Hannibal conspicuously appeared in public, then he went to his stable and selected his favorite horse. He rode out the city gate as though he were taking one of his customary rides on his favorite horse. He took no baggage, as this had been already arranged by Gisco, so that no one would become suspicious of his actions. He rode south for 140 miles, night and day, to a villa he owned south of the military camp at Hadrumetum.

Gisco had arranged to have all of his baggage waiting for him, and Hannibal boarded a fast vessel stocked with his gold and silver bullion, and other valuables, and sailed away. He was recognized in the port of Cercinia where he was hailed as a hero by the crews of many Phoenician ships that were in the harbor. He invited them to a reception party on shore that afternoon, and he cunningly asked the ships' captains to bring the sails from their ships, to use as awnings, to shield the festivities from the strong sun. Hannibal provided many jugs of excellent wine for the celebration, and the crews of the ships drank heartily. Their drinking caused the sailors to sleep late into the next morning, as Hannibal had hoped it would, and they awoke with heavy heads. They were surprised to see that Hannibal had already sailed away, and they were unable to follow him or see the direction that he took. Their ships did not have their sails rigged on them; the sails were on the shore as Hannibal had planned.

Hannibal's fleeing from Carthage made it appear as though he was guilty as charged by the Roman commission. To appease the enraged Romans, Hannibal's enemies in the Carthaginian government declared him an outlaw, confiscated his property, and razed his home. If Hannibal had not pushed through tax reforms, prosecuted so many grafters in the government, and reduced the power of noblemen in government, perhaps this would not have happened. But Hannibal's character, his constant desire for fair play and efficient government, and his patriotism would not allow him to abide the conditions that he found in Carthage. He was used to being in charge and taking necessary actions with fast results most of his life, in the army where he had complete control. He was not accustomed to the slow, inefficient workings of Carthaginian politics which existed for centuries until he changed them. It was against his nature to placate and flatter incompetent aristocrats who ran the wasteful and unjust government.

Gisco and Tarra had an uneventful voyage back to Athens where they had a joyful reunion with their son, daughter-in-law, and young grandson. Gisco's mother was elderly, but she was in good health and she participated in all the festivities. The family business was prosperous, and Gisco found he was able to make significant contributions to many of the large projects that were in progress. He was amazed by the technical competence and knowledge shown by his son in the

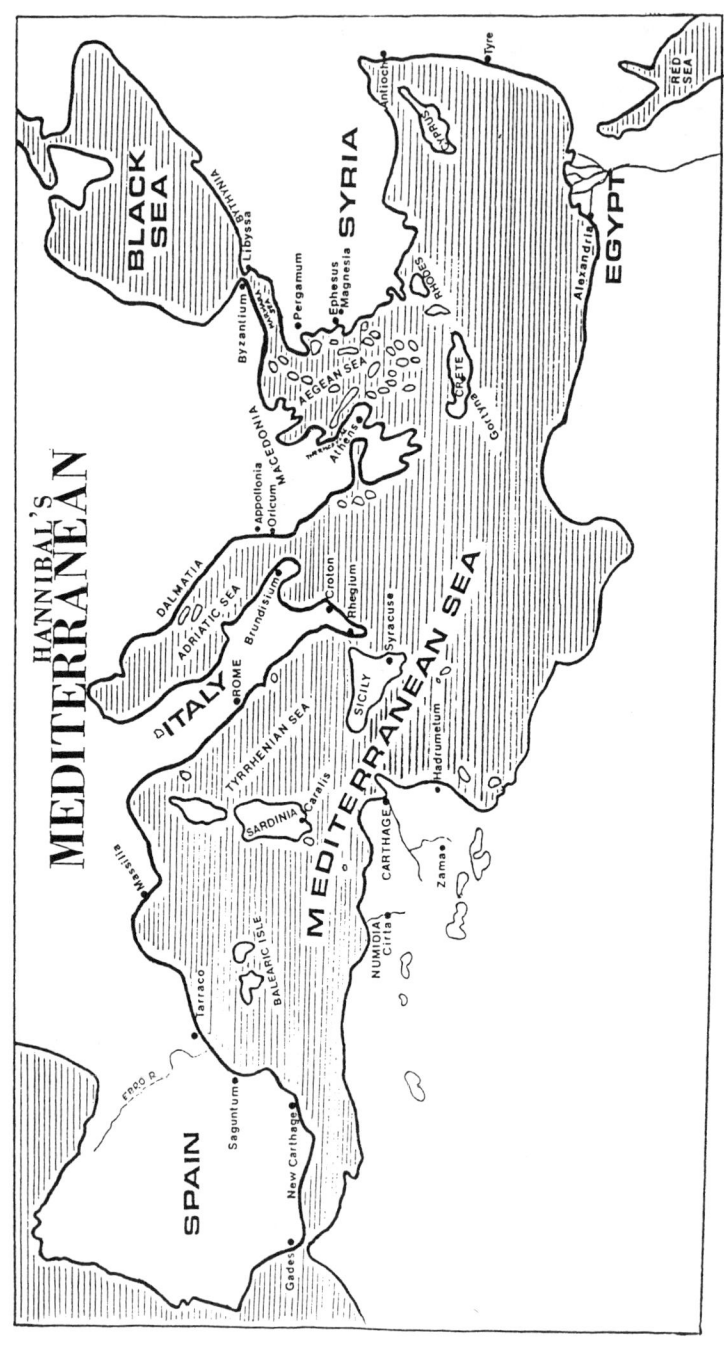

workplace. It was good to be back in Athens and to see many of his old friends again.

Hannibal's ship sailed for Tyre (now in Lebanon), which was the Phoenician motherland of Carthage. Phoenician colonists from Tyre had founded Carthage many centuries before, and Carthage had been one of the Tyrian trading colonies for centuries afterward. Carthage became independent of its motherland when Alexander the Great conquered Tyre in 322 B.C., but cultural, blood, and trade ties remained between the two cities. Tyre was now ruled by Antiochus III, King of Syria, who was trying to reclaim the Hellenistic Seleucid Kingdom that was left by Alexander. Alexander's empire had been divided into three kingdoms at his death: Macedonia, the Hellenistic Seleucid Kingdom, and Egypt.

Antiochus saw himself as the rightful heir to the Hellenistic Kingdom because he was the direct descendant of its original ruler, Seleucus Nicator. Antiochus had originally expanded his kingdom from Syria eastward to India, and he had control of most city-states of Asia Minor. Now, he was looking to take the Greek cities of Europe. He had become fabulously rich. He now controlled the rich overland trade route to the Orient, and he had acquired many huge Indian elephants and fast moving cavalry from his ventures into the east. He now had a formidable military power.

Hannibal had foreseen the head-on conflict that Antiochus was going to have with his old enemy, Rome, as the king attempted to expand his kingdom to include the Greek cities of Europe. Hannibal had corresponded with Antiochus when he was in Carthage to warn him about this serious obstacle to his ambitions, which the king's own advisers had not foreseen. Rome had allied itself with many Greek cities, through the shrewd diplomacy of Titus Quinctus Flaminius, who declared them free and independent cities under the protection of Rome at no cost. Earlier, in 197 B.C., Rome had defeated King Philip of Macedonia and freed Greek cities from fear of the Macedonians.

Hannibal saw it as an old, familiar Roman ploy. The Greek cities welcomed the professed protection of their independence, but Hannibal saw it merely as Rome's first step to get a foot in the door. Rome was expected to continually expand its influence on the cities, from a hegemony to a more tight control. Hannibal warned Antiochus that he would face war with Rome if he attempted to take the Greek cities in Europe. Furthermore, he told Antiochus that he had to beware of the protective alliance Rome had made with King Eumenes of Pergamum. Eumenes was fearful that Antiochus would take his kingdom located next to that of Antiochus.

Hannibal was headed east to offer his services to Antiochus, as a military expert for fighting Romans, and to find a safe asylum from the hated Romans. He had not forgotten his vow to hate Romans, and the Roman commission that forced him to flee from Carthage made it easier for him to remember his vow. He had decided to land his ship at his Phoenician motherland, Tyre, and try to locate Antiochus from there.

Tyrians had closely followed the Italian campaigns of their most famous Phoenician son with pride and emotion. Hannibal was universally admired in the eastern Mediterranean where many feared and disliked the Romans. He might be an exiled outlaw in Carthage, but when his vessel sailed into the Tyrian port filled with Phoenician ships, he was instantly recognized, and word of his presence rapidly passed throughout the island-port. People lined the streets to get a glimpse of him, and he was offered the hospitality usually reserved for royalty. Everywhere, he saw sheets of the famous, expensive Tyrian purple cloth drying in the sun. The purple dye was made from sea-snails, and the cloth had become world famous as a mark of royalty. After enjoying the Tyrian hospitality and adulation for several days while he rested from his long sea voyage, he decided to continue his trip to find Antiochus. He was offered a royal chariot for his journey, but Hannibal wanted to make the 230-mile trip to Antioch on horseback with his small party. Throngs lined the streets as he rode across the causeway, built by Alexander, joining the island of Tyre with the mainland, where he started his journey.

On reaching Antioch, Hannibal passed through the city walls and rode down a colonnade-lined street to the center of the city where it intersected with another great colonnaded street. He was met there by the king's son who told him that Antiochus was in Ephesus (now in Turkey), at the northwest of his realm, 600 miles away. He told Hannibal that he would provide a warship to take him there after he had a chance to rest from his journey. Lute players led the way for Hannibal and his party to the palace that had been prepared for his use. People lined the streets to get a glimpse of the famous general. After resting and enjoying the lavish hospitality provided by the king's son, Hannibal and his party were taken to a warship in the harbor of Seleucia, near Antioch, and he sailed away, headed for the port of Ephesus.

Hannibal's vessel finally reached the harbor of the magnificent city of Ephesus during the summer. The city was considered the cradle of cultural and social civilization of the western world, and it contained many beautiful marble edifices, shrines, shops, and statues. Hannibal had read much about the city during his early studies. He was anxious to see the huge Temple of Artemis, one of the famous Seven Wonders of the World, the largest marble structure ever built, located nearby.

As they came into the harbor filled with warships, news of his arrival quickly spread and people gathered in the streets to catch a glimpse of the famous military genius. Hannibal was anxiously looking forward to an interview with King Antiochus, and he was given a royal welcome by the despotic ruler.

The king, a forty-two-year old Greek, met Hannibal, now fifty-two and after exchanging pleasantries and after a sumptuous feast, he listened carefully to Hannibal's analysis of the strategic situation facing him. Hannibal reiterated his belief that the king's main enemy, as he tried to obtain the remaining Greek cities to the west of his present kingdom, would be Rome. Thus, he advised the king to start preparing for a war with Rome as quickly as possible. The king's advisers had not anticipated this problem in their planning for his campaign to gain control of the European Greek cities. Hannibal told the king that he was the world's leading expert at fighting Romans, as he had fought them for sixteen years in Italy and his army had killed more than a quarter million Roman soldiers.

He told the king that Syrians would need a powerful navy to control the seas if he expected to be able to retain control of the Greek cities once he had conquered them. The most logical way to fight the Romans, who would be his greatest and most powerful obstacle to retaining control of the Greek cities, would be to develop a strong expeditionary force to fight a war in Italy. Hannibal continued, saying that Antiochus, who had more than enough resources to build the necessary forces, should accomplish as many of his objectives through diplomacy as possible while his fleet and his army were being built to the size necessary to accomplish the task.

Hannibal advised the king that there was great urgency to build the necessary military forces, a large, strong navy and an amphibious army. The king should be able strike as soon as possible because Rome had let its navy deteriorate after Zama. Rome's army was currently occupied with fighting tribes in Spain and Gauls in northern Italy. It was important for Syria to strike before these other wars were settled, which would free-up Roman legions to oppose Antiochus. The reason that Antiochus would need a superior navy was to prevent Rome from sending an expeditionary force to Greece to stop Antiochus once war was declared. Hannibal told him about the Carthaginian experience with the strong Roman navy and explained how the navy became one of the single most important reasons Rome was finally successful. If Carthage had been able to control the seas with a superior navy, the outcome of his war would have been different.

Hannibal proposed that he, Hannibal, lead an attack on the Italian mainland to distract the Romans while Antiochus led his army to the Greek mainland. Hannibal's attack on Italy would enable the king to consolidate his forces in Greece and gather Greek allies to enable him to launch an attack on Italy from Greece. This would be the most practical way that Antiochus could secure his holdings of Greek cities from the relentless Roman legions. Hannibal reiterated his view that the necessary key to success of the king's plan to take control of the European Greek cities was a strong navy to prevent Rome from crossing the Adriatic from Brundisium to Greece, and for Syria to control the waters off the coast of Campania. The Carthaginian told the king that for him to make his diversionary attack on Italy, he would need 100 decked warships, 10,000 infantry, and 1,000 cavalry. He intended to take his task force to Carthage where he wanted to pick up more mercenary soldiers, then launch his attack from there on an undisclosed part of Italy.

The king approved Hannibal's plan for striking Italy. However, the military advisers in the king's court who hadn't anticipated the Roman problem, and were jealous of Hannibal, told the king that the threat from Rome was not a serious one. Rather than accept Hannibal's assessment of the Roman threat, which would admit to the despotic king that they had made a grave mistake of omission, they defended their former position that they believed Romans were no serious threat. After all, Rome did not have many soldiers in the Greek cities, they said. Furthermore, the king's court of military advisers, sycophants all, had an inflated opinion of the ability of their military strength that they themselves had developed.

Their army had not been tested against the quality of opposition that Hannibal knew they would face against the Roman legions. The king didn't understand the urgency Hannibal had expressed, partly because his advisers gave him advice that conflicted with Hannibal's. Antiochus was very slow to build a task force as Hannibal had advised. The king's military staff was overconfident and it underestimated the power of the threat from Rome. It didn't see the need for the forces as Hannibal had suggested. Furthermore, the leisurely pace with which tasks were normally performed by the king's court were never accomplished with the same sense of urgency as Hannibal was used to seeing.. The king's men seldom, if ever, did anything urgently, unless it was for a social celebration or party.

Antiochus did act reasonably fast to form an alliance through diplomacy as Hannibal had suggested. On the Greek mainland, Antiochus won the promise of the Aetolians to support him, and he won allies in Asia Minor. He gave his daughter, Cleopatra, in marriage to Ptolemy, ruler of Egypt, to gain his support. But, most important, the king was slow to build a naval fleet, and he didn't start to build Hannibal's task force as he had promised the knowledgeable Carthaginian. Hannibal became angry after months passed with little progress. While very little attention was given to preparations for an invasion of Greek cities by the king's court, very much attention was given to excessive partying.

Again, Hannibal's impatience with incompetence resulted in making himself less welcome by the king's courtesans and military advisers, who envied and feared him. They feared that their positions in the tyrannical king's court were jeopardized by Hannibal's presence. Hannibal was an outsider, being a Semite among Greeks, and he was not as sociable as was necessary to gain their acceptance of him. He kept to himself, ate and drank sparingly, while all others at court gorged themselves at the table of the king's chief advisers. The king's military staff, in addition to being jealous of Hannibal, was not competent enough to appreciate what Hannibal was forecasting for their campaign, even if they wanted to understand it. His staff told Antiochus he would be received in Greece as a savior and that military powers, including Spartans, Aetolians, as well as Macedonians in the north would jump on the bandwagon and help Antiochus achieve his goals. Hannibal knew better, from his experience with the promises of military support he had received from King Philip of Macedonia. Hannibal did not believe that the Greek communities could be relied upon. Hannibal knew that Rome had already given Greek cities a guarantee of their freedom at no expense to themselves, and that the powerful Romans had only withdrawn their military forces temporarily. Nothing that Antiochus intended to offer them could top that, and Hannibal couldn't see what the king was saving the cities from, if he believed he was their savior. The sycophants in the king's court had given Antiochus a vastly inflated opinion of his power and of Syria's appeal to Greek cities.

Hannibal further alienated himself from the king's advisers by his remarks after attending a lecture on the art of war given by a respected philosopher of the king's court, Phormio. Asked to give his opinion of the lecture after he had attended it, Hannibal said he had heard many fools, but never such a fool as the one he had just heard at the lecture. On another occasion, when he was with Antiochus reviewing one of the many parades the king enjoyed, the despotic king proudly asked him if he thought that these soldiers were good enough for fighting Romans. Hannibal replied, undiplomatically, that they were enough for only one mouthful to the tough Romans. Hannibal had worked most of his life where he was in command, with power to take necessary action to correct deficiencies whenever he saw them. In his situation at the king's royal court, he had very little power to take corrective action, and his advice was largely ignored, until it was too late.

The Roman Senate was becoming concerned about the claims that Antiochus was making for his empire to the west of Asia Minor, across the Bosphorus, and the Senate took him seriously because he was rich and powerful enough to try to enforce his claims. The news that Hannibal was in his court as an adviser was also cause for Rome to take him seriously. The Romans began a strategy of delay by overtly trying to solve the problem through diplomatic negotiations, while it rapidly, and secretly, built up its military capability to confront him with military power. Roman envoys went back and forth between Rome and Ephesus, and Antiochus was becoming irritated by the fact that the envoys always claimed they had to return to Rome for a decision on each small matter before negotiations could proceed further. Hannibal explained to Antiochus that these were delaying tactics to allow Rome more time to prepare for war.

Hannibal had sent a Tyrian citizen to Carthage to contact trusted members of the Barca faction with details of his proposed expedition which Antiochus had approved (but had not taken action to implement). Romans had intercepted rumors of his plan. Although Carthaginians denied the plan, it added to Rome's concern and increased Rome's urgency about preparing to fight Antiochus. The Roman Senate decided to send a commission to personally interview Antiochus, as another tool for delay while they hastily prepared for war. Antiochus was not hastily preparing for war because he believed his incompetent military staff of advisers when they told him Rome was not a serious threat against his superior army. They told him Syria had nothing to fear from the inferior Romans, who had no forces in the area.

The Roman commission sent by the Senate, headed by Publius Villius, arrived in Ephesus. Hannibal's old adversary and the victor at Zama, Scipio Africanus, was in this party. The commission arrived in Ephesus at a time when Antiochus was away, so Villius and Scipio decided, at Scipio's suggestion, to pass the time with an interview of Hannibal, while they waited for the king's return. They enjoyed the first visit with the great Carthaginian commander so much that they made many visits to see him, since they had to wait for the return of Antiochus. Hannibal genuinely enjoyed meeting his old adversaries as much as they did him. The two great commanders had a special rapport, and each had great admiration and respect for the other.

In one private conversation between the two, they talked about military affairs in general, and Scipio asked Hannibal whom he believed was the greatest military general of all time. The Carthaginian replied that in his opinion Alexander was the greatest; the great Greek, Pyrrhus, was second greatest; and he, Hannibal, was the third greatest. Scipio then asked him how he would rate himself if he had beaten Scipio at Zama, and Hannibal then replied that he would then have to rate himself as the greatest. Scipio was elated and flattered by Hannibal's subtle compliment to his ability because he had complete faith that Hannibal was being honest.

The two commanders enjoyed their leisurely conversations together, talking about various military campaigns and politics over glasses of wine. Publius Villius was enthralled as he listened to the scintillating conversation the two great men conducted, and he could see that they were enjoying themselves immensely. The wily Hannibal, while he truly enjoyed the visit, had the ulterior motive of getting as much information from them as he could. The Roman visits to Hannibal were carefully observed by members of the king's court, and they told Antiochus about them when he returned from his trip. They noted that though Hannibal avoided associating with them at the king's court, he freely associated with the visiting Romans. The king was severely shaken by the news because he feared that Hannibal was too friendly with them and that he might be giving Romans his secrets.

Antiochus met with the Roman commission as it had requested, ominously, without inviting Hannibal to attend the meeting. At the meeting, the king told the Romans that the Greek cities in Asia Minor and Thrace were legally his, but the Romans countered his claim by saying the cities of Thrace should be free. The Roman commissioners wanted the Bosphorus to be the clear line of demarcation between the influence of Antiochus and the Romans.

After a lengthy discussion between the two sides, it became clear that a compromise could not be reached through diplomacy, and the king impatiently dismissed the commission. Next, he summoned a meeting of his council, again without inviting Hannibal to attend. When Hannibal heard of the important meeting being conducted without him, he was very dismayed. He went to the hallway outside the council chamber where the meeting was being held, hoping to have an audience with the king as he emerged from the meeting room. When the meeting was concluded, Antiochus allowed the disturbed Hannibal to talk to him in private. The king told the Carthaginian, frankly, that he had become disenchanted with him when he learned of his many meetings with the Romans while he was away. Hannibal replied by telling the despotic ruler about his sworn vow at the sacred alter of the Tyrian god, Melkart (Hercules), at the age of nine, to hate Romans the rest of his life, and that he had spent the rest of his life since that time finding ways of fulfilling his vows to defeat them. He explained that his meetings with the Romans were a valuable source of information concerning their intentions, and to determine how resolute they were in their convictions, nothing more. He told the king that if he wanted his help fighting the Romans, he was available, and if not, he would go elsewhere. He told Antiochus he had come to his kingdom because he knew the king had enough resources to defeat Rome. The king smiled a rare smile at Hannibal and told him he would keep him as an adviser.

Antiochus then told Hannibal of his council's meeting and of the meeting with the Roman commission. Hannibal told the king that it meant war with Rome, just as he had advised the king would happen more than a year before. The king agreed. Hannibal had been advising the king to urgently prepare a large navy and army for the inevitable conflict if he continued to pursue his claim to the Greek cities across the Bosphorus, but the king's advisers could not see the urgency. They told the king that Rome had only a few warships in Greek waters and anticipated allies in Greece would be anxious to provide sufficient military forces to help them easily defeat Rome. They grossly underestimated the Roman capability and determination, and they grossly overestimated their own military power. They paid no heed to Hannibal's constant warnings. Hannibal knew from experience the quality of help King Philip of Macedonia would provide, and he did not expect better help from the other professed Greek allies he knew. On the other hand, Hannibal had an intimate knowledge about the quality of the Roman fighting forces that Antiochus could expect to face. The Carthaginian also knew from experience how quickly Rome could build a large fleet to transport many legions to Greece. Information he received from his still active intelligence network indicated that Rome was feverishly working at building its military strength all the while their diplomats had been employing delay tactics to buy the necessary time. Hannibal told Antiochus and his staff about this, but the message fell on deaf ears because they were so overconfident. The king's advisers were so confident that they convinced Antiochus to cancel Hannibal's proposed diversionary attack on the Italian peninsula. The advisers said it would not be necessary. Hannibal told the king he was very concerned about the lethargy and lack of serious preparation for the dangerous campaign upon which the king was about to embark.

In Rome, news continued to spread that Hannibal was advising Antiochus, and it was a great shock and stimulus to the Roman Senate. Preparations were stepped-up, to defend itself against another imaginative attack they expected Hannibal to make on the Italian peninsula. A special defense force was created to guard against an attack on Sicily in the event it was his initial objective. A larger Roman navy was already being built. There was no lethargy or overconfidence in Rome, as there was in Ephesus, and serious preparations were hastily made for a Roman expeditionary force to Greece.

Rome sent the competent T. Quinctius Flamininus to confirm Rome's earlier alliance with the Greek cities. Flamininus had earlier taken away much of the leverage Antiochus had for rallying the Greek cities to his cause. He made a speech at the Isthmian games telling the Greeks that Rome recognized the right of Greek cities to be free and independent, and that Rome would ally itself with them to guarantee their independence. This had been done at the time Philip of Macedonia was attempting to enforce his control over them. Flamininus gave them an offer they could not refuse by offering them an umbrella of Roman protection at no apparent cost to themselves. Why would they respond to an appeal by the despotic King Antiochus to "liberate" themselves when they were already guaranteed liberation by Rome?

Only Aetolians, longtime enemies of Rome located in the north-central mainland of Greece, declined to ally with Rome. They allied themselves with Antiochus. They offered him forces to support his invasion of mainland Greece. The Aetolians did not want Antiochus to allow Hannibal's diversionary attack on the Italian peninsula, as Hannibal had proposed, because they wanted Antiochus to bring his entire military strength to Greece to protect Aetolia from Rome. Aetolians wanted his full protection from Rome because they had openly declared themselves to be enemies of the feared Romans. They did not have the foresight to see the strategic advantage of defeating Rome in Italy, and of fighting the war on Italian soil instead of their own, as Hannibal's vast experience at fighting Romans had convinced him was the best strategy. Aetolians told Antiochus that Hannibal was an adventurer, only seeking advantage for Carthage. This was one of the factors that caused the king to cancel Hannibal's expedition to Italy. The Italians had a better and more accurate evaluation of Hannibal's ability than the people he was currently advising, and the Roman Senate made careful preparations to guard against the much-feared invasion by Hannibal. Rome feared Hannibal more than it feared the Syrian army.

Hannibal accompanied the poorly prepared and ill-conceived expedition led by Antiochus in the fall of 192 B.C. to the fortress of Demetrias in Thessaly. He was opposed to it and he was greatly dismayed by the small size of the military forces with which the king expected to accomplish such a gigantic task. The king and his staff had grossly underestimated the reaction they would receive from the Romans. Antiochus had only brought a small force of 10,000 infantry, 500 cavalry, and six elephants. He had much more military power available to him in Syria. The Aetolians, too, were horrified to see such a small Syrian force, which was inadequate for the mere occupation of Greece, let alone for fighting Romans too. The winter of 192-191 B.C. was wasted while Antiochus attempted to organize the Greek cities his advisers had told him would anxiously join his cause, to be "liberated." Only the Aetolians, already declared enemies of Rome before Antiochus approached them for support, provided support for the Syrian king. Meanwhile, Romans were being allowed ample time to make preparations for an expeditionary force to send to Greece, as Hannibal had advised Antiochus against, and which Hannibal had serious concern about.

At a council meeting in the fortress of Demetrias, Hannibal reiterated his advice that the war must be won on the seas and in Italy, not in Greece. He said that although they were starting much too late, the Syrians should make a maximum effort to hastily raise a large naval force to prevent Romans from coming to Greece across the Adriatic from Brundisium, and to patrol the Italian coast off Campania. Again, none of his advice was heeded.

In the spring of 191 B.C. a large Roman expeditionary army landed in Greece, sailing without opposition from Brundisium, as Hannibal had predicted. It was under the command of Consul Manius Acilius Glabrio. At about the same time, the unreliable Philip of Macedonia, not only failed to keep his promise of providing forces to support Antiochus (as Hannibal had anticipated would happen), but the Macedonian king declared his alliance with Rome to fight against the Syrians. A further blow to the fortunes of Syrians occurred when Aetolians provided a much smaller force, only 4,000 troops, than the incompetent advisers of Antiochus had told the king he would have.

Antiochus was beginning to have more respect for Hannibal's advice, all of which was now seen to be good, whereas almost all of the advice he was getting from his own staff was proving to be catastrophic. In desperation, Antiochus asked Hannibal what he should do now, to make the best of a very poor situation. The Carthaginian military genius told Antiochus he should go to the historic pass at Thermopylae to try to stop the advance of the strong Roman army there. The narrow pass was bounded by marshes on one side and a cliff and hills on the other. Hannibal expected that even the king's weak army could be able to easily hold the pass, with its great natural advantages favoring Syrian forces. Syrians were assigned to hold the pass while Aetolians were ordered to guard against encirclement by the Roman legions if they attempted to traverse over the difficult trails in the hills above the pass.

It took the Romans only a few hours to crumble the king's weak army, and Romans, with very little effort quickly destroyed all of the king's forces that were supposedly protecting the pass. Antiochus was able to escape with only 500 survivors, Hannibal included. They returned to Ephesus.

Back in Ephesus, the once overconfident king was disheartened and told Hannibal he was ready to capitulate to the Romans. Hannibal convinced him that he still had a good chance of preserving his kingdom in Asia Minor if he assembled a strong navy to guard the Dardanelles and the coast of Asia Minor, to prevent Roman legions from crossing the water to Asia. He advised the king to keep a strong army along the south side of the Dardanelles to oppose a Roman crossing as an added security measure, in the event the navy failed to achieve its task.

Hannibal went south to Tyre, hoping to raise a fleet in Phoenicia to augment the existing Syrian fleet that was still too small. Now, the king was beginning to listen to the advice Hannibal was giving, almost too late. The king had only built a fleet strong enough to make the expedition to Greece, but he had a good admiral, Polyxenidas. The king began having heavier galleys constructed with more banks of oars to fight the heavier Roman naval vessels, and he began fortifying the south shore of the Hellespont while Hannibal was in the south trying to raise a fleet to augment the very weak Syrian navy.

Scipio Africanus, Rome's military genius who was the victorious invader of Carthage (over his Senate's strong opposition), was long interested in having a military command in the east. However, he had too many political enemies in the Roman Senate to get himself elected consul. He was able to get his brother, Lucius Cornelius Scipio, elected consul for the eastern area, then his brother allowed Scipio Africanus to direct the operations against Syria. He, Lucius, acted as a figurehead by signing his brother's operations orders. During the years 191 and 190, there were a series of naval battles in the Aegean, neither side gaining a clear advantage, so Scipio Africanus decided against bringing his army to Syria on a long sea voyage. He decided to take a safer land route to Asia which would only require a short sea voyage to cross the narrow Dardanelles.

Hannibal still had many private sources of intelligence information. He soon learned that Romans were assembling a large fleet composed of the combined fleets of Rome, Pergamum, and Rhodes. His hope of a Syrian naval victory with its small naval fleet, and his hope that the Syrian navy could go to the Dardanelles to prevent a Roman crossing there, was soon greatly diminished. The fleet of Polyxenidas, with its lighter triremes (warships having only three banks of oars), was beaten back and blockaded at Ephesus by the stronger, larger Roman allied vessels. At this, Hannibal decided he couldn't wait any longer for more ships to be built in Tyre and other Phoenician ports. He gathered the forty-seven ships he had already obtained and hastily began to sail north to Ephesus. He hoped to break the Roman blockade of the Syrian navy at Ephesus, with the help of the Syrian navy there, then sail to the Dardanelles in time to prevent a Roman army crossing there.

Hannibal's fleet did not reach Ephesus in time. First, strong headwinds slowed his fleet's progress north, and his fleet was delayed as it sailed through the narrow straights in the hostile waters near the Island of Rhodes. Hannibal's larger, slower ships, built to fight the larger Roman ships, were attacked by the smaller, faster triremes of the Rhodian fleet, which were manned by very skilled seamen. The faster Rhodian triremes rammed the slower warships of Hannibal's Phoenician fleet with their strong metal beaks built for that purpose. They inflicted sufficient damage to Hannibal's ships so that Hannibal had to turn his fleet around and return to Tyre for repairs, in spite of the fact that he had not been defeated by the Rhodian fleet. Without Hannibal's fleet to help him, the desperate Polyxenidas attempted to break out of the blockade a few months later, but he was soundly defeated by the Roman navy at the battle of Myonnesus, where forty-two of his ships were either sunk or captured. This gave Romans control of the seas, and Scipio Africanus had his freedom to cross the Dardanelles to Asia without opposition on the water.

Antiochus panicked after his navy was defeated, and Hannibal was not there with the weak king to shore up his confidence. The king unwisely ordered the evacuation of the strong fortifications at the south side of the Dardanelles, which could have given Scipio's army serious, strong opposition as it landed after crossing the water. If Antiochus had left his Syrian army there to fight, it could have had a great advantage by attacking the Roman army as it landed on shore. In their haste to evacuate the fortifications, Syrians left huge stores of valuable supplies in the forts they abandoned. This helped Scipio a great deal after his army landed unopposed on the south shore.

In January, 189 B.C., in a battle at Magnesia, eighteen miles southeast of Ephesus, the incompetent Syrian army was soundly defeated. It wasn't until 188 that the Roman Senate finally approved the peace treaty, after much debate, and after adding conditions to those provided by Scipio. Again, the Senate thought Scipio was being too lenient on his old friend,

Hannibal. The Senate was incensed that, again, Scipio had not required the surrender of Hannibal to Roman forces. The Senate, in addition to many other conditions, required Antiochus to surrender Hannibal to the Roman army. Further, Antiochus was required to: evacuate the east shore of the Mediterranean and retire beyond the Taurus Mountain Range in the east, out of Asia minor; pay 15,000 talents of silver; surrender his fleet and elephants; and make no future war. Antiochus then faded into history, never to be heard from again.

At the defeat of Antiochus, Hannibal heard of the Roman demand for his surrender and sought a safe haven in Gortyna, a small village on the remote island of Crete, which his research led him to believe was sufficiently off the beaten trade routes so that he would not be discovered by Rome. He played a trick on the local inhabitants. He filled many ceramic jars with lead and covered them with a little gold and silver on top to make it appear the jugs were completely filled with precious metals. He placed them in the guarded temple at Gortyna, near his villa, ostensibly for security reasons. Local inhabitants were impressed by his show of good faith, trusting them with such valuables, as he took a receipt for the jars. He put his real gold and silver stores in some uninteresting old brass statues near his house.

Hannibal was now in his sixties. When he took rides on his favorite horse around the countryside of Crete, he could see many of the ex-Roman soldiers he had captured and sold as slaves working in the fields. Rome paid little attention to the out-of-the-way island until a squadron of its navy landed there to capture local pirates operating from the island. The pirates had been interfering with Roman merchant vessels.

When Roman officers learned there were more than 4,000 Romans being held as slaves on the island, they decided to free them. That was enough for Hannibal. They were getting too close, and he loaded his bullion of precious metals on a sailing vessel again and fled.

Hannibal had been in touch with King Prusias of Bithynia (a small kingdom east of Istanbul, on the southern part of the Black Sea). He had met the king when the king was an ally of Antiochus. When Scipio had crossed the straits with his army on his way to defeat the Syrians, he forced King Prusias to become neutral in the war. The king was not very intelligent; he was illiterate, he had no army, and he didn't have much money. Hannibal went there to find sanctuary and to advise the king pertaining to Bithynia's affairs of state. The king was glad to have him, as he liked and admired Hannibal. Hannibal obtained a house in the picturesque, small fishing village of Libyssa, near Nicomedia (about forty miles southeast of Istanbul on the sea of Marmara). Here, except for an occasional ride into the king's court to advise him, he spent most of his time dictating his memoirs. It was while he was here that he sent a message to his old friend Gisco in Athens, using their secret contact there. He requested that Gisco come to help him with the manuscript.

When Gisco arrived, the two old friends spent long hours discussing their poignant adventures. Hannibal told Gisco about his experiences since they had parted in Carthage many years before. Gisco helped Hannibal recall various events, and the two genuinely enjoyed reminiscing about old times. Hannibal told Gisco he wanted him to hand-carry the manuscript to the great library in Alexandria, Egypt, to make it available for all scholars to study, just as he and Gisco had studied the exploits of Alexander and of Pyrrhus before them.

Hannibal told Gisco he wanted his views of the wars with the Romans to be known.

King Prusias faithfully kept Hannibal's presence secret. Scipio learned of Hannibal's whereabouts, but he kept the information from his Roman colleagues to protect his respected, retired adversary whom he admired. The fatal turn of events came when Prusias had a quarrel with his old enemy, the King of Pergamum, who was an old ally of Rome. When envoys of Prusias were summoned to Rome to settle the dispute, one of the Bythynian envoys inadvertently disclosed the fact the Hannibal was a guest of his country. Rome ordered Prusias to surrender the Carthaginian to them, but the king refused. He told the Romans that if they wanted Hannibal, they would have to get him themselves. Prusias sent a fast messenger to warn his friend Hannibal.

Many days had passed since the old warrior, now sixty-four years old, had been warned. He and Gisco worked feverishly to complete his memoirs in the short time remaining before the expected Roman soldiers came to arrest Hannibal. His entire household kept a constant watch for the expected messengers. He had lookouts posted at strategic parts of the route from the king's palace, and they were to give him advance warning when the Roman soldiers were on their way to arrest him. Hannibal had always kept alternate escape routes from his villa prepared to use in such emergencies. One, a secret hole in his garden wall, was carefully maintained. While he was dictating his final words, he was warned by messenger that Romans were on their way. They were expected to arrive within hours. He told Gisco how to finish the manuscript, gave it to him, and told his old friend to depart immediately. He told Gisco that he would follow him later, and that he would get in touch with him through their secret contact in Athens when he had finally settled some place. Gisco left for Alexandria taking a merchant vessel he had arranged to be waiting for him. He delivered Hannibal's scrolls to the library as planned, then he returned to Athens to rejoin his beloved family.

After Gisco left, Hannibal took another sip from his ornate goblet of wine, grabbed a special bag he had prepared for the occasion, and made his way to the secret passage in the garden wall where servants were to have a horse waiting for him. By the time he could get to the escape hole, he was too late. Roman guards had been posted at all exits, including the secret escape hole. Someone had informed the Romans about the hole.

Hannibal returned to his chambers where he had left his goblet nearly full of red wine. He emptied a vial of poison, which he had kept with him for many years for such an occasion, into the red wine. He never wanted Romans to parade him through the Forum as a special exhibit for all to see and jeer. He told his servants it was time to end the waiting that Romans had to endure, for the death of their hated enemy. He had fulfilled his sacred vows to the gods, substantially, and he decided it was time to stop running, and to die. He drank the red wine and died at age sixty-four. He was buried in the hills nearby. It was 183 B.C.

Chapter 12

EPILOGUE

Publius Cornelius Scipio (Africanus), brilliant conqueror of Spain, Africa, and Asia, and great admirer of Hannibal, died at age fifty-three, the same year Hannibal died. He left instructions that he be buried outside Rome because of the unjust treatment he had received from his political enemies in the Roman Senate. His enemies in the Senate, particularly the ugly, redheaded Marcius Porcius Cato (Cato the Censor) who had been the right hand of the senatorial faction (originally headed by Fabius Maximus) that had continually opposed him, charged Scipio with withholding 500 talents from the 15,000 talents he collected from Antiochus. The talents had been withheld for expenses related to the support of Scipio's troops. Cato, who was jealous of the handsome, successful Scipio, charged him with lax discipline in his army (similar to the previous unsuccessful charge he had made against Scipio in Sicily, just prior to Scipio's invasion of Africa), and with furnishing his camp with oriental luxuries. Scipio, in reality a poor man, went before the Senate with his account books and tore them up before the eyes of Senators, telling them to find evidence of his wrongdoing in the torn pieces on the floor. In disgust, he exiled himself from Rome and requested to be buried in a foreign territory.

Events that followed in the years after Hannibal's death vindicated his lifelong concern about the danger

Rome presented his homeland, Carthage. Roman behavior in the years that followed his death justified his lifelong hatred of Rome. His constant warnings, and the warnings and beliefs of his father, Hamilcar Barca, and of the entire Barca faction, were proven to be justified by the horrible experience that befell Carthage in 146 B.C., at the hands of the barbaric Romans. The Barcas had continually warned the Carthaginian people, and their Council of Elders, that Rome was a crucial threat to the safety and welfare of Carthage. Thirty-seven years after Hannibal's death, Roman legions ruthlessly destroyed Carthage with very little provocation. They killed, enslaved, or caused the suicides of all inhabitants of the city. Rome forbade all human habitation of the city for many years, until Rome itself decided to colonize the fertile land years later.

The Roman commander of that despicable crime against Carthage, Publius Cornelius Scipio Aemilianus, was the adopted grandson of Scipio Africanus. This Roman commander was a friend and student of the famous Greek historian, Polybius (200 - 118 B.C.) who wrote what is currently the most famous and accepted history of Hannibal's war (the Second Punic War), in his *The Rise Of The Roman Empire* (available from Penguin Books). The close association of Polybius with the Romans, from whom he obtained much of his information and among whom he lived for many years, may be one reason that his history should be suspected of being more sympathetic to the Roman view, rather than to the Carthaginian view. His history is the most accepted because he had access to contemporary Roman records, he was able to interview combatants who were contemporaries of Hannibal, he claimed to have seen a bronze plaque on which

Hannibal recorded some of his experiences, and Polybius was reputed to have traveled the routes Hannibal traversed.

The next most famous ancient historian to write a complete history of Hannibal's war was the Roman, Livy, born in 59 B.C., 124 years after Hannibal's death. His purpose, in his voluminous writings, was to present Rome in the best light for future generations. Livy's *The War With Hannibal* (also published by Penguin Books) is more biased toward the Roman view, and it is written more in the style of an historical novel, rather than a true history. Other ancient writers about the subject include Plutarch, Appian, Cassius Dio, and Cornelius Nepos, but they are not as widely respected as Polybius who was closest to being a contemporary of Hannibal's times or their works are not complete.

All ancient writers of Hannibal's exploits are in general agreement, friend and foe alike, that the Carthaginian was a great military genius seldom equaled in history, that he had almost unequaled leadership qualities, and that he had a well developed, ironic, sense of humor. The most critical charges against Hannibal's character made by his enemies, that he was avaricious and cruel, were not supported by their own writings. It was generally agreed that he lived austerely and there is no record of his ever being guilty of debauchery. While it is true he kept stores of precious metals, they were used primarily to support his military operations against Romans, to support his vast intelligence network, and to keep a reserve ready to continue to fight Romans. He did not use the wealth to contribute to his personal comfort and lifestyle. Hannibal's constant fight against Rome was one of patriotic support for what he believed, correctly as it turned out, to be in the long term interest of his homeland, Carthage. He did not fight for personal aggrandizement or personal ambition, as his father had taught him to avoid. He was a dedicated, selfless military professional who was completely devoted to his cause. As for his enemies' charge that he was cruel, Hannibal was less cruel than was the custom in ancient warfare, and most of his actions that could be interpreted as cruel had a military purpose to them. He must be evaluated in the context of his times. His kindness toward his enemies caught the attention of Plutarch, and it was recorded by Polybius, Livy, and other writers. He was more magnanimous and humane in war than most Romans and other conquerors.

The great library in Alexandria, Egypt, was destroyed in the third century A.D. by a Roman soldier during a Roman civil war. It was one of the greatest atrocities ever perpetrated against the civilization of the western world. Many valuable and irreplaceable scientific and historical manuscripts, accumulated for many centuries, were lost forever with the Romans' destruction of that magnificent edifice.

Gisco lived a long, happy, successful life until his death in 172 B.C. His wife, Tarra, died eleven years after him. Gisco's grandson followed in his grandfather's footsteps, and he became a pentathlon champion of the Panhellenic games.

THE END

Appendix - i

Selected Bibliography

Abbot, Jacob. *Hannibal.* Superior Print Co., Akron, Ohio. (1900).

Arnold, Thomas (1795 - 1842). *The Life of Hannibal,* with introduction and notes by Henry Ketchum. A.L. Burt Company, New York. (1903).

Baker, G.P. *Hannibal.* Dodd, Mead & Company, New York.(1930).

Bath, Tony. *Hannibal's Campaigns.* Barnes & Noble Books, New York (1981).

Bourne, Frank C. *A History of the Romans.* D.C. Heath and Company, Boston (1967).

Bradford, Ernle. *Hannibal.* Dorset Press, New york (1981).

Canter, Howard Vernon. "The Character of Hannibal". *The Classical Journal,* Vol. XXIV, May 1929, #8.

Caven, Brian. *The Punic Wars.* Barnes & Noble Books, New York (1980).

Charles-Pickard, Gilbert and Colette. *Daily Life in Carthage At the Time Of Hannibal.* Translated from the French by A.E. Foster. Macmillan, New York (1967).

Cottrel, Leonard. *Hannibal: Enemy of Rome.* Da Capro Press, London (1960).

Appendix - ii

De Beer, Gavin. *Hannibal: Alps and Elephants*. Geoffrey Bles, London (1955).

De Beer, Gavin. *Hannibal: Challenging Rome's Supremacy*. Viking Press, New York (1969).

Dodge, Theodore Ayrault. *Hannibal*. Houghton Mifflin, Boston (1891).

Engels, Donald W. *Alexander the Great and the Logistics of the Macedonian Army*. University of California Press, Berkeley (1978).

Lamb, Harold. *Hannibal: One Man Against Rome*. Doubleday, Garden City, N.Y. (1958).

Lazenby, John Francis. *Hannibal's War: A Military History of the Second Punic War*. Aris and Phillips, Warminster, England (1978).

Levin, Bernard. *Hannibal's Footsteps*. Crown Publishers, New York (1986).

Livy (Livinius, Titus). *The History of Rome*. Literally translated with notes and illustrations by D. Spillan and Cyrus Edmonds. Henry G. Bohn, London (1854).

Livy (Livinius, Titus). *The History of Rome*. J.M. Dent & Sons, Ltd., London (1924).

Livy (Livinius, Titus). *The Second Punic War*. Written by James Chester Egbert, The Macmillan Company, New York (1913).

Appendix - iii

Livy (Livinius, Titus). *The War With Hannibal*. Translated by Aubrey De Selincourt, edited by Betty Radice. Penguin Books, London (1965).

May, Elmer C. *The West Point Military History Series -Ancient Medieval Warfare*. Avery Publishing Group Inc., Wayne, New Jersey (1984).

Mellesii, H.E.L. *The Roman Soldiers*. Taplinger Publishing Company, New York (1965).

Morris, William O'Connor. *Hannibal: Soldier, Statesman, Patriot, and the Crisis of the Struggle Between Carthage and Rome*. Reprint of the 1897 edition published by Putnam, New York (1978).

Newark, Tim; McBride, Angus. *Celtic Warriors, 400 BC - AD 1600*. Blandford Press, London (1986).

Polybius. *The Histories*. With an English translation by W.R. Paton. G.P. Putnam's Sons, New York (1925).

Polybius. *The Rise of the Roman Empire*. Translated by Ian Scott-Kilvert. Penguin Books, London, (1979).

Proctor, Dennis. *Hannibal's March in History*. Clarendon Press, Oxford (1971).

Soren, David; Khader, A.B.A.B.; Slim, Heidi. *Carthage*. Simon and Schuster, New York (1990).

Appendix - iv

Wise, Terence; Hook, Richard. *Men-At-Arms Seried: Armies of the Carthaginian Wars 265-146 B.C.* Osprey Publishing, Ltd., London (1982).

Zeuner, Wolfgang. "Hot on the Heels of Hannibal". *The National Geographic Magazine* V 62, P. 22-6 October 1990.